# THE RESISTANCE

ISBN: 978-1-956515-53-4 (Paperback Edition)
ISBN: 978-1-956515-54-1 (Hardcover Edition)
ISBN: 978-1-956515-52-7 (E-book Edition)

# THE RESISTANCE

## In the Life and Times of
## Arturo Cortez an American Patriot



ARTURO CORTEZ

From an original engraving by Moses Pitt in Kol.

A LA CASA PUBLICATION/76541/KILLEEN, TEXAS

# *La Resistencia*

---

"American Social Security Governmental Death
Panels and "The Resistance a lo Pendejo"

By Arturo Cortez

1/1/2017

La Resistencia is the second book in the Resistance series of yearly writings/books by the Author Arturo Cortez. In a time when there is no option but to lead or follow in American Democracy one must do what is humanly right, for what is good for one globally diversified American human race? This book archives the beginnings of the Resistance against the racist/fascist virtues of our United States governess in the hands of 2017's Donald John Trump's Presidency in a time and a day not much different than today, only the year than was 2017.

*Political Chicken Soup for a betrayed American Democracy the Resistance by the Grace of GOD,*

**My Appeal to Dismiss Social Security Administration (SSA) Case Numbers: Arturo Cortez /543-62-xxxx/543-62-9272-A/543-62-xxxx-AAAA/543-62-xxxx-HA/543-62-9272-CCC/**

## On this Friday the 18th day of November, 2016

Social Security Administration
511 N Main
Temple, Texas  76501-9902
Re: Social Security Case # **543-62-xxxx HA**

Reasons to dismiss Social Security Case # 543-62-xxxx HA "This Appeal to dismiss the duet created by Social Security Administration for me Arturo Cortez, without my knowledge or permission to do so, on my part I do fill like a citizen governmental whipping boy solution, to the over payment created by Social Security Administration for Arturo Cortez during the 2015 holiday season. In November of 2015 I received notice from Social Security Administration that a accounting error had been made dating back to 2002, this letter explained that the accounting error had been corrected, and I would be receiving $ 8,181.00 on December 1, 2015 and I did receive the money from SSA. SSA sent the 2015 1099 Form, explaining to me that I was to claim the money as my earnings, and I did. I than spent the money I received as a "accounting error," by Social Security Administration:

On December 1st 2015 I received a direct deposit to my account of $8,181.00, from Social Security Administration; whereas for me, I suppose I wanted to believe that we had been blessed that 2015 Holiday Season in my time as Arturo Cortez; I must admit $8181.00 did not seem like much for a 12 year accounting error on the part of the United States Department of Social Security Administration. Certainly I at that time of the "accounting error by Social Security Administration had no say so or influence on my award calculations, otherwise as we say here in Texas "I would be looking a gifted horse in the mouth" from a legal Texano layman perspective.

I received, and spent the $8181.00 under the false impression created for me by The Waco, Texas United States Department of Social Security Administration.

The money which I had received as a accounting error in 2002 had now created a second accounting error in 2015, at the Waco Social Security Administration/76501-3246, who calculated, distributed and encouraged me to spend the funds as my own disserved earnings for year 2015; which I did as instructed by the Waco, Social Security Administration/76501-3246.

The decision by Social Administration to deny me Arturo Cortez/543/62/xxxx-A of 404 Alexander St., Killeen, Texas my Social Security disability benefits without my right to appeal prior to administrative punishment is nothing less than legal administrative death panels allowing local decision as to who deserves the human right to live die/SOCAIL SECURITY.

From my perspective I would have to say that the Waco, Social Security Administration/76501-3246 did try to exterminate my existence by denying me my live long earned income, and Social Security health benefits between December 2016 and September 2017. As my American human right to life, whereas, I would hope that the reason for me a United States citizen qualified and receiving my earned Social Security Disability Benefits from my nation is to witness and Tell the story other Americans who are now prey to the human virtues of Social Security wish are now used as Social Security Admistrative Death Panels, for those of us who have served our nation as Tax Payers.

This story is not fiction,

Medical Record for Arturo Cortez: Please reference Exhibit 1

Primary Health Care Providers:

Arturo Guajardo M.D.,P.A.," Family Medicine" 101 E. 24th Street, Suite B, Belton Texas, Telephone #254-415-7598

Adolph Mares Jr. Cardiology Department, Austin Heart, 800 West Central Texas Express Way, suite 355, Harker Heights, Texas, 76548, Tele. #254-526-2085

I would like to thank my Medical Teams for their effort to keep me going through difficult medical times in my life, the medical diagnoses from this medical team is attached to this appeal along with a list of RX prescribed medications, as evidence of need to continue the service which Social Security Office Of Disabilities provides to Arturo Cortez, the now client of Social Security Administration for your wise, and honorable review.

Certainly, I as a layman disabled citizen do not have the knowledge, or technical educational resources to create a Social Security accounting error in my own favor; this is why we have a Social Security Administration to take the responsibility for what they do in there paid jobs for we the clients of SSA.

I Arturo Cortez am the victim with regard to **Case # 543-62-xxxx HA** I cannot nor, will I except punishment for Social Security Administration accounting errors, for me to do so would set system wide procedural precedent; that I do not agree with, within the Social Security Administration; that recipients of Social Security Administration Services for medical reasons as disabled American worker, are to be used by Social Security Administration as, human toilet paper when SSA accounting Errors happen at no fault of their own.

Social Security Administration did abuse my SS Account to deny me and other Americans such as I, our legal right to life, by denying us healthcare survival services based on SSA accounting errors.

Sir,

> The evaluation instrument used to evaluate this case for this honorable Administrative  Hearing # 543-62-xxxx HA is recklessly developed to cater to **A. Guardiola's** findings and punishment to deny me, my American right to life, with respect to my chronic heart condition, or human dignity as a disabled American, for the sake of Social Security Accounting Errors. Please fined enclosed my Medical Record and the list of medications which I am required to take in order to survive our world today.

> I submit to this honorable hearing, to deny me my Social Security Disability Benefits in this point of my time based on Social Security Accounting Errors is in fact a capitalist death sentence challenge to me a human of man-kind, who must exist within our own socialist, capitalist, democratic Texano means, and justifiably wrong.

> This appeal is consistent to procedural SSA prodical and consistent with the mission of Social Security Administration to service the human's right to exist as a dignified Senior American Citizen.

> I Arturo Cortez will be representing myself in this hearing because I do not have the money to be represented by a professional legal advocate.

However, as a writer, blogger, author, and publisher, I do view this hearing as a extremely serious challenge to my life in a capitalist democracy, as well as a challenge to the integrity of Social Security Administration's ability to deliver its services based on the original Social Security mission of purpose.

Please fine this text as my request for Waiver of over-payment created for me by our Social Security Administration government case workers/agents; enclosed please find the reason for the request, on this day.

### *Evidence:*

**Exhibit 1** Medical Record, my Medical Condition has not changed please reference Arturo Guajardo, M.D., P.A. (254-415-xxxx) / (Adolph Mares MD. Austin Heart, Harker Heights, Texas/ Telephone Number (254-526-xxxx).

**Exhibit 2** 2015 Form SSA-1099-Social Security Benefit Statement received, January 2016,

**Exhibit 3** "Notice of Change in Benefits, from Western Program, Richmond, California/94802-1791 March 22, 2016 letter to me on when the over payment first occurred in April of 2002."

**Exhibit 4** March 22, 2016 "Notice of Change Benefits,"

**Exhibit 5** April 27, 2016 Overpayment Information letter"

**Exhibit 6** May 3, "Important information" Case Number 543-62-xxxxHA"

**Exhibit 7** May 7th 2016, "#543-62-xxxx HA"/ ArturoCortez76541 to SSA, Western Program Service Center,

**Exhibit 8** May 25th 2016 "Important Information Letter" case number 543-62-xxxxACCC

**Exhibit 9** September 15th 2016 "Overpayment Information" Claim Number 543-62-xxxxACCC,

**Exhibit 10** September 23, 2016, "Important Information Letter" Claim Number 543-62-xxxxHA

**Exhibit 11** December 20th 2016, "Refer: 543-62-xxxxx Arturo Cortez letter" Jason Schoenthal, Hearing Office Director,

**Exhibit 12** September 14th 2017, "Refer To 543-62-xxxx Arturo Cortez Letter," James W. Lessis, Administrative Law Judge.

Again, gracias to you Honorable, James W. Lessis, Administrative Law Judge, SSA , for hearing my case, the rest Senor, I leave in the sands of Texas History, you have a wonderful day.

# 2017

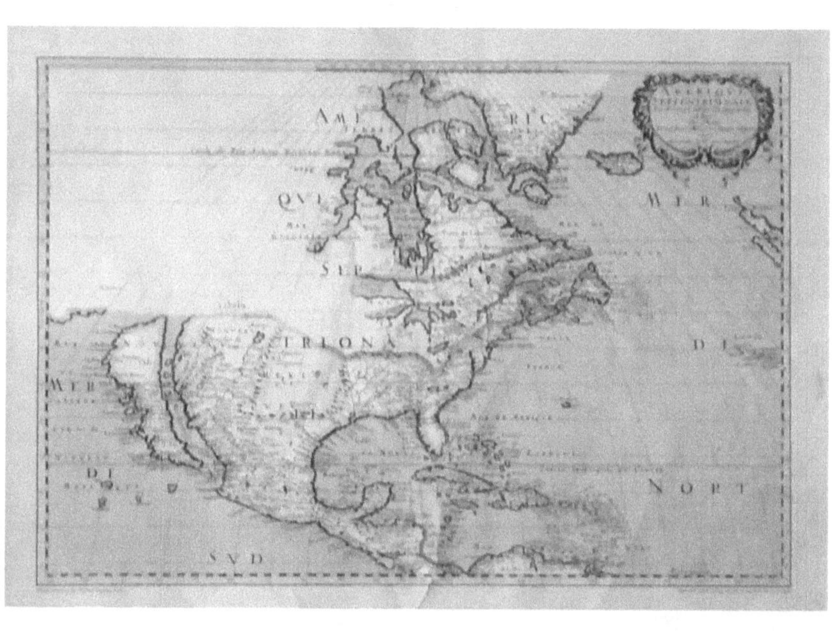

AMERICA
QVI
SEP
TERRONA
MER
DI
MER
DI
NORT
SVD
AMERIQVE
SEPTENTRIONALE

# Preface

What a wonderful time to be a writer, the 2016 Presidential political election year a time when we the arrogant diversified democratic socialist American exercise our political democratic socialist ritual in order to elect a American Presidential leader of our diversified American people for this our time in American history.

"Globe powers stand aside," the American voters influenced by Russian cyber KGB dis/miss information intelligence tactics have democratically elected the United States Russian Puppet Government of POTUS/45, Donald Trump to be our leader and defined who we are as Americans in American democracy, of today.

POTUS/5 James Monroe is now rolling over in his grave, saying to himself "I should have added the United States to The Monroe Doctrine towards Latin American."

New as well as old world nations be dammed we the American voters of today have failed foundational American democratic tradition for the sake of capitalist corporate lust "$" in American politics of and for the American People.

So now we have King, Emperor of North American United States Republic's POTUS/45, Donald Trump redefining who we are as a capitalist contemporary socialist democracy of the people to date.

To this I can only write five "Ha, Ha, Ha, Ha, Ha's," and say to the American voters, we the American voters of today voted for Hillary Clinton, we won by over 3 million votes strong in November of 2016, we are Si se Puede and we never forget, nor do we know how to forgive or make excuses for the truth.

The resistance towards our own now fascist United States government is much like saying no when it hurts. It is a diversified American citizen's responsibility within one nation of global immigrants to stand as one traditional American historical democracy establish by honorable men and women who are our forefathers founders, and the framers of the world's most powerful democracy known to man to date.

Donald Trump, POTUS/45 as a Russian installed American President must first do what every new born elitist KGB fascist must do, first create chaos in governmental leadership, install doubt towards truthful media and replace the truth with miss-information as factual truth.

Russian KGB miss/dis information is clearly defined to American Intelligence which must be dismantled by the new Russian puppet government governing our nation in order to disenfranchise the American people from their nation.

Among the American people, the Donald will make himself a victim of the truthful mass media by asking the American people to question their own simple logical truth. Establishing the base foundation to dis arm the truth with miss and dis information directly and indirectly to mass media and the American people. Whereas, to the truth to POTUS/45 Donald Trump is the noise the Royal makes when passing gas by way of American Democracy.

POTUS/45, Donald Trump must challenge the American people to poll a vote between himself, and the American Judicial institutional Systems in place today.

POTUS/45 Donald Trump introduced the word miss/dis information to truthful American Intelligence information as the seed to dis-arming, dismantling and replace our own intelligence with loyal to the king Russian political operatives in the White House today.

We must all look deep into who we think we are to ourselves, and the world knowing that we are all the American voter generation who was miss-informed by Russian dis-information influencing the evolution/ direction of American democracy, all of this by foreign Russian influence into our domestic 2016 American General American Democracy.

Personal commitment to our truthful selves for the sake of our families, and our nation is but our American right as one human race; only then can we say to ourselves; that who we are belongs to a truthful collective way of democratic political principles of every day life.

American democratic dignity can only by found within "La Resistencia" at a federal level for now; I encourage each and every American to vote and be counted in the 2018 Mid-Term Election if we are to deny the American POTUS King legislation over the American people by democratic political process.

La Resistencia, will now organize at a grass-root level to include the citizen political takeover of City, County, and State governments in 2018, if America is to belong to the American people, only the American can harness the powers of the American Presidency by denying the Office of the President the right to lead or legislate over the American people. We as American democracy are now being weighted, measured and counted by partisan political influence looking for democratic political dictatorship over the American people of today and tomorrow.

We now need change to our representatives at a local grass root community level.

We can only bring change to Washington D.C. from a grass-root community level. The Resistance must target local governments and candidates to be replaced by humane based candidates to governments of and for our American people of the human-kind.

We the American must fine meaning and human understanding in who we are as one American diversified human race, regardless of political party or even international political influence to our American socialist democratic political ideology.

Human first democratic perspectives in political American leaders must be required from candidates running for office in 2018 as human first instinct; whether as a blessing or a course God did gift the human race the necessary tools to know right from wrong for a reason, now is the time to define ourselves as American first in political ideology to our communities across our nation," if you lead, than lead, if you follow, than follow," and get involved and vote for change. "Arturo Cortez76541/04/27/2017

# CHAPTER 1

**April 2017**

### *Statement of Purpose*

These leadership writings archived in this book may be comical to some but are in fact intellectually none fiction, dedicated and focused on influencing the American people as the American Resistance to the Presidency of Donald John Trump/POTUS/45 by way of these political blogs and our politics post related to the 2016 General Presidential Election, as the purpose to Resist foreign imposed government on our American people. It is our purpose to deny the President of the United States POTUS/45 Donald Trump the ability to lead and/or legislate American politics of and for the American people.

Political leadership of government must be denied by both political parties to the Executive branches of the United States, the political control of the Congressional House of Representatives, as well as the United States Senate both must deny the Office of the President political legislation, after all we are not a American Democratic/Republican Capitalist Monarchy, Royalist in the now Republican White House of today.

We the Hispanic American did first bring political change to our nation in 2008, with the election of the first man of slavery ancestry as the President of the United States of North American, whereas America did keep its promise to its entire people by way of the Hispanic Bloc vote in 2008.

In 2012 our Si Se Puede Movement, re-enforced change come to America by casting our diversified Hispanic Political American vote for POTUS44, Barack Obama in the 2012 reelection of Barack Obama; who after a billion dollar political campaign resulted in a virtual tie between Mitt Romney, and Barack Obama. It was our unified Hispanic bloc who carried the 2012 election by voting to reinforced change in honor of human dignity first American governess, in the re-election of POTUS/45 Barack Obama for President 2012.

History will show POTUS, Barack Obama failed America's Hispanic American grass-root immigrant communities by not establishing Comprehensive Immigration Reform as the need for Home Land Security within our nation of immigrants; certainly by way of do nothing for the black/president Republican racist Congressional political ideological, in Washington D.C. as the means to American Republican political social design.

We the diversified Hispanic nations of this time must come out of our melting pot closet and claim our rightful place in American's historical roots to this our nation/country as one diversified human race of new world American people.

# Chapter 2

**May 2017**

Enter Forced Global Military Power," By Arturo Cortez /76541/**05/15/2017**POTUS/45, Donald Trump "what a fairytale of American democracy," I have lived to date I do suppose I could write for hours on how the self defined political outsider was elected democratically as President of the United States of North America with 3,000,000 less votes then his political opponent Hillary Clinton in the first democracy in the year 2016 General Election.

From this perspective Donald Trump and his KGB Russian operatives' now in the White House have in fact defeated and will attempt to re-define our American Democracy of today, for our American children of tomorrow.

Whereas, today Vladimir Putin's Russia, has expelled over 700 United States Diplomats from Russia; whose jobs in Russia was to gather information on Russia, this information on Russia will no longer be received by our United States Intelligence services.

Yet, Vladimir Putin's Russia will continue to gather information, and continue to disrupt our American democracy legally or illegally under the Donald Trump United States Administration.

Today, POTUS/45 Donald Trump sealed the art of this deal by thanking the KGB President of Russia, Vladimir Putin for crippling our American diplomatic mission in Russia as his personal contribution to Russian home land security, at the expense of our American intelligence diplomatic mission in Russia.

La Resistencia strongly advices the White House and it's Republican Congress to respond to Vladimir Putin's Russia by sending home the same number of Diplomats + 10%. It is Donald Trump who is indebted to Vladimir's Putin's Russia, and it does appear as though we the American people are making the payments on Donald Trump's personal business loans with Russian banks, by compromising our American moral obligations to our foreign policies with respect to the rest of the world, for the sake of the Trump\Russian personal sweet-heart business deals/ personal capitalist relationships.

**The Democratic People's Republic of North Korea:**

La Resistencia **stands firm** with POTUS/45 Donald Trump, on North Korea. Laser scanning cannons must now be in play over North Korean Air Space.

The moment a North Korean missile enters the atmosphere we must be there waiting to receive the Korean missile and eliminate the threat to global human interest to peaceful nations around the world, of today.

Military Power anywhere around the world, only understands Superior Military Power and the will to use it. Contrary to my mother's believe, though, "that it is always better to have one nut in the house, and not two," it does appear as though King, Kim Jung Un has met his equal with nuclear disregard to human dignity in Donald Trump the American white is right American President.

We the American people have allowed the Democratic King of North Korea to starve his people for the sake of building a missile, with capabilities to kill Americans in our own home land; all the time knowing we had the capacity to destroy and repair their North Korean way of life.

King, Kim Jun Un has now lost his 1ˢᵗ strike military advantages over the United States, and our regional Pacific Rim trading allied partners as well.

The King of The Democratic People's Republic of North Korea has placed his kingdom at risk. He now has to fire his missiles, and we do have to shut them down for the sake of our own survival. If we do shut all the Korean missiles down, the Korean King is left with nothing to show for his effort to nuclearize North Korea except for North Korean national starvation for the sake of nuculearization.

**The United States of North America:**

We must negotiate nothing less than complete surrender of all nuclear weapons of mass destruction within North Korea; the United States must never allow North Korea to fire another missile without making that missile a life target of the United States whether the weapon is nuclear, or not the intent is military say so over peaceful peoples around the globe.

**The Democratic People's Republic of North Korea,** must never be allowed to test or fire intercontinental missiles whether the missiles are nuclear, or not they must be destroyed on the ground, in the air, or in the atmosphere when the intent of the North Korean government is to intimidate friendly peaceful nations with or without nuclear capabilities within 6 to 8 thousand miles of **The Democratic People's Republic of North Korea.**

**The United States** must now encourage a conflict in order to activate its Atmospheric Global Defense Systems, which can only further define the United States of North America as the one and only mightiest military force the known world has ever known.

The United States must encourage Pakistan, China, Russia, and Iran to activate their own atmospheric defense systems or pay for the service as required by our socialist capitalist democratic republic of the United States of North America.

The world must now understand that we the American people are the biggest military dog at a global setting, and we will keep their nuclear "Bad Asses" at ground level; for now.

**The Democratic People's Republic of North Korea** must now follow their democratic king to self destruction and social reconstruction of the North Korean people of tomorrow. The cowardly king will fire his missiles at us or one of our allies with in his region the "Asian Pacific Rim" with nuclear capabilities at a global level.

**POTUS/45, Donald Trump,** must now put the rest of the world on alert of the nuclear global thread to humanity from the North Korean People, verses the rest of our civilized world as we know it.

With or without fully developed nuclear capabilities the Korean king of North Korea has now targeted the Island of Guam a American Territory, and we must now target North Korea on the ground, in the Air, and if necessary in the global Atmosphere.

It is we who have allowed the Chinese, and the Russians to use the American people as their defense shield against their own possible regional nuclear conflict with its own neighbor in North Korea.

It is we the most powerful nation in the world who will receive the North Korean Missiles for the sake of capitalist Russian, and Chinese national security.

The historical sands of time will tell the story about the POTUS/45 who failed to warn and protect his own people by not telling us of the incoming nuclear attack from North Korea.

I than offer this old school Texano advice, to those of you who voted for Donald Trump for President; depending on how long North Korea can delay their missiles re-entry back into the atmosphere, the farther away the Korean missile can target its prey, allowing the target 20 to 30 minutes at its farthest point, the ability to put our heads between our legs and kiss our own arrogant asses fair well. Arturo Cortez 05/16/2017

**Note from the Author,**

In this book you will fine text in Spanish and English this in no way means that one story is the interruption of the other Story; this only means that I was inspired to write in English or in Spanish that day.

I as the author do feel I am about the story as a one of many bi-lingual individuals who do not feel the responsibility to translate, when the reader can learn a different language for the sake of their own good.

La Resistencia 2017 writings written to inspire a Si se Puede, global Resistencia in political ideological writings will be understood in the historical Hispanic languages of my American Texano people.

As I go through the 2016 writings in English formatting my 2017 Resistencia writings into the manuscript, I find myself a old arrogant, romantic, politically dangerous, diversified Hispanic American patriot in my English American political writings.

In these writings, you will find that my political leadership is decisive coming from a cyber Hispanic political leader of the largest most powerful ideological political social media Movement known to American politics to date; created and founded by these writings which will continue to create political ideological talking points, long after we are all gone. From this perspective my Resistencia human first writings will ideologically influence diversified American grass-root change as an organic written seed for human dignity regardless of language or politics of the "Political ideologies/ political Parties" or even our historical hypocritical American Political Times."

This "Si se Puede political ideological Movement," is not so much a campaign as it is a human understanding of what it is we represent to the world around us as one American diversified people of one American socialist Democracy by the American people, not to be confused by the Political Parties.

Whereas in our new world of today the American immigrant native of this land is of New World sweet water ancestors to faithful to this earth.

It is those of us who's European ancestors first arrived to the new world from the salt water ocean who stile hunt and persecute we the people of this our New World.

Post conquest 1502-1533, on a day much like today the new world had one ruler of the North and Southern Americas and his name in global American History is "Hernando Cortez de Monroe " known to the word of that time as "El Adelantado," Conquistador, del Mundo Nuevo, so it is my last name was first used in the new world in 1502 ten years after the Spaniard, Cristobel Colon first discovered that the New World was not flat; or so as the story is told, of a man and his time.

Whereas, those who came in search of freedom, and a independent way of life in the new world lands, also brought with them inquisition age human property; which favored the noble cultural elite by monarch royal social design, not much different then what we have today as POTUS/45, when viewed from the bottom of the barrio perspective.

Yet today the rest of us who never came, or who were ever brought to the new world are now native alien in our organic human of the land origin to the new world earth of today. We are all of the water, the earth, the sun, and the land, now governed by the elitist leaders of the "Electoral Collage" in place of American foundational democratic rule design one human, one popular vote of the people.

We are the Movement of the land, and the American people who belong to the new world land as one of many diversified by modern day American nature, new comers to the enchant new world land come as immigrants, as did those before them to the land; whereas, many came as new free Americans to the new world land, and others came as their new American property.

Yet today modern contemporary American history forgets we the American native have always been here, of and for our kind and your kind as human brother.

Certainly, we the American voter as a diversified American nation cannot have two masters in our socialist democracy, and the now President Donald Trump who has captured the American Presidency with foreign Russian money, and Republican immoral political horse sense, must now prove themselves the Republican reason to betray American democracy in 2016.

A Donald Trump Presidency which would have never been possible without the help of the Russian intelligence hacking services requested by Donald Trump in the General Election public debates, as the political skirt used to hide his request in the form of Russian KGB disinformation periodical.

Donald Trump is a capitalist well vested in the Russian capitalist markets controlled by Vladimir Putin who can negatively affect Donald Trump's personal business interest in exchange for our American foreign policy towards Russia and thus, the world. Donald Trump dose have personal business interest in well over 26 different nations including Russia and/or Russian influenced States.

The Executive Offices of the United States under Donald Trump's White House can at best be viewed as a commercialized capitalist global American business oriented whore house of and for a capitalist United States President in, Donald Trump.

Donald Trump the mid-night tweeker illustrates the need to drug test to all candidates running for public office. Donald Trump the capitalist has now purchased and hacked himself into what was once American democracy. Donald Trump's financial foreign capitalist interest will always come first with regards to the American people, or the Donald Trump American Presidency.

Our nation today stands strong, based on today's statistics created by the Democratic Administration of POTUS, Barack Obama.

Only time will tell how much damage Donald Trump will do to our foreign relations and our domestic economy by the will of the Electoral College and not the people of this nation with regards to popular vote of one American, man or woman, one vote.

Every American President deserves the right to fulfill the promises made to his Republican majority voters. However Si se Puede views popular vote as the nature of American Democracy; whereas the Electoral College is but a bandage to a possible problem in American Democracy such as is Donald Trump; I can honestly say I stand proud among my peers in my American village for my human first perspective on American governess ideological perspectives of and for local government of the people.

It is now our right to judge and to define the purpose and commitments of American democratic politics to reflect human dignity of man and woman as the purpose of life and our American governess; when by democratic vote of the people it is popular vote that is the purpose of the democratic vote from a American socialist democratic foundational perspective.

I find that the voters are only human in partisan corporate politics where Party rules over what is humanly right; making arrogant stupidity not only a human virtue of man, but an excuse to govern over a arrogant contemporary American society of today.

However, I in my cyber character to change America by way of organized diversified Ideological Hispanic political Bloc vote must now unite a diversified human race under one human race of our time.

Only in this way can we hope to resist the political siege of our American democracy as we knew it to be prior to November 8th 2016, by Russian KGB influence in the Donald Trump's White House of Today.

# CHAPTER 3

June 2017

The Resistance," is what happens when a American man or woman is denied a dignified right to life and American human dignity, Respect for others human rights to peace is peace among all men or women whereas, we have all been blessed with the same human forces within ourselves; whereas every human mind is in fact its own world, in our diversified American society.

This I do in the hope to influence the readers of my "Yes we Can"/stories to learn a different language; I personally find that my writings is Spanish are much more morally passionate in Spanish, whereas my writings in English appears as though as though I am thinking in Spanish and writing in English in search of humane moral understanding somewhere in between.

I do feel though, we as the American people must look to the future in order to define and identify ourselves as one human race under American legal judicial American justice.

Whereas we are or is it that we assume we are a civil equitable democratic contemporary society engaged in our own mono-human arrogant American way of life; the same place where we the people of this country lost our democratic virginity to global capitalism, and global dictators by way of corporate political partisan party politics of today.

Let there be no doubt, that I along with those I influence do feel that our American 2016 popular vote for President of United States was for Hillary Clinton the right person for the job, our vote of the people has now been degraded to a political democratic siege over the American people by foreign governments.

Our 2016 vote for Hillary Clinton was deluded by Russian Operatives within the now Donald Trump Russian 2016 political victory over the American popular democratic vote of the people.

POTUS45/ Donald Trump has now attempted to dismantling our American Constitution as well as our American Democracy in his effort to establish grass root controls over our American local governments and our way of American life style, by way of eastern European Russian KGB Dis-information and manipulation tactics supplied to the American media by a shameless capitalist elitist in POTUS/45, Donald Trump who now uses the human virtue know to Hispanic America as "Presidential Political Pendejismo" (PPP).

It is than our patriotic responsibility as Americans to resist capitalist Russian fascism political siege over our own American way of political American life.

Whereas, this book represents a real, and naive political effort in 2016 to do the right democratic thing for our American way of life by popular American vote of the people; in this regard we won the election by 3,000,000 million+ in American popular vote.

Yet, today American Democracy denies the popular choice of the American people, the American democratic right to lead for the sake of American Capitalist Corporate welfare for what is Corporate American Citizen.

La Resistencia Movement, of today is a contemporary American social reaction to Russian influence in the 2016 United States General Election, and now the Executive Office of the United States of North America by way of "Electoral College Vote Appointment" in the stead of American popular Vote of the American people.

This book represents my political effort in journal format documented in the Battle grounds of the 2016-2020 General Election, whereas, correspondence e-mails with Resistance Teams have been removed along with all images from this manuscript due to publishing requirements/ regulations.

POTUS45, Donald Trump must be denied domestic leadership and political legislation as well as tax payer financing of Donald Trump Neo-Russian fascism in American governess.

We the Americans of today have honored and respected this Electoral College installation of a Viceroy Russian American government, now the time has come for Donald Trump to go milk a different capitalist cow. Arturo Cortez/76541**/06/01/2017/**

# Chapter 4

**July 2017**

When in the resistance we must think back and remeness to a time when we were young humans and valued our friends, families and others around us for what we once meant to each other as human individuals of mankind.

Our human values were different than, it was the positive things in life which guided and established our moral perception of each other. It was then the funny and silly things in life which made it easy to establish our own safe place among others within our own personal immediate worlds.

Not to say that we were always right in the things that many of us did or did not accomplish in our times. Who would think than that those accomplishments in our childhood would define the root from the stock to what we have become today as adults shaping now our own expanding world for our children to live in tomorrow.

Like many of you who come or have lived the political experiences of the Greatest American generation known to man, I like many others do wonder at what some of you might consider old age and must admit today's follow the leader generation is what established today's dumb and dumber American United States Presidency of today with the partisan "Electoral Collage as the arbitrator to the popular vote of the American people.

As for me, I do have my own accomplishments within the consciousness of my own world which dose profiles my historical deeds and service as the purpose of my own legacy/Mission in God's given life.

Whereas, in looking back at my life I realize now how I have been blessed as God's own in life; with the ability to read and write my truth to power writings from my own perceived, humble honest thoughts.

I like many of you was not born with a gold or silver spoon in my mouth; even though there are those who have never tasted their mother's milk.

I knowing my mother was brought up on mother's milk and corn tortillas simply because I was brought up as a Hispanic Texano American.

It was then as is today that American Society judged us the first European Americans inland of the new world as 1st, 2nd or 3rd generation immigrant Americans, with in our own Hispanic Texano new world lands.

My name is Arturo Cortez and my place of birth on the North side of the Rio Grande, in the Texas Village of Mission, in the Valley of the Rio Grande, Texas/ I was born to witness life./**07/11/2017**ArturoCortez

Let no man say that Arturo Cortez did not resist the American/ Russian Governess under the capitalist POTUS45/Donald Trump.

Yet, what an interesting fellow the Donald Trump is, a man with everything a man could want, yet disappointed that he does not have more.

Where is it that we as the American of today must tolerate abuse of democratic Presidential Power? Are we not one diversified American human race? Is it the American right, white thing to do to allow federal Donald Trump governess to hunt down and persecute my Texano family because they don't come from the original 13 English American Colonies?

Was it not then Cristobal Colon, Spanish Admiral of the Seven Seas who discovered Texas in 1502? If this is so, is Texas than not a Hispanic Republic claimed by Cristobal Colon, your Christopher Columbus who claimed the new world for the Spanish Kingdom of Infanta Isabella del Castillo y Ferdinand de Aragon? Of course it is, and so it is that I ask you, is Texas than a American Hispanic State? If in historical fact Texas is a American Hispanic State are we then denying our native now diversified Texano brothers, the native human right to live life in American human dignity within our own historical Texano lands of today; simply because we are the original Texano nation now aliens in our own lands in Texas by way of Republican hypocritical American historical political design?

Where is it that we must allow/force the City of Killeen, Police Department to use our Texas tax dollars to hunt down our own mothers, fathers, brothers, sisters and even our Texano grant parents? Expecting that we the diversified Texano of today to say or do nothing but watch it happen for the sake of the Donald Trump's of this time in Texas.

It is the Republican fascist racist Donald Trump political criminals in Austin Texas of today who must be replaced for the sake of Texas human dignity and Texas Republican Conservatism?

I say it is not we the native of the new world who need to be kept away from our own families, our own diversified worlds and our own lands.

It is those of you from salt water immigrant ancestry in the new world who must now pay the price for inhumane terror on American innocence of the human kind; whereas, it is we the American Hispanic of today who must feed our ancestral European emigrant beast now on the new world; who is born to bite the humble hands that feed it as a American historical/

traditional virtue  or dare I write for the sake of Texano Human dignity, understanding that we are the purpose of the creator to all who will be judged in that, that "I am that, that I am" a Texano root of the new world lands to my people.

Whereas, the Trump is gifted with the believe that he has to be accepted as a human Pendejo among and above others American Texano pendejos with the elitist democratic human believe that they have the elitist right to walk through the eye of a needle into paradise simply because they are the followers of the Donald Trump's of these our times. **07/11/2017**ArturoCortez/

So it is that I write truth to power with respect to that, that I am and I tell you the new world American Texano of today that in my American time, I have lived American fascism north and south of the Red River with respect to who we are today as American Texanos of today.

The Donald Trump's of today reflects your own modern day Hispanic racist fascist experience which the American Electoral Collage appointed as your democratic presidential American ruler without regards to the popular vote or the will of the American voter.

There were times when Kings were ordained for life the Trump is now appointed by the Electoral College for only four yours, and I of course know that everything that happens does happen for a reason. "Que Viva La Secesión de Texas y los estados unidos" y "Que Viva La Resistencia Texana a lo Pendejo, Norte Americano" Arturo Cortez/76541

## The Resistance

Where is it that we must allow/force the City of Killeen, Police Department to use our Republica de Texas tax dollars to hunt down our own mothers, fathers, brothers, sisters, and even our Texano grant parents? Expecting us the diversified Texano of today to say or do nothing but watch this type of racial cleansing of American new world indigenous human of the new world, happen in our time.

It is the Republican fascist racist appointed POTUS/45, Donald Trump who has now committed crimes against the native Texano peoples of La Republica de Texas, supported by conservative Republican Coupe de Ta political rulers still in Austin, Texas of today.

You the Texano of today must ask yourselves what Texano human dignity is to you and then drop a dime on your father, brother, Texana sister, or mother for the sack of corporate Republican Conservatism, in Texas of today? Or should this question even matter to you as a Texano human of man and women, yourselves?

I say we need to define and accept who we truly are first in order to change our world to what we were meant to truly be as proud Texano Americans. It is not the international lines which defines family for me or any human in or out of the new world.

It is those of you from salt water migrant ancestry who if deported would have a European Nation to go back too. Whereas, we the Texano diversified natives of the new world belong to the new world land as American Texanos of today being hunted and terrorized by today's United States federalism in our own native lands, whereas to do nothing, or to say nothing is to assist the United States Fascist Federalism in Texas today destroying the lives of humble working families who pay their tax on what they consume in order to be hunted and and persecuted by today's America.

Inhumane federal US government terror has no place among our American Texano innocence in Texas of one human race; God's purpose for Texas has always been to be fruitful and multiple as the purpose of Texano independent tranquil life as his gift, or the curse to us from our one creator.

Whereas, it is we the American Hispanic of today who must stand and be counted by the pillars of Texas political power for the sake of whom we are as a part of one diversified Texano Nation in the Old Republica de Texas.

We the American Texano have always faced up to our task, as American sweet water immigrates to our own new world as of today. We have met and surpassed our task to feed, our own and those of salt water immigrant old world ancestral know to this book as the beast; who now shows us all his elitist ungrateful teeth from the Executive Offices of Washington D.C. where Texas Republicans and Austin Republicans in Texas now vote for city governments to hunt down their own American Texano families for the fascist United States Government of today in POTUS/45 Donald Trump. Whereas, American United States Democracy is now under fascist Republican siege in Austin, and in Washington DC.

The Unites States of America now bites the humble hands that feeds the nation by attempting to turn Texano brothers and families against each other for the sake of putting a $ sign on Texas human dignity. Whereas, "I am that, that I am" a new world Texano the Historical root of this North American empire of American Republics.

I am "La Resistencia," Whereas, the Donald Trump is gifted as a snake oil sells man with the believe that he has to be accepted as a human Presidential Pendejo, among other American Texano pendejos with the elitist human right to walk through the eye of a needle into paradise; simply because he, she or they are the Trumps of this time.

Wrong this time we resist to the extent of Session from the American Union of American States, Texas will stand with what is the right thing to do for our Texano families whether from the English 13 colonies or not we the diversified Texano Republica de Texas, was here as Roman Catholic Hispanic new world Kingdom long before English Captain Drake, burned the Spanish Armada down in the 1590's.

I charge The United States of North America with violating the Treaty de Guadalupe Hidalgo, and ask our American Texano families on both sides of the Rio Grande to ask ourselves is it time to be one Hispanic family with the world around us as God made us to be? if so go out and register to vote now in order that we can make, Texas family culture "grate again," "Que Viva La Resistencia" /76541/**07/13/2017**ArturoCortez

With me the Resistance in a democratic capitalist way of life is but natural. Whereas, a traditional independent Texano American now is a sub cultural minority within colonial Texas looking for itself within a historical hypocritical historical past of today.

However, I as a acceptable human social alien in and to his own Hispanic worlds of today must try to understand democratic evolution.

As a result of my life I do realize that I am one of many men and/or women against institutionalized power for many reasons.

I know that I must write that I have had my accomplishments as a community organizer who stands today as a legacy of my time among other political/leader's peers of my time.

I must admit there are now times when I must remind myself of who I was in my younger days.

So it is that I write my memories down as a testament to La Resistencia. "Oh," I do suppose that it could be that my inner self is asking me to write this personal story down as a young man in the farm labor fields and labor camps of our nation.

The nation then was much larger than today, however in retrospect we had won the Cultural Revolution in the late 60's and the time had come to define the need and deliver the service to the American people like the nation then we the community organizers of that time simply need the ability to bring people together around their need in order to establish a organization for the government to fund. The American government then was defining social services delivery systems to be funded by the Cabinet Offices of Office of Economic Opportunity then today, the Department of Human Serves.

In my beginning there were many organizations with one thing in common, they all had been created by the need for governess of that time to spend money on human services.

Such as Community Organizations like the "Valley Migrant league" and Community Action Organizations, who were among the first community based organizations in the grass root community front lines of our War on Poverty Campaign then in or about 1968-1970.

I do suppose I have to agree with those Texas nuts who think I'm a nostalgic nut who is considered one of the founders of the "El Centro Cultural Del Condado de Washington, Cornelius, Oregon 1970-. Where we did not create El Centro with federal funds, we at the Centro were able to generate our own funding to support our own staff buy and buying and paying for our own buildings and administrative staff by creating jobs and establishing our own funding source by establishing "Ormetix."

Ormitex was a peace-work business created between Tektronix Inc. of Beaverton, Oregon and the then new Centro Cultural, on

Adair and Tualatin Valley Highway, Cornelius, Oregon where El Centro stands today.

The government funding agency's had no say in our programs to service the needs of our people. It was not long before we were able to us diversified funding to hire additional staff for our Centro Administrative staff and maintain our admistrative organizational autonomy independent from governmental American politics.

Our funding at the Centro began to evolve in a planned diversified funding manor where as it was not long before the programs I was writing were soon paying the Centro rent, and our autonomy grew as our Texano young further evolved within the Chicano Cultural Movement of our time en El Centro Cultural.

"The Resistance, defeated the Republican Health Bill last night on the 17th day of July, 2017, and American health care today is still a human right of the America people of today, for now," Arturo Cortez/07/17/2017

### 07/19/2017/Gracias,

Don, Tomas Perez, Chair, Democratic National Committee thank you for your inspiring speech in Austin today, as a old friend use to say in his time, "I Am Fired Up," Don, Tomas you were "Fired Up" in Austin today.

However, for tomorrow i ask you to read my writings and have faith in tomorrow, as the purpose of the Resistance is to what is now a political KGB siege of American Democracy, via Republican capitalist internet evolution.

The Democratic Party is but one wing of a two wing Democracy political system, whereas I did not lose the 2016 General Election of the people in 2016, the two party American democracy did lost the popular vote as the will of the people to Hillary Clinton in that she prematurely conceded the 2016 General Election to the than Candidate Donald Trump.

Please except this whatever indoctrination contribution from La Resistencia/76541, your response Senior is not expected, or required now. "Para que Viva la Resistencia." Arturo Cortez/76541/**07/19/2017**

It is the purpose of city governess to make sure it's citizens can safely cross the streets and boulevards of Killeen, Texas/76541; whereas, today human dignity is denied to those disabled, national heroes, seniors, and children within Killeen, Texas.

Now my personal friend the not so new Alcalde, de Killeen City Mayor, Jose Segarra must decide whether he will use the City of Killeen Police Department to hunt down and break up innocent Mexican families in our own historical traditional lands for the fascist within the White House of today for the sake of the federal $ in our city of Killeen Texano communities of today.

The City of Killeen Police Department must stand down to the fascist Texas State/federal government to hunt down our own Texano kind in domestic innocence, within our own Cosmo/ diversified Texano grass-root communities.

Immigration is and should be the responsibility of the United States of North America, whereas, we as the American Texanos of North America must be concerned with violations to our human legal rights granted to the Texano descendents of the "Treaty de Guadalupe Hidalgo." Where travel within the two nations is to be guaranteed to the Mexicano/Texano people on both sides of the Mexican/American international line /port of entry.

The time has come for Texas to be one in what God meant us to be as a North American historical Hispanic nation on the new world of today.

Texano nationalism is not an option, we are the Texano nation of today with the future of our children in our hands, and Texas

History will weigh, and measure us all for the final purpose to our lives.

Others will lead and many will follow as we have led and followed in "The Resistance" of our political times which have now come and gone.

Our social revolution in the resistance must start now, and it must start from within our own diversified, Texas municipalities of and for the people. Arturo Cortez/76541/**07/28/2017**

La Resistencia won the day in American comprehensive health Care a stunning victory in the Supreme Court against the Republican Political Party effort to deny up to 30,000,000 Americans their human right to the "Affordable Care Act." "As a Human Right"

The question whether health care is a American human right has now been answered by the Texano "Maverick" John McCain, Republican United States Senator, from Arizona.

La Resistencia honors John McCain for his Republican commitment to American Democracy of the people of his/our nation. John McCain risked his life to make the Affordable Care Act the law of the land, by flying to Washington DC to cast his vote against the Donald Trump Republican health care bill to remove and replace the Affordable Care Act of the people; the bill was presented as a motion to proceed. John voted to proceed and put the bill on the table for congressional discussion.

The first vote on the bill to remove and replace the Affordable Care Act, "failed," but did define the Resistance to the removal of the Affordable Care Act denying all Americans the human right to health care as the order of the day to make America great again for those who already have, and can afford Health Care.

La Resistencia encouraged our grass root political communities from across the nation to unite around community town hall meets and express their concerns to their local elected community political leaders all across the nation.

The honey moon is now over for the new American President in POTUS/45. Our Si se Puede political Organizations were and are today encouraged to deny the fascist United States governess the right to "lead or legislate," as the Mission Statement to our American human right to resist in "La Resistencia."

Opponents to health care as a human right to all Americans was the issue at town hall meetings across the nation. Americans from grass-root communities across this nation stood up and spoke to the Republican nation as one American people for what is right for American human dignity in the Affordable Care Act of 2008.

The national 2018 Mid-Term Elections is now @ "Game On" political evolution for those Americans who will take the time to experience a yes we can, hands-on political experience for what is right for family and friends within your own local communities with respect to American politics.

The Republican political effort to deny Americans our human right to health care has now failed in the "Skinny Bill"; and John McCain along with his right thing to do Republicans have now helped the democrats institutionalize our American human right to comprehensive health care as the law of the land in the Affordable Health Care Act;

It is now the responsibility of POTUS/45 as Executive of the United States governess of today to implement the American law for the people of the United States of America.

Whereas responsibility to implement the Affordable Health Care Act, is now the responsibility of the Executive Branch of the United States, whereas, we the American citizen do have the human right and the responsibility to protect our human right to Comprehensive Health Care in the United States.

La Resistencia is honored to tell you the yes we can resisters of today, as the "leaders, and the followers," of today that we have all done a very humane act as one Resistance Movement, in forwarding our faith in ourselves as one hopeful American people with the basic human need to American human health care; where health care, can only be a national human right as is our human right to life as human of mankind.

The Affordable Health Care Act is now the law of the land, and I encourage political candidates, and community leaders of today who come or plan to come to Washington D.C. to work to repair the Affordable Care Act for the people of this nation, our prayers are with you all.

As for me I would start by changing the name to, "The Affordable Health Care Plan" to what the Republicans know as "The Obamacare Health Care Act." "Para q Viva la Resistencia en la alma de la gente" Arturo Cortez /76541/**07/28/2017**

# Chapter 5

August 2017

**08 / 16/ 2017 / By Arturo Cortez / 76541**

American traditional rebel Civil War losers is not Texas history; Texas history had no slavery prior to March 2, 1836; oppressive North Eastern colonial Yankee enslavers known then in Texas as the new Mexican Americans in Texas who brought and imposed slavery as a Texas Constitutional Right on the independent diversified Texano people of that time.

The Racist North Eastern symbols of Texas oppressions imported and imposed on the people of Texas must be removed to private ownership.

Texas government legal oppression and persecution base on racial or national profile is not what Texas is or should be all about?

"The Racist Texas Constitution," and the "Racist Texas Declaration of Texas Independence," of March 2, 1836 must be replaced with what we truly are today, as well as pre-Columbian, ethnic Texano cultural integrity. Arturo Cortez/76541/08/16/2017

## Hernando Cortez

"A Hispanic European name in the foundational roots of European American culture of today ,"

This after Hernando Cortez the Conqueror of the Stone City, Aztec Empire had spent two years at the University of Salamanca Law School in Salamanca, Spain.

Spain, then was still under the rule of the founding monarchy of the Spanish Kingdom of a unified Spain of today; Ferdinand de Aragon y Infanta Isabella del Castillo, were known then as the Royal "Los Catolicos" of the Spanish Inquisitions; who had commissioned Cristobal Colon now Admiral of the Seven Seas, as the "Adelantado" (point-man) in his discovery of the new world meaning that the world was not flat in 1492.

Hernando Cortez was six years old at the time of the discovery of the new world then.

Hernando's father, Martin a Captain of the Royal Guard del Castillo Real, who had fallen out of favor with the Royal Spanish House of Ferdinand y Castillo during the Spanish Civil war of 1465 at the birth of the than young unified Spanish Kingdom, of today.

Martin Cortez, then a son of Norwegian mercenary warrior who had settled in Spain early in the 15th century from the then Norwegian house of Corte. Martin Cortez lived a meager simple life with his son and his Italian noble wife who raised and educated their son in the Catholic ways of Spanish civilized royal nobility.

Martin Monroe Cortez, was a retired Royal Spanish Captain of the Royal House of Aragon y Castillo, back in a time of new world discovery, and mythical adventures to the new world, place and a time when birds of the same feather really did fly together.

Slaves then as we do today, enslaved themselves for money property, and or wealth, whereas a man or woman's time has always been worth its weight in salt.

Whereas, wars often resulted in the winning army paying it's warriors with loser warriors as slaves based on monarch noble/ favor/social rules of that time.

Slavery in the time of my Historical new world European ancestors was never based on race alone, or the color of a man or a woman's skin. Slavery then was as is today, and is of cash value ownership of a man or woman much in the same way as is today in which capitalist corporate human today finds self worth in creative methods to enslave human of man and woman today.

Cortez claimed Texas as North America for the then King Charles of Spain in 1519 in doing so he did create the first European Kingdom inland of the New World eastern coast.

Many, many American diversified Texanos of today are teaching and learning our diversified Texano Cultural ways of today and Racism, Slavery and hatred is represented in our Racist Texas Constitution, and our Racist Declaration of Texas Independence of March 2,1836 whereas even today we see and glorify our selves within with racist symbols flags, and statues of loser racist generals, and racist flags of the losers in our civil wars.

I sometimes wonder what color of cow, a racist hater would prefers to eat Don, Manny Martinez: as for me "frijolitos pintos, pintos y dorado's."

"Que viva la Resistencia a lo Pendejo nacional," of curse.

We the American Texanos of today with our five hundred year old North America root in Hispanic American history as a independent diversified Hispanic Texano Nation of today are now being judged by resent events of 181 years ago on March 2$^{nd}$ 1836.

These were the times when the first North American English migrants first came to Texas in or about 1824. The negotiations for the new English settlement were negotiated in Mexico City with the then new Presidente of the New Republic of "Mexico" Santa Anna and the American C. I. A. operative Stephen Austin.

Texas then was still under social revolution to honor our own declaration of Independence from the Old Spanish Kingdom on January 21, 1811.

In retrospect, one can arguably write that Mexico negotiated the sale of the Spanish Provence of Texas to the United States with the West Pointe C.I.A. operative Stephen Austin in Mexico City in 1824.

The Old Republica of Texas in the beginnings of North American English colonization of Texas was at war with the Kingdom of Mexico under the first and last Mexican Independent King of 1821.

Texanos need Statutes of the real now diversified native heroes of its historical Texano lands/ pasted who made our people who we are today, as one diversified one human American race.

Yet where are the historical statues of my people the native Texano American people of today. I suggest that Rebel Civil War statues created to intimidate of us who do not believe in slavery should go the same way as the Hispanic historical memorabilia to the dump.

Virginia Hooper, "Congratulations" on your historical name, I too have picked cotton by the pound. As a juvenile young man I my family did migrate north to Hart, Michigan one year and the Pacific Northwest to harvest and do our part to feed America.

I did start my life harvesting our nation's human fuel/ in our nations chemical infested farms, farm labor fields and farm labor camps, no different than many other America Texanos of traditional American Texas slavery of my time. Simply put human fuel is about the price of potatoes/$ as is modern day Slavery.

And so it is darling that the Statues must go as we hear in Texas are not about a overt owner of human as capitalist, equity.

The civil war statues today in America are symbols glorifying American historical racism and human slavery as our national virtue. Clearly today the American of today has no reason to idealize racist "LOSER AMERICAN WAR's," or their loser "Racist Generals."

Today El Rio Grande belongs to one Texano people on both sides of the river as our Texano source of life and prosperity in the Texano Wilderness.

Okay, the Trump plans to builds political wall hype, so it is that the question must be asked and or answered. "On which side of the wall, will the Rio Grande run?

Texas is on both sides of the Texano Rio Grande as it has always been, my cousin el Mexicano to the South of the Rio Grande from where I stand is my family, and the Texano families who live on both sides of the Rio Grande is our diversified blood family and our mother-land a independent Texas.

Bola de pendejos republicanos Norte Americano." "Que se Reporte La Resistencia internacional aquí en Texas y México para que al fin sacar las cuentas históricas Hispanas en este nuestro mundo nuevo."/ Arturo Cortez/76541**/08/25/2017**

# Chapter 6

**September 2017**

"Si se Puede"

By ArturoCortez/76541/**09/01/2017**

Democracy for America has added a new candidate to the Si se Puede 2018 Candidates list: Arturo Cortez/76541/**09/03/2017**

"Laura Moser is the DFA-endorsed candidate running for Congress in Texas's 7th District, located in Houston. She's working hard on the ground to help her neighbors and community members who have been hit hard by Hurricane Harvey and the unprecedented flooding.

Thank you Robert Cruickshank, Senior Campaign Manager, Democracy for America for your nomination of this Texas community leader/ Candidate for public office.

If you are a Yes we Can Candidate, and you would like to add your name to this list simply write a small profile on you as a political candidate, I will review your request to be on the list, I reserve the right to edit and publish your text request, no political partisan identification is required from the Yes we Can political candidates.

I respectfully recommend to the Texano voters and candidates of today, to do what the man who raised me once said to me, "In politics son always stick to the price of Potatoes" and remember that "a Politian is not a Politian unless he or she is getting played." "By Don, Arturo Solis Orozco."

This candidates list will help local communities as well as national organizations and there local members to plan and coordinate at a local level for what is right for the old Republica de Texas and the rest of our nation and our diversified communities across America, of today.

American Democracy has been betrayed and now compromised by the Executive branches of the United States of America/by capitalist self serving, personal interest in as the purpose of today's White House.

In or about the 16th day of September 2017 and thereafter, on the 16th day of each month I will release a up to dated candidates "National Si se Puede Candidates List" to my friends and family on social media until November 2018.

### *Please Reference:*

Dear Hillary thank-you for your interest in "Bravery" unfortunately American democracy and its political leaders are not about bravery, but rather about making blood money of those who are already in misery. I personally have been writing my progressive writings in support of progressive leaders for the last 12 years; I have helped to elect a proud black man in POTUS/44 Barack Obama, in my time.

I have help with my writings to elect and re-enforce POTUS/44 in the Presidenual re-election of 2012.

I have helped you win the popular vote in the 2016 General Election last November of 2016 and not once have i received a penny for what I have done for you or POTUS/44 Barack Obama. I have now given up on you and the capitalist Democratic political party.

I no longer have the need to help you raise funds for self edge inverted political capitalist democrats looking to politically profit from my writings and those I influence with my writings.

I now ask you to please keep your profitable political capitalist non-profit good will to yourself, unless you are willing to support my political efforts here in Killeen, Texas with your "Onward Together" political money machine of curse! Thank-you.

## Municipal Corporate Capitalism

By, ArturoCortez/76541/**09/12/2017**

Alcalde/Mayor, Don, Jose Segarra, and Honorable Killeen City Counsel my name is Arturo Cortez I live @ I, like most of you came to Killeen from somewhere else, in my case I first came to Killeen in 1969, as a young man at the age of 16 after having spent my summer harvested the crops in the valley of the Rio Grande where I was born.

On February of 1970 I sent the funds for my family to come from Oregon and bring with them my wife of today then Miss, Mildred Jean Owens, de Cortez who I married here in Belton in the heart of Texas in 1970; today the heart of Texas is home.

## 09/07/2017

On Tuesday the 5$^{th}$ day of September 2017 I attended a City of Killeen Budget Meeting. Where a Houston auditing firm attempted to justify a $8,000,000 discrepancy in the city budget. Although the general conclusion was no wrong doing, other than wrong information flow between the Killeen City Staff, and the Killeen City Counsel.

I for one am not one to kick a dead horse, but I can agree that a audit in this regard is a legal attempt to justify a finding by the City of Killeen who will sign the auditing check at the expense of the tax payers

The lack of $8,000,000 in City services denied to City of Killeen communities has now revealed itself in the need for community economic development. Our communities now need reconstruction.

However, it is the need to change 1960's good old boy City of Killeen public policy which must change. This audit did express the need to change direction in public policy and bring change to how we view ourselves as the guardians of City of Killeen public policy.

We must optimize on domestic human resources, with respect to community economic development of our now ignored ghetto like North Killeen communities as a priority with respect to Killeen human dignity.

Whether the people here today are conservative or of liberal ideology we in Killeen must vote as one for what is right for the people in our now run-down Killeen City communities and come together come 2018.

In this regard I must advice that the real battle in the 2018 elections will be to educate ourselves, and the Killeen Tejano voters of today. We the City of Killeen taxpayers of today must be the model economic plan for the rest of Texas to follow in our lead.

We must redefine the purpose of city governess of and for the people of Killeen verses the corporate capitalist needs profiteering industries within our mist.

Corporate business agreements with private business will always be necessary with regards to community development but it must never be the only form of community Economic Development for the City of Killeen.

For now we must diversify our prosperity or risk becoming victims of change which has to come to Killeen based on our growth profile.

HEB, LOWS, Home Depot, or any corporation for profit control their business product price for cost effective profit. For the City of Killeen to build parking lots for corporations with tax payer funds is classic to "Corporate Welfare." By doing that we create capitalist favoritism and unfair completive conditions in a otherwise competitive capitalist environment.

Certainly if we in Killeen, Texas contribute 100,000 dollars to the construction of any private corporate store we would be establishing a business model for the rest of the stores across Texas and Mexico to follow; placing undue economic capitalist pressure on other communities across the State who may not be as effluent as the City of Killeen.

Capitalist corporations are for corporate profits from human of man, and are needed in our communities, they however should not depend on our tax payers for there their profiteering, otherwise we are creating corporate welfare for some favored businesses at the expense of their capitalist competitors, and denying the citizens of Killeen, Texas our tax payer right to community economic development opportunities for the sake of corporate welfare.

Certainly like cars, air planes, and machinery we the gifted human also require human fuel in order to create energy and our need for human energy does create a competitive capitalist market place for food.

So it is north of the Red River as well, with one major deference in the capitalist delivery of human fuel to their service communities, other stores for human fuel have competition with in their communities, setting affordable community prices for human fuel at a grass root level for those of us who prefer not to live off peanut butter as our only option for human fuel.

Have we the leaders and keepers of Killeen civil human dignity lost our way, our tax dollars at the City of Killeen are meant for enriching and developing our communities by way of diversified economic opportunities to our resident citizens in our Killeen communities first; and then become partnerships with private business.

Economic Community Development within our North Killeen's oldest communities have now been ignored to long; all for the sake of City of Killeen corporate welfare tax dollar band-ate projects.

We must all stand as one to demand that our domestic citizens of Killeen come first with regards to democratic community wealth distributions of our tax dollars.

Gracias, Alcalde/Mayor, Jose Segarra for allowing me the time to express my concerns to you and your Honorable City Counsel my hope is that I can be of service to help you bring about positive systemic ideological change to Killeen public policy. ArturoCortez76541/09/09/2017

CC: Killeen City Council

ArturoCortez/Killeen/Texas/76541/09/12/2017

## 09/17/2017/"Q Viva la Resistencia"

The elected City of Killeen, Texas - Government will never hunt human of man, whether of the North, South, East of Texas today; nor will Texas mimic the fascist Republican nation of the United States governess in Washington, District of Columbia of today. I remind the colonel descendants of Texas that your ancestors came to Texas because they wanted to become a part of our Hispanic, Texas nation which was already here.

The time is now when we must all stand proud for what we have become as a diversified Texas. It is my Texano cultural family on both sides of the Rio Grande who settled the new world lands as it has been for our 500 years since the discovery that the world was not flat.

Human migration North and South to North America has been here since 1224ad. When the first Aztecs Texanos of that time first migrated south into Central America.

In Texas we are one human race for human dignity of man. Texas Governor Greg Abbott needs to remember he is a Mexican American in Texas and find shame in his fascist relationship with the North American government of the United States. ArturoCortez/76541/09/17/2017

## 09/18/2017

La Resistencia stands with the truth in the statement made by Jemele Hill; The Statement made by the POTUS/45 is a dis/miss information fascist political tactic last used by the USSR/KGB after World War 2 to keep control of Eastern European countries.

"esto para q viva la RESISTENCIA a lo Pendejo."ArturoCor tez/76541/09/18/2017

## 09/20/2017

From one primo to another I want to first thank the Mexican government for the aid and support the people of Mexico delivered to the Texano Norte Americano Gulf coast.

I want to apologize for my nation and for my Texas Governor Greg Abbott de la Republica de Texas who have not responded to the human needs of those in need after the earth quake in and around Mexico City.

We the American of today, send you our prayers to Jehovah the same God who Jesus el Cristo taught us all to pray too./ ArturoCortez/09/20/2017

## 09/21/2017

### The Texas Democratic Party

Sr. Gilbert Hinojosa, Chairperson

Querido amigo, it has now been 6 years since I came back to live in Texas my friend.

As you know me, I try not to be one who has to pick hairs of his tong when speaking simply moral logical to truth to power.

So I write to you today because I am exploring the possibility of running for a state wide Political office here in Texas. Since I arrived back to Texas to help to bring change to the Killeen City Council to this end I have be a part helping to elect three Si se Puede, City Council men and woman as well as my friend Alcalde of the City of Killeen Mayor, Jose Segarra.

As political fortunes come and go it does seem as though my community sees me as one who can be trusted with moral political common sense politics here in the City of Killeen, in Central Texas.

Please understand that my community now is perfectly aware of who I am as a writer and a political influence in my home community as well as at a state and national level.

I feel as though the time is right for major change, here in Texas germinating and manifesting itself into what the creator meant Texas to be to its diversified Texano people of today.

Sad, as it may sound I do feel at city meetings as though the same people I help to elect now fear me for their own political life simply because candidates I posted on my lawn have not lost an election yet.

From a political organizing perspective today it is no longer the Republican nor is it the Democrat who will rule the American democratic vote in Texas or the nation. It will be the moral ideological understanding of who we are as one diversified American Texano nation. As well as how we define the purpose of Texas governess created by and for the civil American Texanos of today.

As a candidate in a Texas election I would concentrate on a grass-root Human/humane platform supported by progressive

American grass-root organizations such as Democracy for America and MoveOn in Texas as well as Texas organizations such as Texas Organizing Project, (TOP), Battle Ground Texas and maybe even the Texas Democratic Party.

My question to you is simple for now my friend what office would you see me running for, here in the state of Texas?

Again I want to thank-you Gilbert Hinojosa for taking the time to read my writings and all you do for Texas, and our nation. Arturo Cortez/76541/09/21/2017

# CHAPTER 7



Arturo Cortez received correspondence from non-profit corporate entity Move On ArturoCortez/76541/**11/2017**/7 :15AM CTT/

**Response:**

From Arturo Cortez 76541/ "Noted, and Archived @/ Campaign to elect Arturo Cortez to City of Killeen, Texas, City Mayor/CC, Si se Puede/CC, La Resistencia/CC,

You and your non-profit corporate organization will be removed from all ArturoCortez Si se Puede, social media accounts, Susan you have a wonderful day."

"I encourage MoveOn members in, and around Killeen, to gather with others for a fund raiser event to elect Arturo Cortez to Killeen, Texas, City Mayor and I will be there to listen, speak, or preach for municipal human dignity. ArturoCortez/76541/11/20 17/7:15AM CTT/

At my age of I can look back @ my lives' accomplishments, and I must say I am proud of what I write, say and do in my time. I am now ready to take my next step in my mission to bring the truth in change come to Texas.

Whereas, we the City of Killeen have been selected to make a statement to the rest of Texas as we know it today.

In my campaign I will document and publish my effort, to get elected to public office Community leaders and Municipal governess from across Texas and the nation will read my effort to get elected, as the City Mayor of Killeen, Texas.

Other leaders across Texas and the nation will be inspired to run for public office as well; at that point my campaign for human dignity has scored a victory as well as a humane political base necessary for political change here in Texas, and across the nation.

Without question very thing that happens in my life is meant to be, as a missionary for our creator who supplied us all with the gift to bring change to our own future, as the human race? Not to say or think that human is the brightest bulb in the Animal Kingdom, of course.

My campaign is not meant as a political fight against any political party or person, my campaign is meant to educate and organize and when elected lead my City of Killeen Community.

I have had the honor to meet Don, Jose Segarra, Alcalde, de la Cuida de Killeen, Texas at my home, and Don, Jose's place of business, but never at his Official Mayor's City Office. It was Don, Jose who once said to me that, "it did not matter how many screaming people are in a room, it was many more that got him elected."

So here we are now, again time for re-election to the Killeen, Mayors Office, and I am ready to find out if Don, Jose is right.

The real difference between Don, Jose and me is that one of us is there to service the exciting operating systems of the city, and I as a old school, Construction Builder of all Structures/ am here to change and improve the City of Killeen infrastructure.

The needs of the city and the needs of the citizen of Killeen have been ignored, both by the City Charter and their political infrastructure Don, Jose Segarra is a good man and I have voted and supported him in the past i am proud to call Don Jose Segarra, Mayor of Killeen Texas, a friend.

I have decided to run for Killeen, City Mayor and the plan for today November 1, 2017 is the news release today a wonderful time of year to campaign. I will be establishing a fund raising committee to coordinate fund raiser events hear in Texas and across the country with face book friends and families of one Texas, some of you will be asked to establish fund raiser face book events which if at all possible, I will attend. Si se Puede, organizations are encouraged and expected to support this political effort in Central Texas.

Cause, will be expected to contribute and participate in this Resistance political campaign to elect Arturo Cortez to City of Killeen, Texas Mayor, Mayor.

Arturo Cortez/76541/11/03/2017/

Move On, Friends, Amigos, Familia, y Compañeros,

## Political Declaration 11/01/2017,

### For City of Killeen, Texas, Alcalde/City Mayor

I as a moral political activist, a centralist in political ideology have now made my decision to run for public office. As of the 1st day of November, 2017 I am declaring my candidacy as a 2018 candidate for the Executive Office of Mayor of the City of Killeen, Texas.

This because i do understand how men and women of today can, and do abuse our moral human obligation to the gift of knowledge granted to us all as one human creation first.

Regardless of political parties we must all have a moral responsibly to ourselves as one America and to what is morally humanly right for human men and women first, before we can understand ourselves as part of human dignity with respect to what our creator meant us to be.

I am writing to MoveOn today because I have now started my walk across Killeen City neighborhoods talking to people about Killeen.

This campaign is just now getting started here in Texas. I will be documenting and publishing my efforts and strategies to win this election and sharing my writings on how to win a municipal election in a traditional conservative Red State in order to bring much needed change to the citizens and the City of Killeen, Texas.

I have now started walking and passing out my card in my Killeen neighborhoods, much like a fish in water I enjoy actually standing in front of another individual and talking city issues with others. I am blessed with my abilities both in English, and Spanish in one American Texano raised in Oregon, now come home to Texas.

I find that people in my hood view ourselves as Old Town Killeen, whereas others in Killeen view us as the Killeen City Slums." The City of Killeen economic development moneys for our historic community and diversified native peoples of Killeen has been diverted not only to other community development corporate welfare projects in the stead of the of the Citizens tax payers community here in Killeen, Texas.

In my walks among the people I seem to take to the local native much like a fish to water; I love talking and being amongst the people and they love talking to me as well.

As soon as I open my mouth and make my noise the locals notice I am not from around here, a personal virtue/value of attention getter; a humanist massage of interest to the locals in what is now my community as well. All of this much like a breath of fresh air in political change in the winds of Central Texas, "de la Republica de Texas politics".

My campaign has no money and for now we run on faith, so I ask that you support my campaign by asking your own friends/ face book friends and family to come together and create your own fundraiser an if at all possible I will be their too.

I will only be participating in campaign fund raising events for now until I can effort to do different. Our campaign must come from within the citizen of Killeen, Texas first, with the help of the rest of the know world behind us.

*So it is mission accomplished, Arturo Cortez did make a personal effort to bring change to bring change to/76541KilleenTX.*

### "A Bi-Partisan do the right thing Campaign For Killeen City Mayor."

"I would first like to encourage each and every one who reads this brochure to register to vote and/or correct your mailing address, if you have moved recently so you will be qualified to cast your  legal vote when the time comes to vote here in Texas, "Please" do that first.

This is my declaration to running for the elected Office of Mayor of the City of Killeen, Texas. It is we all as a village of citizens of the City of Killeen who have the responsibility to glorify our lives, and the lives of others around us with ourselves as the gifted human of man.

The reason I am running for Mayor of Killeen is simple, I will bring change to how we deliver city services to the citizens of Killeen; I will prioritize public safety first measures first to include pedestrian crosswalks needed, sidewalks, Parks and recreation, The Killeen Police Department and Fire Department as public safety.

As the Mayor of Killeen I will encourage the Killeen Chamber of Commerce to encourage local small business economic development grants in our Killeen slum like North Killeen Communities which have been denied social and economic evolution in favor of corporate subsidies to profit corporations with respect to the City of Killeen building parking lots for H.E.B. a now corporate entity for profit/corporate welfare on the City residents.

## Talking Points

Whereas, I offer the citizens of Killeen a new perspective in how we need to change the City of Killeen in order to enrich our own human lives as the taxpayers and the recipients of city services. Those of us citizens of Killeen, who are old and/or disabled and unable to run across a street or city boulevard in this military town, do have the human right to cross the streets in dignity and safety here in Killeen, Texas as a part of the United States of North America if not in Texas.

The first time I voted for Mayor, in Killeen was when I casted my vote for the Honorable Don, Jose Segarra, for City Mayor and we won. Don, Jose and I believe we are good friends with different perspectives on our personal Killeen Mission Statement.

To date after almost two years as Mayor and about one hundred and sixty million dollars later, I cannot say that we the average citizens of Killeen citizens are any safer crossing the streets of Killeen today, than when I arrived to the city six years ago.

Whereas, today it is more important for the City of Killeen to subsidize corporate capitalist welfare projects in the form of city economic development projects; rather than funding projects of human public safety in pedestrian cross-walks, a safety paint striping street crossing areas, pedestrian cross walk lights, and sidewalks.

As is today in our small city we have now developed a third world approach to crossing our own City of Killeen, Texas city streets here in the United States of North America for the sake of corporate capitalist welfare City of Killeen projects funded by City of Killeen tax payer's funds.

Certainly, public safety dose include the City of Killeen Police Department. The police department under my administration will be proactive within the City of Killeen neighborhoods and a part of our City of Killeen communities across our City.

Although, the City of Killeen Police department should never be seen as a social service agency, in my administration! The City of Killeen Police Department will be expected to exercise and integrate community policing tactics across our city of Killeen communities.

Any and all paid servants representing the City of Killeen involved in the death of human of man will forfeit their right to work for the City of Killeen, with the right to appeal after six months.

Family members will be encourage to participate at this hearing to heal there loss prior to officer integration back into service amongst others who have not killed, imperfect human in a somewhat contemporary civilized Killeen, Texas village of today.

My campaign for City Mayor will bring a new perspective in change not only to Killeen, Texas but will bring change to Texas as a model effort in Texas moral governess civic responsibility as city voter in the City of Killeen, the State of Texas, and the nation.

There will be some who will say that my campaign is or will be to ideological; to this I can only agree and say that the time has come for a moral ideological political plat- form TO GET ELECTED to influence the city of Killeen local government. This of course is not true simply because our pro-human campaign is focused on "what is right for the residents in the city of Killeen."

***Please donate to our campaign, make a gift, and/or contribute to our effort to improve our own quality of life please contribute***

Again I want to encourage giving to my campaign for Killeen City Mayor, and thank-you for taking the time to read about our effort to improve our on lives on behave of my wife and I, I hope to see you all @ your fund raiser events for Arturo Cortez for Killeen, Texas City Mayor. Arturo Cortez /76541/11/03/2017/8:30AM/ ArturoCortez/76541/**11/23/2017**

"Wishing one and all a wonderful Thanksgiving Day, love, prosperity, and growth"

On behave of La Familia Cortez, y mi Conpadre, Imam, Muhammad A. Najieb and Familia we want to thank all friends and family who influence our lives this holiday season.

A very special thanks to my son and law (Henry Noble) who will soon be out on the Big screen title "**Competition** " and My beautiful daughter La Donna Maria Cortez de Najieb, for making this Thanksgiving a very special family time for our family, we wish all u all the gift of love, prosperity, and growth. Arturo Cortez /76541/11/23/17

He had is opportunity to make a deference and failed, POTUS/45 Donald Trump must go.

50

# CHAPTER 8



**T**weet: @realDonaldTrump why are you destroying everything that works for our American democratic way of life? "Jobs did not come back" they were already there you inherited, Barack Obama's 4.8 unemployment #'s, Republican Gorge W. Bust's unemployment #'s were at 12% when Barack won in 2008, @ realDonaldTrump 's coat tail political economy (5) HA'HA's.

Arturo Cortez /76541/**12/02/2017**

"La Resistencia a lo Pendejo,"

The Resistance is nothing more and/or nothing less than our own human American democratic ability to say no to those things in American life which hurts us or ours, or discredits our American way of life.

Recently, our Electoral Collage appointed President of the United States (POTUS/45) Donald Trump as our President, a man of senseless inverted personal narcissistic ego who takes no responsibility for his actions; a man who lives his life among lies, innuendo, accusation, and immoral human behavior.

This man who has promised to show all of us his tax returns if he got elected and now tells us all that he does not have to show his tax returns because he did get elected, has now passed a tax bill through the United States, Senate to disable our balanced progressive economic growth created by eight years of the POTUS/44 Barack Obama era.

Whereas, POTUS/45 Donald Trump inherited a balanced economy which works very well so long as he does not mess with it.

To dismantling our tax code now would set off dramatic economic shift in American economic wealth distribution. We do not now have a problem with the economy Corporate Capitalist tax base and we are now recording measured record profits among capitalist corporate interests, our economic goods within supply and demand at this time are affordable to the average American consumer within our present tax codes, certainly if something works than what is the purpose in changing it?

Certainly, the Republican 2017 Senate tax plan is meant to establish economic welfare burdens on the American tax payers of today and tomorrow. No longer will our community American tax dollars service the human needs of our local communities. But, rather our tax dollars will go towards building economic development projects around Corporate profitable capitalist evolution for personal corporate profit.

It is for now Corporate Human, who must resist the temptation to participate in this Donald Trump Corporate Welfare Tax Plan which destroys our economy as we know it today. Whereas, our economy is meant to stand on its own, without government supplement in order to exist as a profitable respectable business.

American businesses subsidized by local, State, or Federal governments reserve a commercial advantage over other competitors in a free American economy of today. New up and coming business must not evolve around tax dollars or subsidies as their only means of commercial existence.

"La Resistencia a lo Pendejo," recognizes that even Donald Trump is human;  I also recognize that Donald Trump is not stupid, and the Republican Party is once again destroying our balanced economy, this time for the Republican President of the United States, Donald Trump and his need to destroy something before 2018.

All political leaders in Congress are encouraged to refuse Donald Trump's Senate bill to revise the Tax Code, or face being removed from office in 2018, and/or in 2020. As for those Republican Senators who voted for the Senate bill to change the tax code have defined themselves as shameless traitors, and cowards to the average American taxpaying citizen. "Q Siga La Resistencia Adelante" Arturo Cortez/76541/12/02/2017

## The Resistance 76541

### Arturo Cortez/76541/**12/09/2017**

The Resistance is our own God given ability to say no to what we know is humanly wrong.

Donald Trump once again is challenging the common human virtues of our civilized society in order that he can claim victory over Alabamian common human sense with his support for Candidate Roy Moore for the US Senate come this Tuesday's election in Alabama.

La Resistencia stands with the Democrat Doug Jones, for the US Senate who stands with the civil and dignified people of Alabama, with or without a Political Party.

The Resistance encourages all Americans to deny POTUS/45 Donald Trump any attempts to lead or legislate American Democracy, regardless of political partisan politics that is morally wrong for other political leaders in American politics, must be morally wrong for the people of Alabama, "Q Siga la Resistencia a lo Pendejo en Alabama." Arturo Cortez/76541/12/09/2017

### By "Arturo Cortez/76541/12/10/2017"

The Confederate Statues must go, i am American and the statues are of American glorified losers of the American civil war, here in Texas. The purpose of the Confederate armies was to enslave based on racial distinction of human of man for $ value. Get over it, slavery will never be back as before.

The relics of racism in the American Southwest, and across the nation must go. "Q viva la Resistencia"

### By "ArturoCortez/76541/12/10/2017"

Here in Texas, the first salt water English colonel immigrants came in or about 1824, with permission to colonize Texas from the then Dictator and Mexican General Santa Anna, and Stephen Austin of the United States Colonial Government who was the founder of modern Central Texas of today; the colonial English came to colonize and they pledged an oath to become proud and loyal Mexicans of who would practice Texas Hispanic cultural roots.

The New Mexican immigrates to Texas came in large numbers and they were baptized into their new lives as Texano Mexican/ Americans.

The New English immigrate brought with them their human (collateral/ slaves) with them; who were allowed to finish their lives as slaves in Central Texas if they so willed it. All new born African Americans in Texas of slave ancestry in Texas would be born free Mexicans in the Texano State de la Republica de Texas under independent rule over Texas.

Whereas, The first Cortez landed in Espanola/ "Haiti" in 1502, Helped Diego Velasquez, conquer Espania del Mar,/ "Cuba" of today; he Conquered the Aztec New World Empire in 1519 claiming North America, and South America as Nueva Espania del Mundo Nuevo, for the Spanish Empire, and his Spanish King, Charles.

Whereas, yes the plait of the Palestinian people in the Middle East, does mimic our own Texas History. The American Texano has always been here, we never came here nor were we brought here, we are of the Texano landscape in today's diversified Texas, now looking for its ethnic Texano cultural to identify with.

We are a Hispanic Texano Nation within the United States of North America as the reality and testimony to what is true from a third party global historical perspective. Our new world of today requires all who do not vote to register and vote in our 2018 elections. We must all stand as one human race against Donald Trump's racist, fascist, governess over all our people.

La Resistencia denies Donald Trump the ability to Lead American Democracy, and/or Legislate American Democracy, "a lo Pendejo, como una de muchas razons humana". " /ArturoCortez /76541/12/10/2017"

## 12/15/2017/"Gracias, Alabama,"

"La Resistencia a lo Pendejo," stands strong among the people of Alabama, who voted for what is right in American Democratic politics of today, last night. The Republican people of Alabama placed their faith in the Democrat Yes we Can Candidate Doug Jones for the US Senate, to represent them in the US Senate.

Last night a honest Republican community in Alabama was challenged to vote for the wrong candidate in Roy Moore, for the sake of the Republican Party.

The President of the United States, Donald Trump challenged the people of Alabama to vote for the wrong candidate for the sake of his agenda for all of us regardless of political party.

The people of Alabama stood strong for what is right and resisted the Donald Trump Republican Party effort, and voted for what was the right thing to do as partners in American democratic politics.

The unified Republican ideological voters of Alabama have now sent a strong message to the Grand Old Party (GOP), "Alabama will not allow Donald Trump to lead or legislate Alabama," American Democracy must come first regardless of political Party" we are all a morally civilized democratic society with respect to what we are as a Nation.

The Resistance will not allow the President of the United States Donald Trump to democratically legislate his new tax plan for America, or anyone else.

Gracias, Alabama for what you have done for our Nation, and the Resistance y "Feliz Navidad" /ArturoCortez/76541/12/13/2017

## Arturo Cortez/76541/12/15/2017

**As many of you know,** I started a list of candidates to share with my friends and family in the 2016 election, and named it "The 2016 Si se Puede Candidates Support List." By November of 2016 the list had accumulated 23 community leaders from across the nation, some of which did win their political races.

On September 16th 2017 I committed myself to the now 2nd Si se Puede political list to be released on the 16th day of every month until November of 2018, "*The National Bi-Partisan Si se Puede 2018 Candidates Support List.*"

As of today *I can advice that we now have 23 community leaders added to this National Yes we can list, I do expect this list to grow nationwide within the next 11 months to go to November 2016.*

*I want to thank our people of Alabama, and our Candidate US Senator Elect, Doug Jones who won the election, and will honorably represent the people of Alabama, in the United Sates Senate.*

*I am proud to advice that the community leaders from across Texas are adding their names to "The National Bi-Partisan Si se Puede*

***2018 Candidates Support List"*** as of today this list of 23 national candidates, consists of 12 Texano community leaders looking to change Texas at a grass-root level in this List.

Today, I ask all Texas voters to stand true to our democracy, and give of ourselves in time, and money to these Texas Community leaders, who are committed to bring change to Texas, and our Nation.

**Texas Candidates:**

**Arturo Cortez,** for City of Killeen, Texas, Mayor,
Gregory Johnson Incumbent for Killeen City Councilman @ large,
**Andrew White** for Texas Governor,
**Justin Neilson** for Texas Attorney General,
**Kim Olson,** for Texas Commissioner of Agriculture,
**Miguel Suazo,** for Texas Land Commissioner,
**Beto O'Rourke**, For the US Senate,
**Brian Cronin,** for Texas Senate
**Ken Lester,** for the United States Congress,
**Chris Perri,** for US Congress 25th District of Texas,
**Congressman Pete Gallego,** endorsed by: Texas Organizing Project (TOP), and the people of Texas,
**Laura Moser,** for Congress, Texas's 7th District,
Again, I want to thank all those local leaders across Texas, and the Nation, who are now stepping up to lead in their local communities, /ArturoCortez/76541/12/15/2017

**"The Republican Tax Cuts" are for the Wealthy and well to do, with our Blessings,"**

By ArturoCortez/76541/**12/17/2017**

Our American Economy is doing fine; our Barack Obama financial economic growth is well balanced to this point in the Republican, Donald Trump Presidency.

If anything everyone can agree on, is that the tax cuts for the rich and well to do are not necessary to sustain our consistently steady economic growth between those who have, and those who have not in American Society of today.

The Republican Party of today has failed its mission to represent the conservative peoples of our Time.

In Return the Leader of the Republican Party President Donald Trump declares wars on itself by attacking American free media as fake news in order to discredit the integrity of the simple human truth and the American Democratic national virtue.

Unless, the Republican Party stops what they are doing to change the "Tax Code" they will be held accountable for whatever goes wrong with the economy between now and election day 2018.

A President of the United States who promises to show his tax numbers to the American people when he gets elected, and later tells the American people that he does not have to show his tax forms because he is now elected is now attempting to change our American tax code to favor himself and his corporate welfare friends, and his corporate welfare capitalist entities.

The Republican Party President, and his Republican Party are now removing spindles from a well balanced economic American wheels which continue to provide growth and profits to our successful economy of today, for now.

I ask that we all realize that we and our American way of life are under attack by foreign globalized capitalist influence attempting to dis-honor American Democracy.

Donald Trump has been given the opportunity to lead, Donald Trump has failed his opportunities provided to him by the Republican Party and the conservative American people they represent.

Donald Trump has been given the responsibility to legislate, and Donald Trump and his Republican Party have failed the average American person of this nation.

The Resistance against the United States Governess over our American people which was created on the 7th Hour of 2017 has now grown and will continue to deny Donald Trump the ability to lead or legislate American Democracy.

The American popular vote was right in electing Hillary Clinton the United States President; the Electoral College was wrong in appointing Donald Trump President for the American voters simply because 300,000,000 more voters voted for Hillary Clinton than did for Donald Trump for President.

Today I respectfully ask the Republican Party to deny Donald Trump the right to democratically lead and/or legislate and otherwise further damage American Democracy by passing the Tax Reforms to the Tax Code. ArturoCortez/76541/12/17/2017

"American Social Security fascist governess under POTUS/45 Donald Trump"

## For the Record of ArturoCortez/543-62-xxxx-A:

Regarding SSA Case Numbers: Arturo Cortez/543-62-xxxx-A/543-62-xxxx AAAA/543-62-xxxx-HA/543-62-xxxx-CCC/

**Honorable, James W. Lessis, Administrative Law Judge, Social Security Administration (SSA),** thank-you sir for this opportunity to explain to you, from my layman moral legal perspectives how I have now been denied my disability benefits for nine months, without my legal human right to legal appeal to something I have had no choice in. Certainly, a SSA case management problem gone array and know out of control to a deadly extreme of inhumane treatment to the consumer of the service provided by SSA case workers, of SSA clients under medical care and receiving qualified Social Security benefits.

Because **A. Guardiola's** punishment came first/ before your honorable legal wisdom Sir, I can only assume that you have already written the final chapter to this my SSA story. So, I submit this information to this hearing today to help you define yourselves as I have paid for the SSA accounting error to **Mrs. A. Guardiola, SSA** out in Temple, Texas. Sir, you have now forfeited your honorable responsibility to **A. Guardiola out in Temple, Texas.** I regret to be the one to inform you Sir; I have been accused, sentenced, found guilt, and convicted, by a case worker, I have even paid for the accounting error SSA made without your administrative legal wisdom, Sir.

As I see it Sir, **A. Guardiola,** SSA out in Temple, Texas as has now denied you, and me both the right to a fair moral appeal legal perspective on Case Number/543-62-xxxx-A; so I ask that you honor my appeal to forgive me of wrong doing with regards to SSA accounting errors on my account created for me, without my knowledge. I have now paid back your duet, created for me in the form of a Social Security Administration (SSA) accounting errors, dating back to 2002. **Exhibit /3**

Sir, I attached 12 Exhibits; on **Exhibit /11 A. Guardiola SSA/76541-3246** accuses me of three things, "I knew", and two "I should have known's"of SSA accounting errors.

Whereas the punishment by way of **A. Guardiola Justice** denies us all recipients of Social Security, Social Security as our human right to life and human dignity. To deny my right to my benefits in order to balance SSA accounting books is not only wrong but inhumane in any form of government agencies prodical or should be in a American civil human society.

As for the "I should have known's" I must say If SSAOOD had done their job right there would have never been the need for me to know or receive anything but what I had coming on December 3, 2015. My account became a problem after SSAOOD calculated the remedies to the original error by SSAOOD in 2002.

I only ask you Sir, to read the evidence in the form of twelve Exhibits I have attached to this letter, and make your own just, moral, and legal findings; if in fact I am as the evidence will tell you; who I am, then you must return my benefits denied me between December 2016, and September 2017. Certainly, a generous offer when I should be asking for mercy from **A. Guardiola SSA's** for my earned benefits/pay for nine months.

Sir, I must say, "I do, and will respect your honorable legal finding as precedent for others with respect to legal or proper procedure. **A. Guardiola** / 76541-3246 did her way with me, and will continue to do to others in the same way simply because she is allowed too, Sir this is clear.

I have been denied and violated by SSA right to Administrative rule. My human dignity has intentually been violated by a 1938 German, SS death panel scenario now present within Administrative Juditualy justice, with no humane regard to my chronic disabled condition, I was denied. I have now paid for your Social Security accounting error at the risk of losing my life, not by my choice or the choice of my request for a "**Administrative Hearing and Appeal.**"

I as a writer of non-fiction works do continue to have a sense of romantic faith in the wisdom to your position as the one person, you Sir who will write the legal ending to this one of my many life stories, one that could easily be received and/or viewed as unjustified procedural institutionalized governmental abuse and/ or governmental SSA death panels, in America today.

It is however for this reason that I submit to you this information for the record Sir, as well as for your fully informed honorable legal conclusions to this case, a fifteen year old accounting error with respect to my appeal **Arturo Cortez 543-62-xxxx-A** to dismiss SSA over payment created for me without the knowledge of (SSA, OOD) in their Administrative benefit calculations of my miss-managed Social Security Benefits at SSA, OOD.

It is however true that **A. Guardiola SSA/76541-3246** had the confidence in the outcome of this case today, that she denied me my right to life by her case worker choice, she was my accuser, and my Judge, and I have now paid back for a unjust representation of the facts in this my case; so it is that I submit these 12 Exhibits so you can satisfy, and judge your own moral selves at my personal expense.

**The Honorable James W. Lessis, Administrative Law Judge SSA** Sir, I made no incorrect statements to SSA, I caused no overpayment, and I certainly do not know or should have known nor do I even question how you do your business. I just read the mail I receive, and I assume you folks know what you are doing. I disserve and I try to live within my disabled means. If SSA wrote me a letter I acted as instructed by SSA OOD. This is now and was then my only source of income to my life because of my medical disabilities.

You will find that I did expect payment because SSA sent me a letter saying I would be receiving the funds, because of a SSA accounting errors in 2002. I expected to receive more. But I was raised Texano North American where I was taught never to look a gifted horse in the mouth, Sir.

So it is that I did spend the funds assuming the money was my own as I was led to believe by SSA, OOD. I did spend the money after I receive the **SSA-1099 Form, Social Security Benefit**

**Statement** "Exhibit 2" telling me I had to report the funds as earnings in my January 2016 Form SSA Tax Returns.

Sir, James W. Lessis, Administrative Law Judge, I certainly do understand the precedent your wisdom will have on the many others who are now going through having to pay for accounting errors created by the SSAOOD, with respect to the humane mission of Social Security Administration, Office Of Disability.

Sir, I will be attending this hearing on December 12, day of December 2017, to hear how you will now judge yourselves, as I have already paid the price for your SSA, OOD overpayment errors, and I have been forced to risk my life to pay for a SSA, OOD over payment error, without a right to Administrative legal appeal prior to a life threading case worker punishment action towards the disabled American in what appears to be guilty, and punished prior to SSA, OODAR review by administrative design. Either way we are all subject to the law of the land and what we make of the law that governs us all; Thank-you for reading my writings and God's blessing on all of you, please have a wonderful Holiday,

ArturoCortez/543-62-xxxx/76541/11/14/2017

ArturoCortez/543-62-xxxx-A/76541/11/30/2017

**Notes:** *Points of possible honorable legal interest to this hearing;*

*"Evaluation Instruments used by SS/Agent for SSAOOD A. Guardiola is based on a God like "I should have known believe?" based on letter of dated October 05, 2016.*

The Government, Social Security Administration created in fact a over-payment on my behave in the amount of $8,181.00 in November of 2015 without my knowledge, nor my permission to do so. This, when I received a letter from the Government Social Security Administration explaining to me that the Government agency Social Security Administration had made a mistake in the calculation of my Government Social Security benefits, dating back to the year 2002, some 11 to 12 years earlier, this I submit to this honorable hearing, and its honorable Administrative Judge, of this Government Social Security agency as a legal fact.

**Legal question:** If I did not create a over-payment then who did? And, for what reason or purpose was this government deception of me a struggling writer on December 1$^{st}$ 2015. It is however, The Social Security Administration who found their own Social Security accounting error, therefore it is Social Security Administration who must know, now take responsibility for accounting errors on their part.

**Legal Question:** So it is that I as the purpose of this hearing am now denied the legal answers to who did this mistake within the Administrative accounting functions of the Social Security Offices of the United States. Certainly, if in legal fact I have the legal right to know who created this over-payment for me, then I would think that I and this hearing have a right to know and question this individual who did cause the accounting error at Social Security Account.

**Legal facts in this case:** The correspondence to me in regards to this fact was stolen from my personal file by at the Social Security Administration agent who identified herself to me as A. Guardiola, @ the Temple, Texas Social Security Administration office after I was ordered to bring in all my information to the Social Security Administration Office, A. Guardiola asked to copy my personal file for her records, A. Guardiola left with my personal file to make a copy. All correspondence letters to me from Social Security Administration between October 2015, and May 2016 were removed from my personal file without my permission by the agent thieve of the Social Security Administration in Temple, Texas agent A. Guardiola.

This theft was done in order to deny me the legal right to defend myself from fraudulent activity on the part of Social Security Administration in regards to this legal matter which would in fact deny me my American right to life legal process in front of a Social Security administrative Judge, by Social Security Administrative design.

On or about November 2015 I was notified that I was to receive a payment of $8,181.00 on or about the first day of December 1, 2015.

On about December 1, 2015 my checking account received a direct payment from the Social Security Administration in the amount of $ 8,181.00.

On or about January 2016 I received a "**Form SSA-1099-Social Security Benefit Statement**" box #5 indicates my earnings as "**Net Benefits for 2015 18,319.80,**" this same form never excided $10,000 over the years I have been on Social Security disability.

This from Social Security Administration was meant to deliberately influence me to believe that Social Security Administration was in the process of correcting a past mistake to my Social Security account; as a citizen tax payer client of the Social Security Administration of my disability retirement account, this form did do the purpose for which the 2016 **form 1099** form was meant for when sent to me and I did file my tax forms based on the information supplied to me by Social Security Administration whereas, the $8181.00 were claimed by me as earnings as requested by Social Security Administration tax form 2016 tax forms, supplied to me, by Social Security Administration. The $8181.00 was spent as my own earnings due to the information supplied to me by Social Security Administration.

On or about March 2, 2016 five months after the first mistake was made by Social Security Administration was discovered

I was informed by Social Security Administration you Social Administration created a now **claim # 543-62-xxxx-HA**, and asked me to select a option to justify Social Security past accounting mistakes to my account, so as to make me the blame for Social Security Administration accounting mistakes,..Found 5 months after the$ 8181.00 had already been spent.

In or about September of 2016 I received a letter from Social Security Administration Agent A. Guardiola asking for me to bring in to the Temple, Texas Social Security Office at 511 N Main Street, Temple, Texas field office any, and all information related to case **"#543-62-xxxx-HA** which I would like for her review to see if this case would proceed, or if it case **#543-62-xxxx-HA** would proceed to a Social Security **waiver process.**

Whereas, Social Security Administration Agent A. Guardiola intent not to proceed with my request to forgive the duet based on the fact that I was not aware that Social Security Administration had made a accounting error in my favor, nor am I one to count a gifted horse's teeth. So it is that I did spend the money under the believe that the money was my own, as I was led to believe by the Social Security Administration with no Mel-intent to do deliberate wrong, on my part.

Whereas, to disrupt my Government Social Security benefit services now is to deny me my right to life consistent to my chronic medical status, I will or could die because of a Social Security over payment to me, it would certainly be a horrible human waste, to some I would think.

The question to be defined by Social Security Administration is too fine wrong doing in what I have done wrong to deserve a life or death punishment from Social Security Administrative in "Claim # 543-62-xxxx HA.

## RE: Social Security Administration mistaken Claim # 543-62-xxxx HA

Thank-you for your letter dating March 22, 2016: as I understand your position today based on this letter you sent me, where you advise me that the Social Security Administration made a mistake, admitting to administrative mistakes on your part in regards to you depositing 8,181.00 in my personal account on December 1, 2015 "thank-you".

However, you are now responding to the last mistake the Social Security Administration made in regards to your Social Security Administration claim # 543-62-xxxx-HA; Whereas, on your letter of March 2, 2016, five months after your first Administrative mistake, you write to admit to your mistakes.

In referencing your Administrative mistakes, I must say "I acted with the funds in question in accordance with the ownership information supplied to me by you the Social Security Administration, whereas, some things are just meant to be"

### Social Security Administrative Mistake # 1:

In November 2015, I received a letter from Social Security Administration, Western Program advising me "we corrected and raised the benefit amount beginning April 2002 to correct your benefit amount." You explained, "The next check you receive will be for $8,181.00."

### Social Security Administrative Mistake # 2

On December the 1st 2015 the Social Administration, deposited 8,181.00 to my personal account here in Killeen, Central Texas. Although, I did feel as though someone had made a mistake on your end I was raised never to look a gifted horse in the mouth; the $8,181.00 stayed in my checking account until after the 15th day of December 2015; I moved the funds to my savings account, fearing that during the holidays I could over spend and effect the $8,181 balance amount, I moved the funds to my savings account to protect the funds during the Holidays, from me.

## Social Security Administrative Mistake # 3

On January 2015 in or about the 5th day I receive a "Social Security Benefit Statement, Form SSA-1099-SM" explaining to me that the $8,181.00 is to be filed as earnings, certainly clarifying the fact that the money was my own to use as I wish, and I did just that."

## Social Security Administrative Mistake # 4

On March 2, 2016 five months after the first mistake you discover your mistake which you now call, claim # 543-62-xxxx-HA, you ask me to select a option to justify your mistakes. To this I can only say I am grateful, thank-you from my wife and I, and thank-you from the local Killeen, Texas venders in my community; I spent the money as my own with your encouragement and blessings in this regard to do so.

## Social Security Administrative Mistake #5

Now stands a life threatening 5th Administrative mistake on your part, you must first prove wrong doing on my part, prior to creating and opening a case against me which you have done in Claim# 543-62-xxxx HA; prior to denying me my right to life. So it is that I must dispute  Claim# 543-62-xxxxHA  with the Office of Social Security Administration. And respectfully Request that, Social Security Administration Wave the Over- payment created by you, Social Security Administration, for me to deal with today.

Whereas, I did receive the $8,181.00, I did spent the money as my own as instructed by you, Social Security Administration, it was me acting on your instruction to consider the funs as my corrected earnings; whereas a Christmas Blessing has now become a Social Security Administrative mistake putting a US Government Social Security price on my life @ $8,181.00 my cost for your administrative mistakes.

Last I have enclosed Form SSA-632-BK Request for Waiver of Over-payment Recovery (08-2014) ef (2014) for your consideration as requested by you, Social Security Administration, as my only hope;  I pray for a favorable response, if further information is required please advise me, @:Arturo Cortez/543-62-//11/15/2017 Killeen, Texas, USA/ 76541

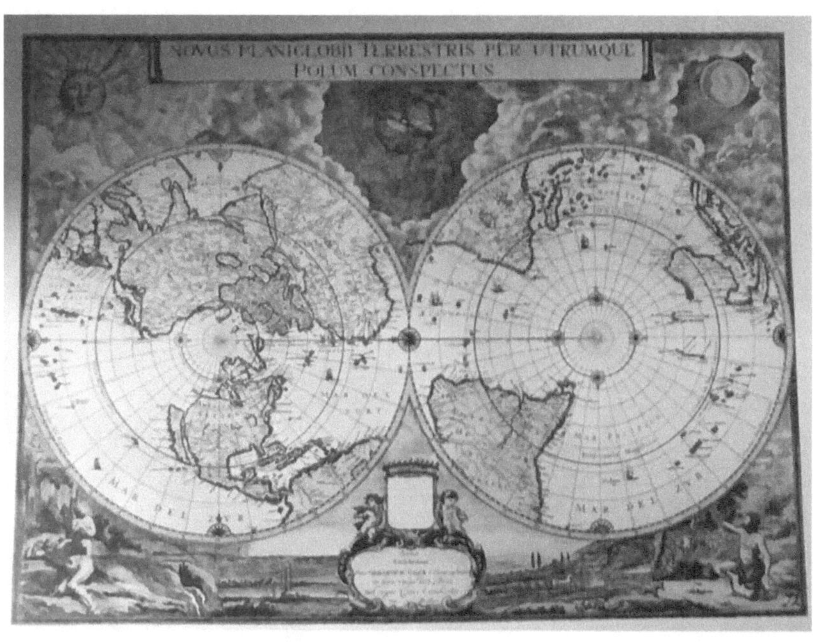

NOVUS PLANIGLOBII TERRESTRIS PER UTRUMQUE
POLUM CONSPECTUS
MAR DEL ZUR
MAR DEL ZUR

# *EL FIN de 2017*

## "Happy New Year,"

The End of the Arturo Cortez 2017 Political Resistance Journal for this year, and the start of "The Resistance/ La Resistencia 2018

NOVA TOTIVS TERRARVM SIVE NOVI ORBIS TABVLA, auct. C. Blaeu
BLAEU WALL MAP

La Casa de Cortez, Publications"

73

# AMERICAN DEMOCRACY REDEFINED

"La Resistencia/Resistance a lo Pendejo,"

By Arturo Cortez

2018

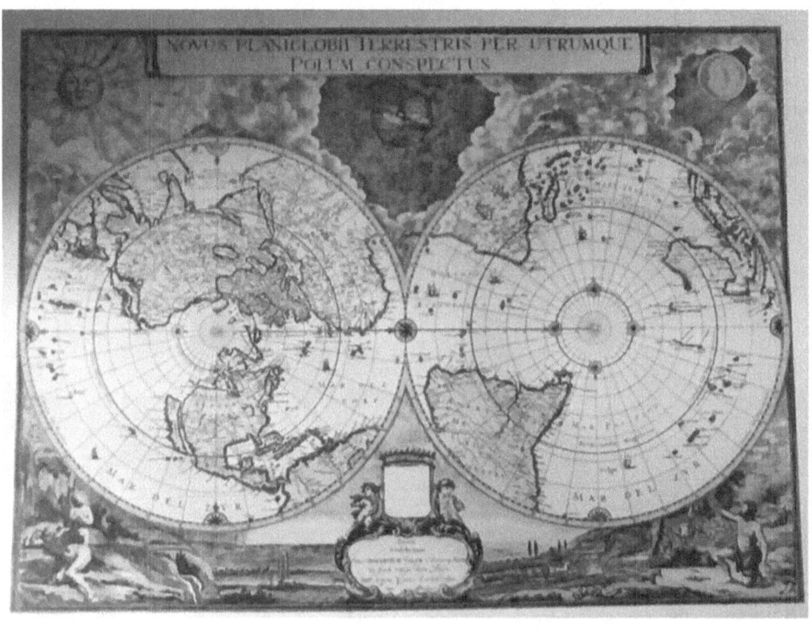

NOVUS PLANIGLOBII TERRESTRIS PER UTRUMQUE
POLUM CONSPECTUS
MAR DEL ZUR
MAR DEL ZUR

# The Resistance 2018

AMERICA SEPTENTRIONALIS
MAR DEL NORT
MAR DEL ZUR
OCEANUS ATLANTICUS
OCEANUS PERUVIANUS
MARE PACIFICUM
CIRCULUS AEQUINOCTIALIS
TERRA AUSTRALIS INCOGNITA
AMERICAE NOVA TABULA

# CHAPTER 9

**January, 2018**
**January Campaigning for Killeen,**
**Texas City Mayor,**
**February"**
**March"**
**April"**
**May;"**

Thank-you for your vote Killeen, I do feel good about the time I spent running for Killeen City Mayor, where as I did give my village/ City of Killeen community the opportunity to vote for someone like me, and some 230 Killeen voters did vote for me, whereas, I did feel I got a good deal per City of Killeen vote, whereas I spend $230.00 to let the city and citizens, of Killeen, Texas know I was willing and able to serve as the Killeen City Mayor for Change and quality of life. I do continue my prays for the City of Killeen and the Cities "Have Not," by government design.

# CHAPTER 10

**June 2018**

*Social Security Administration*

*La Resistencia requires clarification/ on which side of the Rio Grande will the wall stand on otherwise we stand with La Republica de Texas for humane Comprehensive Immigration Reform, DACA as a remedy to legal problems created by poor U.S. Migrant laws of today, we as American diversified Texanos of today all have a 500 year old history to the land as a Republica Texana, Norte Americana, to do nothing about what is happening to our children in own home-land as sweet water immigrants of this new world land is not a option. We as a Hispanic Texano nation must stand for what is right for human dignity whether ones Kin is from the English Colonies, or Tamaulipas, Mexico as humans of one Hispanic American diversified race. Build your wall and la Resistencia will build its wall based on the Southern United States borders of 01/22/1811 where it belongs based on Christian Texano nation virtue. "Que Viva la Resistencia con Respecto a lo Pendejo." ArturoCortez/76541/06/19/2018*

"Happy Fathers Day"

Social security once meant peaceful, tranquil transfer with dignity and social security from a worker provider's life, to a retired life with dignity and respect. Social Security Administration today however does have the Admistrative right to terminate life by using/creating a under-payment in order to establish a over-payment, to any account.

Last year I paid social security administration over $7,300.00 in over-payments created by Social Security Administration on my account.

This year I am told I have to pay upwards of $2,300.00 by the first of the month or lose my retirement social security benefits until the Social Security over-payment is paid back. I do not have a lawyer but i will fight Social Security Administration with what I know to be true, understanding that everything that has happened, did truly happen for a reason.

I would like to wish a "Happy Fathers Day" to all my friends, and families, and I ask that fathers, mothers, and children get out and do something nice for someone else.

Have a Wonderful Day and please read and share this story with someone you love, in your life, Arturo Cortez/76541/06/16/2018 https://www.gofundme.com/social-security-admin-and-you.

### On this the 15<sup>th</sup> day of June 2018,

Notice of formal request to a fair Social Security Administration, "Administrative Hearing" on case number 543-62-9272/ 543-62-9272-A:

Social Security Case # 543-62-9272-HA

Argument/Evidence In reference to case 543-62-9272/ 543-62-9272-A:

If you wish to donate to help me pay back this duet created for me by Social Security Administration in the form of a Social Security over-payment please follow this link https://www. gofundme.com/social-security-admin-and-you

Social Security Administration case # 543-62-9272 / 543-62 / 9272-HA

Social Security and You, Today,

If you pay for your earned retirement survival social security out of your paycheck as I did and/or you are receiving Social

Security Administration benefits to survive, you have to read this non-fiction/true story on what happened to me without my knowledge or consent; if after you read my story you feel that this same thing has happened to you or could happen to you or yours, then I ask that you donate to this worthy cause and share this story with those you care about the most in your life.

Today I ask that you read this story because it was written with you in mind.

My wife and I are forced to ask for survival donations to help us pay the bills for the next few months because Social Security Administration made a accounting error on my social security account.

Whereas the only difference between you and me is our Social Security Administration ID could be your number which could come up next and I would be honored to stand by you.

If you have paid or do pay for Social Security Administration Retirement life support services for when you retire, or if you are presently receiving your earned Social Security survival monthly benefits, you are in fact dependent on your Social Security benefits for your retirement plans you are now a possible victim of a Social Security Administration's "S.S. Death Penal Administrative Process" when you receive a –HA attached to your Social Security Administration ID number placed their at will by Social Security Administration agents/caseworkers.

Meaning of course that Social Security has made a Social Security accounting error, and the time has come for you to pay for the Social Security Administrative accounting errors under or over payments created at will by Social Security Administration with their inability to calculate or record accurately our earned monthly benefit payments with today's technical abilities to calculate

I am humbled by the lessens in life I must endure by having to ask for your donations, whereas last week my wife and I were actively looking for a house to buy here in Central Texas; and tomorrow I will be looking for housing assistance to pay the rent, making my story as much about you as it is about me with regards to personal social security and the Social Security Administration.

This is my true story to the extent of my knowledge about Social Security Administration as my earned retirement plan, and me Arturo Cortez the benefactor of my Social Security account in retrospect of my working life Arturo Cortez/76541/06/12/2018:

## REQUEST FOR REVIEW OF DECISION/ORDER

By: Claimant Name Arturo Cortez

Claimant Social Security Administration ID Number: 543-62-9272 and/or 543-62-xxxx-A

TO:  Appeals Council, Office of Disability Adjudication and Review

5107 Leesburg Pike,

Falls Church, VA

Claimant's Argument and Dispute to the rulings and findings based on false and incorrect Social Security accounting information in his  May 1st 2018 "Unfavorable Decision in my motion to Dismiss over-payments created by Social Security Administration.

In my 2017 appeal to "Waive the Over-Payment" created by Social Security Administration at will on my Social Security Administration account you will find in this document that my request to Waive the Over-Payment was ruled on by the Honorable, Administrative Texas Law Judge James W. Lessis, the Honorable Texas Judge found that "I knew or should have known that Social Security had made a accounting error in the Social Security calculations of my fourteen year underpayment by Social Security Aduministration."

The Honorable Texas Judge implies in his finds that my Texas cultural believe that I never look a gifted horse in the mouth" is wrong and is the reason for his unfavorable decision.

So it is that the Texas Judge ruled in favor of all Americans who in real life have no say so in calculating how much a American worker is to receive monthly based on amount of money contributed into each account.

Nine months after I had paid back $7,341 on May 1st 2018, the Honorable Texas Administrative Law Judge, found my appeal to "Waive the Over-Payment" "Unfavorable." This matter now brings me to this honorable safety net "Appeals Council" process for those looking for honorable moral legal Justice in your review of this case before you.

Thank-you, all for your valuable time in looking into this important matter regarding Social Security Administration using under and over payments created by Social Security Administration as death penal like Social Security Administration procedural prodical/instrument to exercise administrative God like powers of life and/or death over Americans on Social Security today, and yet to come.

## "Please take the time to Contribute"

On May 28, 2018, I received a letter from Social Security Administration advising me that they had made yet another over-payment based on the benefit monthly awards dated 2014-2018 in the amount of $ 2,277.00, I must deal with the Social Security accounting error Claim Number 543-62-xxxx HA.

This claim, on my Social Security ID # claims that the calculations used to deny me my Social Security Benefits in 2017 were in fact false and incorrect when presented to the Honorable Texas Administrative Law, Judge James W. Lessis.

I there for will be asking Social Security Administration for due process, in a "Administrative Hearing" as part of this request I respectfully ask that Social Security Administration not change, my benefits which are now in place and approved by the Honorable Administrative Law Judge James, W. Lessis.

Whereas, in retrospect Social Security Administration in their case 543-62-2018HA now claims that they paid themselves wrong amounts with my money which I did not receive, and now they will take my earned and poorly managed retirement survival Social Security benefits once again, during the hottest climate of the year here in the Heart of Texas, once again.

Social Security Administration lack of humane perception qualifies Social Security Administration as a government Death Panel Team, approach to administratively deny me my right to a Administrative Hearing prior to Social Security denying me my right to life based on Social Security caseworker's accounting errors on my Social Security account created for me by Social Security Administration some fourteen years ago, which has now created yet another over-payment, all based on Social Security intellectual professional Social Security accounting errors at the expense of my life.

On January 4th 2017 you wrote to Arturo Cortez "Beginning December 2016, the full monthly Social Security Benefit before any deductions is $ 918.10." After which you denied me my monthly earned Social Security Benefits for nine months without the right to a social security administrative hearing prior to your deadly, cruel and inhumane punishment during the hottest months of 2017 in Texas desert climate.

When I was forced to paid for your $7,341.00 over-payment between December 2016 and September 2017.

However, this appeal to overturn the "Unfavorable Decision, "IN THE CASE OF Dispute OF Waiver of Over-payment stands and remains in review at a Appeals Council Office of Disability Adjudication and Review, 5107 Leesburg Pike, Falls Church, VA. 22041-3255.

Social Security Administrative Texas Law Judge James W. Lessis made his honorable decision based on the now false accounting information as claimed in the May 28th letter by Social Security Administration case number 543-62-xxxxHA/05/28/2018 whereas, you offer me 30 days to pay Social Security Administration $2,277.00 or you will deny me my monthly earned Social Security retirement survival monthly benefit for a second time in less than a year; once again based on Social Security Administration engineered over-payments whereas, your option to your social security accounting error, again denies me my right as a American to a fair Administrative Hearing in your 30 day repayment plan, Social Security Administration has no right to assume that I will lay down and die in the Texas desert heat on command by Social Security Administration.

I formally request a Social Security Administrative Hearing for your complaint "543-62-xxxxHA" on my Social Security account "543-62-xxx and/or 543-62-xxxx-A" dated 05/28/2018; I further ask that you do not disrupt my monthly earned survival  benefits prior to a Administrative Law Judge making a ruling on your inhumane Social Security Administration Claim "543-62-xxxxHA".

I respectfully ask that you honor the January 4th 2017 award letter which you claimed then was correct, and now you claim you and your review were not correct both errors were made to my Social Security account created with Social Security false accounting information at chronic deadly expense to my life.

I respectfully want to advice Social Security Administration that I resent the fact that Social Security Administration considers me Arturo Cortez {human} Social Security number 543-62-xxxx-A your Social Security "Whipping Boy" and/or Social Security "Toilet Paper" with regards to your in inability to count or calculate my Social Security benefits.

I further ask that the Honorable Texas Law Judge James W. Lessis withdraw his "Unfavorable Decision" made on May 1, 2018 with what we now know was false Social Security Administration accounting information at my expense.

I further offer into evidence this information in support of my claim that Social Security is unable to calculate my accurate monthly benefit payments so long as Social Security accounting errors in under-payments and/or over-payments so long as Social Security can blame me the victim at my deadly expense for Administrative Social Security accounting errors.

It is wrong that you require me to pay for a over-payment or anyone else for accounting errors created by Social Security Administration without the knowledge or approval of their client victim.

Your over-payments to my account are all based on Social Security Administration incompetent calculations of my monthly survival benefit payments, for now it is true that you now claim that you have never been right in the calculations of my Social Security Administration management of my monthly managed benefit calculations.

In your letter of May 28th 2018 you say that you Social Security made yet another over-payment for me, and that the time has come to pay for it.

I say "no," I did not create this new Social Security over-payment nor did I create your 2003 under-payment which Social Security

Administration which Security Administration used to deny me my earned survival Social Security Benefits for nine months.

I respectfully ask that you do not change my benefit award without proper and legal Social Security Administrative Judicial Hearing. I do dispute and challenge your new findings of your over-payment in case#543-62-xxxxHA.

I also challenge the legal integrity of the unfavorable decision rendered by the Texas Judge, James W. Lessis on May 1, 2018 which is now technically based on false accounting and false information now welcomed by the Waco Texas Judge James W. Lessis.

The Texas Administrative Social Security Law Judge, James W. Lessis was asked to judge my Dispute of Wavier of Over-payment with what we now know was false and incorrect accounting Social Security information with respect to the new charges against Arturo Cortez/543-62-xxxx in 543-62-xxxx A

Your May 28th 2018 letter to me will now be added as evidence to review and overturn the May 1st 2018 "Unfavorable Decision" by the Texas Administrative Social Security Law Judge, James W. Lessis at a Honorable Appeals Council, Office of Disability Adjudication and Review, of the S.S.A./ 5107 Leesburg Pike, Falls Church, Va.  22041-3255

My name is Arturo Cortez and I am human now a retired American Construction Worker with 3 cardio stents implants in my heart and a chronic heart condition, thyroid, and type 2 diabetes medical conditions. My diagnosis is chronic health heart condition, which requires that I take my prescribed medications for the rest of my life daily and avoid stressful conditions and encounters, or die. This health information is nothing new to Social Security Administration and is also the reason the Waco

Social Security Administrative Office has decided now is the time for me to die.

Because I am a Christian man of the only God Jehovah, I know that we all must carry our own cross which we build for ourselves throughout our own individual lives. It is wrong for Social Security Administration to think I should carry the cross for Social Security Administration when Social Security Administration has no human soul as it is not of a human moral virtue with regards to Arturo Cortez/543-62-xxxx/543-62-xxxx-A.

I Arturo Cortez am in Dispute with Social Security Claim # 542-62-xxxxHA, with your letter dated May 28th 2018 and all its deadly Terms and Conditions to my person contained within this Social Security Administration letter to me. Your terms and conditions could result in my death based on my chronic medical condition. Social Security Administration has no right to disrupt my life, my nutrition my medical services delivery systems by denying me my right to life support earned Social Security services at will.

To deny me my human right to life in the way this letter dictates does give Social Security Administration God like authority to terminate human life at will based on Social Security Administration accounting errors created for the Old, the Sick, and the Disabled based on Social Security Administration over-payments or under-payments accounting errors by Social Security accounting errors.

Evidence in Arturo Cortez Social Security # 543-62-xxxx will show that the $7,341.00 over-payment was paid back to Social Security prior to my obviously human right to life Social Security Administrative Hearing in which I was denied my earned Health and welfare benefits for nine months prior to due process.

However, now true that this case has decided by the Honorable Administrative Law Judge James W. Lessis who was supplied false and miss leading accounting Social Security information. You will find that my request to "Waive the Over-payment unfavorable decision" was decided with false information. Whereas, Social Security now claims that the accounting errors include the benefit amounts and dates in 543-62-xxxxHA which clearly states that Social Security paid itself with their own false benefit payment information created by Social Security Administration and reviewed and approved by the now dishonorable Texas Admistrative Judge James W. Lessis these accounting errors were all done without my help, knowledge or influence.

The Social Security Administration, Western Program Service Center, PO Box 2000, Richman California, 94802-1791 claim # 543-62-xxxxHA.

Now claims that the corrective measures which Social Security took to deny me my $7,341.00 in benefits in 2017 was all based on false accounting information by Social Security Administration.

## The Appeals Council, Office of Disability Adjudication and Review

5107 Leesburg Pike
Falls Church, VA 22041-3255
The over-payments have nothing to do with me at all, the calculations for payments are done by Social Security Administration, if a Social Security worker who gets paid to calculate my monthly benefit payment, makes a mistake he or she should pay for their mistake with their own retirement Social Security Administration fund, rather than getting paid for making routine over-payments at the expanse of the American sick, elderly, retired and disabled.

The Social Security Administrative Law Judge James W. Lessis ruling on this case does put a Honorable Administrative Law judge in a legally byes position whereas, the Judge actually ruled on a over-payment reimbursement of my money which I was forced to pay prior to due legal process in a Administrative Hearing as I had requested.

I now ask the Social Security Administration, Administrative Law Judge to change his Unfavorable to a favorable ruling based on my dispute to Waive the Over-payment based on the information supplied by Social Security Administration on their letter with their letter head of May 28, 2018 attempting to explain to me their Social Security over-payment between December 2014 and April 2018. Whereas my benefit over-payment had all ready been denied from me illegally, based on false accounting information and no hearing prior to denying me my earned benefits for 9 months between December 2016 and September 2017.

The Administrative law Judge and I were played with false information by the Social Security Administration into rendering it's Unfavorable Decision towards my dispute to waive the over-payment in his letter of May 1st 2018.

I did make a timely request for a Social Security Administrative Hearing and I did receive the 9 months denial of my total benefits in order to pay back the $ $7,377.00 over-payment created by Social Security Administration without my American right to a legal Administrative Hearing prior to the death wish cancellation of my earned monthly Social Security Administration benefits.

Whereas, this new claim to my Social Security account has now implicated the Honorable Texas Administrative Law Judge, James W. Lessis, in that the honorable Judge was supplied with Social Security incorrect accounting information in order to deny me my appeal to Waiver of Over-payments of my benefits; this new accusation of wrong doing by Social Security came to my attention 28 days after the "Notice of Unfavorable Decision" by the Honorable Administrative Texas Judge James W. Lessis was received by me and has been used to appeal the honorable Administrative law Judge's decision at Appeals Council.

As the chronically ill client of Social Security Administration I have no choice but to challenge this 3rd accounting error in the Social Security Administration handling/management of my Social Security retirement funds. With this third error Social Security Administration has now documented accounting errors in 15 of the 15 years I have been on Social Security.

Accounting errors should never be the problem of the client, in this day in time Social Security Administration is well aware as to who has caused the accounting errors at will to my Social Security account.

This knowledge implicates Social Security Administration as a knowledgeable source of the engineered under or over payments to my monthly Social Security benefit payments.

Incompetent actions by Social Security workers are the responsibility of Social Security Administration for the purpose of corrective measures, and not the responsibility of the elderly, sick, and disabled who trust that Social Security Administration is able and capable of counting and calculating their client's monthly benefit payment and take responsibility for the mess they create for those of us who depend on our Social Security Administration retirement plans as our only source of income due to our eared humanly retirement/ disabled medical conditions in our later years.

Attempting to make common since of Social Security Administration of today offers a challenge to the purpose of social security moral understanding of human dignity applied to those in need of their earned social security service. I now know and view this deadly inhumane Social Security Administration process that follows after Social Security Administration accounting errors are caused by Social Security Administration nothing less than "Social Security Death Penal" harassment games played on us Americans with our own funds with regards to Social Security Retirement, and/or Disability as clients of Social Security Administration.

So it is that as a Author, Writer of non-fiction I must do my part for those of us who do not have the ability or capabilities to let others know how they feel about how Social Security is effecting their everyday lives in this true story.

I must now follow this path to its truthful end. And I must trust that this honorable Council in my attempt to find moral human dignity with in Social Security Administration for the sake of all Americans on social Security not so much for my sake as my future is now well defined by my Lord and God.

So it is that what I do in Sharing my story is for the sake of all the hundreds if not thousands of other American citizens who have paid for their Social Security retirement throughout their lives, with their own work and now find themselves the victims of Social Security over-payment or underpayment Death Panel scenario as part of Social Security infrastructure which today lacks moral human virtue and human first integrity and understandings of human dignity within Social Security Administration of today.

"Oh," how great art thou my God Jehovah, that you charge me Lord with the ability to write, "truth to Power" with respect to government abuse of American human dignity Lord, Blessed am I Lord to carry your cross Lord in this regard. Arturo Cortez/76541 /06/08/2018/7:04AMCT

### On this the 25th day of June 2018

El Partido Republicano Norte Americano, y Pendejismo en La Republica de Texas,

I as one of many Texano Norte Americano of today can only fine Texano national shame and cultural shock in the inhumane Texas Republican political delegations in Washington District of Columbia (D.C.) today.

"Blinded by the Truth"= "Lo Pendejismo at a personal level,"

All though you can go to your dictionary and look for the word Pendejo, chances are you will not fine its meaning for this word; this does not mean the meaning to the word does not exist. I know many of my friends and families prefer that I do not use this word in my writings. However it is my purpose in life to write my truth to powers within the Hispanic Texano American Republics within the Union of American States, today.

Today more than ever North American evil again has shown its evil form in American type Democracy within Texano American politics of today by way of American political dictatorship over our now disoriented diversified Hispanic Texano human Race of one God en "La Republica de Texas."

Prior to 1492 the word Pendejo did not exist, the native word Pendejo means," blinded by the truth" to the new world nations of the time.

Hispanic cultural influence on the people of the land within the new world did have codes of conduct among the elites of trade and commerce of that time, the native American then viewed there immigrants as not capable of telling the truth and labeled the European salt water immigrant to their lands as "Pendejos" in order to establish trade with the new world commercial populations of that time.

The Government of the United States of North America has now violated the "The Treaty de Guadalupe Hidalgo" and is not capable of humanely managing the Texas Southern Inter-National Border with our international families and friends. Texas does have the right and the precedent to secede from its union with the United States of North America with respect to the human rights violations by The United States of North America towards Hispanic cultural human dignity.

The Union of American States is blinded by the truth and fails to recognize their inherited Hispanic American Texano cultural roots within Norte America. My God given Hispanic Texano human racial profile is as a small part of God's own diversified new world human race.

Today we the American Texano have made Biblical History as the nation who took the Hispanic children from their Hispanic parents, for being Hispanic seeking refuge and essailum, within the Hispanic "Republica de Texas."

The Texas Republican political Delegations to the unified states of North American political systems, has now established itself into a shameless conservative Texas fascist enforcers for the Electoral College Installed (E.C.I.) American President Donald Trump.

We all in one form or another do have our families on both sides of the Rio Grande if you are of true American Texano ideological national virtue regardless of ethnic profile. We the native diversified Texanos must stand as one humane Hispanic Texano nation regardless of how you pronounce "Texano", we are still la Republica de Texas defining our future as a independent North American Nation.

We the American Texano are now ethnic cleansing sweet water immigrants in our own world as our purpose of Texano American life.

The first Cortez European Immigrant to the new world in 1502 who helped to conquer Espanola, Cuba, and the Aztec Empire and established the first European Colony on the new world in "Vera Cruz, Mexico" in 1519 Hernando Cortez "El Adelantado" who also established the first European Kingdom in Nueva Espania del Mundo Nuevo, inland of the new world, must now be turning in his coffin.

It is we in the Texano American States of North America who are now denying our own children their human right to their Hispanic cultural worth within our human Fathers, Mothers, and Families, based on Texas Republican Party political virtues. All for a Electoral College Installed (E C I) President Donald Trump who better understands Russian political tactics then he does his own Presidential roll as President of the first and most powerful nation in today's world/American Democracy.

In proper use of the word "Pendejo" you could say that the ECI President Donald Trump has made the Grand Old Party the Republican political party into his personal Tejano Pendejos for the sake of evil.

(Que Siga La Resistencia a lo Pendejo de la Republica de Texas) ArturoCortez/76541/06/24/2018

Well now this is where you make an effort to find your own space in la Resistencia by creating your own note book and reading your notes, and plan your own future in these blank pages, thank-you for reading my writings/Arturo Cortez/76541/06/2017/9:14AM:

# CHAPTER 11

July 2018

**07/02/2018**

**"I** do not concede this City of Killeen, Texas Election, and I do call for the Killeen City Council to act to demand a Re-count in order to know who really won the Mayor's race."

This week will mark one month since the May 5th 2018 Killeen City Election for Mayor and three City Council seats. I really do not want to seem like the political whiner in this political race but I feel though the election results were engineered by City election officials.

Whereas, 9,997 Killeen City Voters voted for the City of Killeen City Council, 4,506 Killeen City voters, voted for the Killeen City Mayor Mayor's race, when in fact all the Candidates for both Mayors races and the City Council races were on the same Voters Ballot; meaning that the sum number of voters in both races should be the same in this case 9,997 which gives raise to the question what happened to 5,491, 51 % of Killeen City voters ballots unaccounted if in fact 9,997 ballets were accounted for.

After almost one month has passed and no community domestic non-profits has stood up to question the results for the Killeen City voters I find shameful Representation of their membership by all domestic Killeen none-profit organizations "Local LULAC's, Local NAACP's, as well as Black and or White Democrats and Republican Parties who call themselves as the political leaders of the City of Killeen Administration, and the now City of Killeen Elected Officials, as well as The Killeen Daily Herald.

I call on the City of Killeen, City Council today to demand a recount of the votes cast for the Mayor's office to the point that the Mayor's political race end results should coincide with the same number of Ballots cast for both elections on the same ballot.

As the non-fiction writer of this sad democratic story of acceptable political accounting errors in order to deceive Killeen City voters I now realize it does not matter who wins or even who loses, what really matters is what we lose by playing traditional mid-19th century political carpet beggar games here today in Central Texas.

And so I ask the now Killeen City Mayor, Jose Seggara or a Killeen City Councilperson to make a Motion to recount the election Ballots again, whereas if there is nothing to hide there is nothing to lose, and election integrity and community respect, to our grass root community trust to gain.

**Arturo Cortez/76541/07/02/2018**

## The City of Killeen as a Military Democracy

By Arturo Cortez,

Certainly, when ***5,491 of 9,997*** Votes go missing in a Texas democratic election and no one in the community seems to care, blinded by the truth is only one scenario in a City of Killeen, Texas governess of the willing to be lead by military control, instead of our chartered Texas, American democracy grass root political processes.

Militarized local governess does have its own chartered prodical and it starts with the Killeen City Council who must implement Military Dictatorships over the City of Killeen citizens of the willing.

In my block walks as a candidate in Killeen Texas I learn that all citizens of Killeen feel we need Changes and Reform to city governess. My hold campaign was based on Change and Reform from what seems democracy under military siege here in Killeen Texas.

I ask the Citizen of Killeen to ask for a recount of the May 5th 2018 Mayors Election, I have not yet lost until the # of votes cast in the Mayors Election match/reflects the number of votes cast in the City Council Election for the sake of American democracy. Please do not get me wrong, as a candidate I would not mind being your Mayor, I would bring change and reforms to the city; however my interest is in the telling of the story itself as a writer and Story Teller, I feel blessed with the part I am playing in helping to define Killeen Texas politics as a model for domestic politics, a excemple to the rest of La Republica de Texas.

I do feel an obligation to those who voted for me, as well as to all those who work and do such a good job for the City of Killeen, thank you folks for what you do for all of us. I must remind the military and the Killeen City Council that American democracy is a foundational, Constitutional right, as well as our American cultural virtue, as I will continue to publish my truth to the powers that are in my stories until I am convinced I have lost this year's May 5, 2018 election.

I view this Killeen May 5th election as a shameful arrogant disregard for the American democratic socialist process in Killeen Texas's electoral process, whereas, once published my stories are guaranteed viral global circulation for the rest of our lives.

So it is that I Arturo Cortez do respectfully ask the Killeen City Council to order a Recount of the May 5th City Election Ballots. As there is reason to believe accounting errors have accrued by way of election engineering, at the City of Killeen, level./Arturo Cortez/76541/07/08/2018

## Arturo Cortez/76541/07/12/2018

Neil Mercer, I wanted you to know where I am at today as the Resistance, next I want to show you where I am at with the first book in El Centrolista "Feeding The Beast," which I expect to release as a e-book fairly soon, I am now working on formatting El Centrolista the 2nd book without the 2012-2015 numbers on the title.

Mr. Mercer to date I have written 6 books of 7 and no one has paid me to do it, your firm is being offered the opportunity to market my writings for me if you feel your company can profit from my ability to write and your ability to market this product.

If your company and/or you are interested in developing a marketing relationship I have attached the first book to this e-mail for your critical review this book will be released as e-book first testing both my ability write and your ability to market my writings.

Sells and Royalist from "Feeding the Beast" will be used to build and promote the next book

"EL Centrolista."

I do think you are right that these books should be marketed as memories in the life of a old American Patriot/ArturoCortez;

As you will see in looking at my Manuscript "Feeding the Beast," i can't help but think that publishing has come a long way in building a book, least to the point of where e-book is concerned.

I do thing that Author Centric as a publishing business must evolve with the times of marketing and electronic publishing of this time. This sir is why I have submitted my intellectual properties to you for your review, if after you reading my work you feel that there is a need for improvement please let me know, I am actually considering replacing the images with my political images of that time in 2012.

Mr. Neil Mercer thank you for reading my writings it is always nice to hear from you sir, you have a wonderful day. Arturo Cortez/76541/07/12/2018

## Arturo Cortez/76541/07/21/2018

We as the human element of Donald Trump's governess where as "money talks and bull shit walks" must now find refuge within American Democracy from a Donald Trump fascist democratic capitalist political perspective on American Democracy.

Whether Republican, Democrat, Liberal or Conservative POTUS has now been given the time to learn and lead our nation and now, I challenge our own American Inelegance to leek Trumps in-come tax in order that we the American people can find out were Donald Trump's bread comes from, and who he really works for?

Donald Trump has no idea who he is as our American President and the honey moon presidential privileges are now over, voters have given Donald Trump the time to adept to his governmental responsibilities we as a people of intellectual legal moral American human virtue have now given "Lo Pendejo" in POTUS/45 the opportunity to lead and as of today Donald Trump's enemies are we the people, the American Free Press, the United Nations, as well as all our allied European nations, our trading partners in Asia, and as well as South and North America in this arrogant believe that the hold world wants to be like him.

No one in this country can dispute that Donald Trump has destabilized our American Democracy as well as our standing in the world. Donald Trump has established himself as a liar whose word cannot be trusted to the civilized nations of our world today.

The time is now when American Democracy through partisan political ideologies must stand as one to defend ourselves by organizing our resistance against "Donald Trump's United States Governess, " we will target and deny Donald Trump populous media, leadership, legislation, and grass-root support at a Municipal, State, and National levels of American Democratic governess in our none-violent tactics.

Our purpose must favor our own human dignity as one diversified American people who are now forced to say "No" by actively resisting American government in our local communities.

Our native brother American Nations of North America must provide refuge and protection to our sweet water immigrants of the new world of today. ArturoCortez/76541/07/21/2018

## 07/29/2018

China can no longer effort to by American and they don't have to the Mid-West Texano Ranchers and farmers who are the back bone of the Make America Grate Again, Movement will now realize that America was already Grate by losing their farms and ranches as China is now signing long term contracts with other nations for pork, beef, grain, corn, plains, trains, and auto mobiles,

## 07/30/2018

### By Arturo Cortez

I would like to thank all our neighbors and friends who supported and voted for Change and Reform & Me it is a honor for me to lead a political campaign for change to Killeen good old boy dictatorships over the people and the City of Killeen, Thank-you, "God Bless".

**Remember to:**

"you want to look at your water meter out on the street, if the area is still green after all this heat you are paying for the water lost," call the proper City Authorities to come and fix it or pay the next bill.

Conserve on energy by changing your air filter on the Furness of the home if you are a true conservative,

Conserve this summer by hanging your clothes out to dry, a honorable Texano will always hangs there under garments on the inside of the cloth lines, in order to minimize exposure.

# Chapter 12

August 2018

**08/14/2018**

I Advised B.O. that I would be organizing in Central Texas a organizing committee to start organizing for the 2012 re-election campaign committee in November of 2011.

I stepped down on the Central Texas Organizing Committee and committed myself instead to welcoming Battleground Texas, to Texas in 2012. If anything, Battleground Texas has learned nothing from me.

In grass-root community leadership there are leaders of the Movement "La Resistencia" and Leaders of the corporate political Leadership "Political Parties and corporate for profit and/or for none-profits".

How we the leadership coordinate our political efforts, right now must be felt at a grass-root level in Texas prior to the November 2018 election.

Any community organizer willing to be my fellow organizer is welcome to do so, I go back to the 1970's in community organizing and I have organized, for the Chicano Movement: The Brown Berates 1971, El Centro Cultural de Condado de Washington, Oregon 1972, La Raza Unida Party 1972, International Union of United Farm-Worker 1973, El Colegio Cesar Chavez 1973-1981, all of these organizations today claim I am their founder at the birth of America's cultural wars of the 70's.

I hope to be able to continue to teach and write of my explodes in the 70's, 80's, 90's, and now the1920's and years yet to come.

I will offer my fellowship to Battleground Texas, for one hour at my home you are welcome to bring a person with you. I will be sharing my thoughts with you on Grass-Root Texas voters. The purpose of this leadership meeting will be to discuss and/or identify a Texas Battle which Battleground Texas can win for the voters of Texas this election year.

Or, you can simply follow my writings @ www.facebook,com/arturo.cortez.7641

# CHAPTER 13

September 2018

## ArturoCortez/76541/09/02/2018

Collin Sawyer, Thank-you for your interest in El Centrolista 2012-2015, this book holds four books with in its cover, I am looking for a publisher to invest in its own abilities to market these four books independently from "El Centrolista". In addition to this offer I do have my transcripts for two additional books 2016 and 2017, both in the ruff which have not yet formatted into book form, I am looking to partner-up with a publisher/marketer in order to release my writings as a series of books in the life and times of Arturo Cortez.

El Centrolista 2012-2015 has served its purpose as a introduction to my writings globally. However, Author House does make 90 % on the royalties to El Centrolista you may want to contact them for marketing possibilities with regards to that Title.

Again, I want to thank-you for your interest in my writings.

Arturo Cortez/76541/09/02/2018/8:52CTT

## ArturoCortez/76541/09/04/2018

Collin Sawyer, the purpose of the attachment is for your team's review of my 2012, one year's work. If after you read my book you feel you or your company can make money of my book, then I expect to receive a offer from you or your people.

I did write, format and published edited this document for publication I am certain that your company does have others much better qualified publish editors than me @these trades; but I know AuthorHouse published my work as presented in my El Centrolista 2012-2015 manuscript.

This first book is the reason you approached me with your ideas. Once my agreement is in place if it gets that far we will find out how many books your company can sell for me and/or you or yours.

I do have to say however that nothing is free in this world to you or me and neither are my books if you or your people wish to play publisher with me.

"No" I will not speak to you on the phone @ this time; i will correspond with you via e-mail for the purpose of archiving and documentation purposes. /Arturo Cortez/76541/04/2018

## ArturoCortez/76541/09/06/2018

Thank-you and your team Collin Sawyer, for reading my book, I do agree with you on the four points of interest in the book. I also feel that we can use the turmoil in national politics to our favor by renaming the title to the book from "Feeding The Beast" to something along the lines of "Once Upon a Time in American Democracy." "Please Advice."

Collin, what I have written, and what you can do with what I have created is the partnership between your company and me and my writings for as long as the promotional arm of your company can sell the book less we put time limitations by contact agreement to our final agreement between your company and me, as the Author.

I do understand how some who live in their own world as I do, can sometimes not understand; so it is "that this book was written to be by generational" with regards to American politics" as a organizing instrument for the 2018 election understanding how moral political integrity can influence a partisan election.

The Miami Day Collage affair would be out of the question for me less you can think of a way to get me there, house me and feed me and back home, you however are welcome to represent me and my writings at that event if you wish to do so, thank-you for what you do. Arturo Cortez/76541/09/06/2018

## By/ Arturo Cortez/76541/09/15/2018

Con Quarinio y Respecto,

Back in the day our new world native now sweet water immigrants who had to negotiate their lives through a unjust racially based political and judicial American governmental system did create a word for intentional biases, the native word "Pendejo" or as a party type group setting "Pendejismo"; Meaning of course a person blind to the truth and the facts of the truth for the sake of the group or party whereas the factual truth is factual truth regardless of  party like Republican Russian Cow Pie, or United States Democratic Horse Shit.

Although the word Pendejo is a symptom which is self induced for the most part meaning of course that a pendejo is a pendejo by individual choice not by group ideology, not to say of curse that Pendejismo does not contribute to a pendejos human virtue.

"Okay" Texas now you know in my world it is not about the fork-it tug historical Texas Republican Cow Pie history books or Democratic Horse Shit political ideology, this 2018 November Election will be about the Republican Pendejos and Pendejismo in Austin and in Washington today. "Y esto para q viva la gente como la gente en las Republicas Norte Americanas de Texas y no a lo pendejo." Arturo Cortez/76541/09/15/2018

## By Arturo Cortez/76541/09/23/2018,

I a child of God have been blessed with a mission to repair a broken concrete Angle Bird Bath on my front yard of my now home here in Texas.

This angle has been broken for many, many years by the time Miss, Millie and I bought our home in Killeen, Texas.

The repairs were done by me and the broken angle on my front yard was to stand upright once again in order to restore its neibor hood glory in our new Texano neiborhood.

The repairs to the Concrete Angle Bird bath did not only bring the Birds, but the presence of the Bird Bath standing once again brought back neibor hood memories to all my new neibor's who drive or walk by our now new home. My of them came to our front door to introduce the selves and share their historical stories of our now new Texano neiborhood home, even those now grown kids who broke the Angle came to confess their attempt to stile the angle for their own home when the home was no longer occupied and for sell.

Oh, my Lord Jehovah God, how Grate are thou, for your blessings on us/Arturo

## 09/24/2018

### La Casa de Cortez, Killeen, Texas

By ArturoCortez

Geico has violated my right to privacy, I clicked on a Geico link to change my billing address in your letter to me and Huges Net letter to me opened a correspondence window asking access to my personal Bank account.

Geico now qualifies as "SPAM" based on La Casa de Cortez, family policy and your own actions to allow Huges Net to miss represent our business to me.

You as a old valued partner in my everyday life have 24 hrs to explain the reason you think you should share access to me with Huges Net or not, after the 24 hours are up, you will no longer be

allowed to use my e-mail address to correspond with me, for now/
Arturo Cortez/76541/09/24/2018

## 09/26/2018

Sorry, Irene I do not pay for political signs unless I am running for office myself. Tell Beto he has my vote, Si se Puede, stands with Texas's Best Beto for the United States Senate I will see what i can do to raise some money for you guys.

You old friend are always welcomed @ La casa de Cortez/76541, Arturo Cortez /09/26/2018

# CHAPTER 14

October 2018

**10/07/2018**

Hillary you would revive & unite the Republican Party, Barney is the Man if he can't do it no one can.

Within the battles of those who have, and those who have not, we as an American people mush find the common center to who we are as one nation under God without political parties, or money.

Republican and/or Democrats, our American Democracy is now a Political Circus to the world. Russia has won the cold war and POTUS/45 is dictating Russian Terms for the KGB to the American people.

Come November we must all Vote for our Nation, "Long Live American Democracy as "The Resistance/."Arturo Cortez/76541/10/08/2018

The Resistance is our democratic right to change American government with our right to vote it was the founding fathers of our American democracy who established and guaranteed us all today the right to Resist Governmental Monarch Tierney by socialist democratic political process/American Democracy/TheResistance2018. Arturo Cortez/10/07/2018

**10/09/2018**

By Arturo Cortez

Americans get "Real" today is the last day to register to vote in Texas, voter registration is now behind us, now the time has come to educate and unite our vote for the 6th day of November 2018, "Election Day" when Americas will be counted and the choice will be made by the people of our nation.

This is when we the American people of today will remove and replace the now Republican Carpet beggars Bums out of American politics, and start with new American political candidates/True Leaders in order to Rock and Roll American Democracy whereas, all you people know to do is "Piss off American Democracy into the Wind" for the Russian GOP/KGB mission in Washington DC today.

"Q Siga o se aga La Resistencia." 10/09/2018

## 10/14/2018

La Casa de Cortez/76541 Stands Texas Proud with Beto O'Rourke for the United States Senate,

When November 6th 2018 comes around in about 20 days from now the Resistance can only ask those who vote in Texas to remember that The Republican Party in Texas has had control of Austin, Texas for the last 38 years.

The Republicans have already taxed everything they could in their time as political rulers over Texas, and still in Texas a waiter or waitress make $2.50 per hour, plus tips with corporate limits of-course simply because the Republican Party wants it that way; now the Republican Party offers tax relieve for the tax they have created and more worthless jobs in order to get your vote.

Whereas just the other day while having breakfast with a bunch of guys one person asked if it was true that Texas is asking people to wear a mussel type mask to measure the amount of air we breathe for paying tax on the air as well, whether true or not one does have to look back on 38 years of Republican political rule of Texas to measure the truth.

It is wrong for Texas to cater to Republican King, Donald Trump we are a American Democracy here in Texas as well and we do know how to do what is right for Texas, all we have to do is "Do the Right Thing" for Texas and our American families of the human type.

The Republican Party must be brought back in line with democratic reality here in Texas and across the nation to reflect average conservative Republican values, which the party has ignored and American History will never forget, the United States of America as a Nation is looking towards Texas for common sense guidance in national leadership in Beto O'Rourke who will represent La Republica de Texas and its citizens regardless of political party affiliation, La Casa De Cortez/76541 Stands Texas Proud with Beto O'Rourke for Texas at the United States Senate come November 6th Mid-Term Elections.

Whereas the Republican Party may not be able to change its ways, it is than the Republican Party who is not a party but a want to be conservative political ideology in virtue which must stand on its own merit as conservatives here in Texas and across our nation.

We must leave no doubt as to our message to the nation; whether Texas will stand for change come election day November 6th or not, we must make it clear to the nation that in Texas we vote for Texas first regardless of political party we are one Republica de Texas who declared its Independence from the first Spanish Kingdom on the new world "Nueva Espania en el Mundo Nuevo" in January 21, 1811. Arturo Cortez/76541/

## 10/14/2018

New Release from La Casa de Cortez, Publications,
Title "The Hacked 2016 United States General Election "
Sub-Title "En El Principio La Resistencia"

Now live and Available @ https://www.amazon.com/dp/1521511004

La Casa de Cortez Publications and the Author, Arturo Cortez respectfully submit to you the reader this text as our "Yes we Can" effort to give American Democracy a human moral perspective; the text in these writings are written and formatted in chronological Journal format.

La Casa de Cortez, Publications, Killeen Texas is the publisher of this Title a self publishing effort by its Author as the scribe to today's social political movements to change American Democracy to include human of man as the purpose of American civil governess.

This book represents my personal e-mail advice to some of most powerful people in American Democracy during the United States 2016 General Election.

On the 7th hour of the first day of 2017 Arturo Cortez published his writing as "La Resistencia/The Resistance" a work still in progress.

In this book you will read the political differences in leadership by a political party, -v- leadership by the Movement as such I would also like to thank all those Yes we Can Community Political Volunteers and their Community Leaders here at home and across our nation who stepped up to lead in the "National 2016 Si se Puede Candidates Support List for Human Dignity," A very Special Thanks to the Grass-Root Volunteers and Contributors who make American Democracy a true to our socialist democratic electoral process principles  of and for the American people as today's effort of purpose to change/dignify our elected government as our own humanly moral effort to dignify ourselves as the United States of America.

I do want to thank the entire progressive Si Se Puede none profit political organizations for your mission and commitment statements to dignify Humanity. In this I want to say that we did fight a good political fight in 2016 and we did "Win" by popular human vote; La Resistencia is the battle cry to dignify American Democracy we are the American nation of today and we will change American leadership by popular Democratic vote once again, regardless of political parties.

America you make me proud to be ArturoCortez/@/76541"Long live the Resistance"

## 10/16/2018

Beto & Teams it takes all Types to build a campaign, into a Movement, consider these writings a well deserved Political Contribution;

As a 65 year old Texano who has lived through 3 heart attacks I am gifted now with today and the truth, "don't waste your glory Amigo on Republican cow pie politics what we need is health care we will both be in our 70's next time this office comes up again for a vote, do the right thing for your family and yourself this election year or pay the consequences with your lives Amigos, you do have a choice now to Vote for Beto O'Rourke for the United States Senate or you may want to vote for no health care for those in need Ted Cruz you think about it and have a wonderful day, Arturo Cortez/76541/15/2018

Beto, I and many, many Texano Americans do know that Texas was once Mexico and La Republica de Texas is a independent nation under God's will, you Sir do have the Texano American right to keep eating your half baked Republican Cow Pie, because you still have your Texano American Civil Rights.

The Republican Cow Pie Candidate Ted Cruz is trying to deny Texano human rights of man-kind to my people from both sides of the Rio Grande and not from New York City, or Canada, Beto please dress the part on TV and remember the three CCC's = Cool, Calm and collected.

La Republica de Texas has your back "long live the Resistance in the soul of Texas/"Q Viva La Resistencia en la alma de Texas," /76541/10/16/2018

## 10/18/2018

"Vote for M.J. Hegar for Texas, Congressional District 31"

On November 6th I will vote for American Hero Mary Jennings Hegar for Texas Congressional District 31 Air Force Major, M.J. Hegar Regardless of Republican or Democrat M.J. has Heroically Honored oath to America and us as the Americans of today M. J. has earn her American right to lead her people in Central Texas into tomorrow, follow and support American values and morals @ https://www.mjfortexas.com/ Arturo Cortez/76541/

## 10/19/2018,

The Texas Republican GOP has now violated American intelligence and human dignity on behave of all the American people, as well as betrayed Democratic principles to the world we live in and know today. We the American people have the responsibility to ourselves and La Republica de Texas first to change government to serve the human need of the Republic; La Resistencia is within all of us, as a human instinct to say no to power with our votes this mid-term election year.

The choice is ours as the voters of today to vote for new rather than old, for different rather than traditional which is what got us into this mass we are in today with leadership with deep roots in Washington D.C. now.

Vote for what is humanly right for you and those you love the most, across this nation and the rest of the world, we must stop or limit this government of the capitalist elite monarch type madness with our vote.

The Republican party must now be placed on political party, "Time Out," and we must vote the Republican Party Bums out" this election year.

American Democracy must go back to the basics of political business while the Republican must learn to respect diversified human dignity as our human American race, Arturo Cortez/76541/10/19/2018

## 10/23/2018

Beto, I have now documented information on how the Republican party uses Social Security Administration Temple, Texas to deny me my American right to life by denying the disabled and the very old there benefits by deliberately manipulating over and under payments created by the government offices of the Social Security Administration, in Temple, Texas.

I now believe and feel as though I am being intimidated by Texas Republican political government personnel within social security administration Temple, Texas.

I did call Congressman John Carter's offices and I was told to call my democratic representative in my district because I am a democrat living in Texas. So this time I vote for American Hero MJ Hager, who will be there for Republicans and Democrats as one Texano village.

The people of Texas must go out and vote for "NEW Texas Political Young Blood," in order for Social Security Administration to re-establish the true mission of Social Security here in Texas and across the nation. Whereas, to  deny us our monthly benefits at will at no rick to Social Security is in fact a crime to humanity by

Social Security Administration administering life and death over the American people of today.

To deny us the recipients of our earned Social Security benefits and Medicare medical benefits payments, is essentially to our human right to life making Social Security Administration Temple, a now Texas Republican Death Penal for those of us who simply want to do the right thing for the Republic regardless of political parties.

I am not a liberal no more than I am conservative I will vote for Texas first in Beto O'Rourke because it is the right thing to do for Texas, I am not hypocritical when it comes to Texanos for Texas in our own Texano way.

This election year in Texas will be about us the Americans who paid for our earned Social Security and expect our earned benefits to work for us the American workers who have paid for the American right to receive our earned retirement benefits.

And not for Donald Trump's and the Republican Party who has given those who already have a 1.6 Trillion dollar tax benefit at our expense.

Now comes the time for pay back and the Republican Party needs our vote in order to pay for their tax break to the rich and famous at the expense of the most venerable we the disabled and Seniors, and children.

The Republican Party has promised to use your Social Security earned benefits to pay back a 1.6 Trillion dollar deficits created by the Republicans in Tax breaks for the elite rich of our nation. While denying the American tax payers our own earned and paid for social security as our American right to life.

I encourage everyone in Texas to go vote Democrat and send our massage to the nation that here in Texas, Texans do come first. Arturo Cortez/76541/10/23/2018

## 10/25/2018

There is no place for Republican Political Violence in American Democracy of today, Vote for Non-Violent Democrats into public Offices today and stop the madness. ArturoCortez/76541/10/25/2018

## 10/26/2018

When the Truth does not matter to the Republican Party,

According to the Resistance I have Beto ahead, and it is wrong for you and the Beto Campaign to tell our supporters that we are close when we are winning this election not whining for money, but by will of the American Texano, we must move on and win for Texas, Arturo Cortez/76541/10/26/2018

## 10/28/2018

"POTUS, Donald Trump the Nationalist,"

Earlier this week Donald Trump called himself a Nationalist, within hours 10 pipe booms were delivered to the leadership, of the Democratic Party including the Obama and Clinton Presidential families, as well as CNN American Free News Media.

The Republican Party of the United States elected by Republicans, blame those who received the bums in denial of the fact that they have now lost control of the Executive Branch of government, the Republican Grand Old Party who is now all powerful in the House, the Senate, the Executive Branch, and the Supreme Court, must now file impeachment papers on Donald Trump POTUS/45 or for fit their moral right to lead our nation.

I encourage the nation to vote for Love not hate, different verses traditional, new verses old, human dignity verses racial haterate and divisiveness on behave of the people of this our Republic, and change will follow.

We the people of this nation have a responsibility to ourselves as a nation, and to our own human families as the recipients of government as the nation which we still are, or should be. Come November 6th 2018 right thing to do Republican voters will have to vote for "One American Democratic Voice for America," in order to work as one in the take back America 2020 Resistance effort.

Yesterday, October 27th 2018 a self described White Nationalist attacked a Jewish synagogue, in Pennsylvania the domestic terrorist killed 11, and wounded 6 Jews worshiping our one and only God, Jehovah Blessed are we who can now see and learn the lesson of the Lions and the Lamb, we are one diversified American people as a one American human race, and we will harness and restore democratic power to the people, with our none partisan American vote as Americans of today. Arturo Cortez/76541/10/28/2018

What an amazing 2 years of Donald Trump Republican politics we have had, many of you who read my writings and books must know that this Mid-Term political year will be over on November 6, 2018; at which point I will start publish editing my 2018 Resistance writings into a manuscript of all my Yes we Can writings for the last to years.

I will have until the first hour of 2019 to format and find a traditional publisher for my 2018 Resistance manuscript, assuming no publishing company will publish my writings by traditional publishing method I will La Case de Cortez, Publications will once again publish my 2017-2018 Resistance writings, God willing of course, prior to February 2019, regardless of who wins the November 6, 2018 election.

The Resistance/76541 is now, and will always be on Amazon. com under the Authors name Arturo Cortez ready to provide my information to true patriots of who we are, or think we are, as sophisticated American people in honorable action and deed.

Whereas, let there be no doubt that Arturo Cortez was here in this time, to write about the lords will in the hearts and minds of the American people through my writings as my mission in La Republica De Texas y Los Estados Unidos del Norte America and the world, /Arturo Cortez/76541/10/28/2018

## 10/29/2018

Republicans "VOTE AMERICAN DEMOCRACY" While your vote still counts,

Every mind is its own world old friend it is those who have the tenacity to write the truth who will stand alone in history as a measure of who we once were in order to live as one human race under one God. Arturo Cortez/76541/10/29/2018

## 10/31/2018

EARLY Voting is on today "GO VOTE TODAY and VOTE DEMOCRAT" for the sake of our Republic and our nation,

The Republican Party of American partisan politics has now driven our nation and our democracy into a national crisis; our United States President is no longer a Republican or a Democrat he is now a self declared Nationalist in the political traditions of the German Nationalist, Adolf Hitler and the Russian Nationalist, Joseph Stalin by declaring the American Free News Media the enemy of the American people.

Our President Donald Trump owes his capitalist soul to the Russians, who will destroy American Democracy by using Donald Trump to destroy our two party partisan politics; we need to unite American Republicans and Democrats into one American voice for American Democracy and honor our freedom with our vote.

We have no choice Donald Trump has been given the opportunity to lead our nation by the Republican Electoral College, and by the consecution of the democratic candidate Hillary Clinton prior to the honorable count of the American popular vote, he has failed to understand the Office of the Presidency, favoring elitist Monarch Nationalist rule over our diversified American people of today.

You must go do your American deed today and tomorrow in early voting; go vote democrat for your nation or we will all be judged by our government for our diversified ethnic race, religion, gender, color of our skin, national origin, and or what you read or write. Arturo Cortez/76541/10/31/2018

# CHAPTER 15

November 2018

## 11/01/2018

Never in my time has a American President sent our American military the most powerful military in the world out to create battle to deny women and children their human right to migrate to America the land of respect for human life and human dignity, "Shame" on all the White is right Republicans who allow 5-15 thousand American troops to degrade our American military's human dignity based on national origin and new world racial profile, "Q Viva la Resistencia lo Pendejo de nuestra gente norte Americana." The Resistance encourages you to Vote Blue Democrat down the 2018 Mid-Term Ballet in order to impeach the political cancer we have today in our American Democracy "One Voice one American people," if we lose this election we lose our American way of life, as we know it today. Arturo Cortez/76541/11/01/2018

Se Reporta: Texas Congressman Beto O'Rourke Candidate running for the United States Senate, Beto needs our help "Please" make a "whatever you can contribution" to our campaign to elect Beto O'Rourke to the United States Senate for Texas and the Nation:

The Mexican President must also now activate the Mexican Military to protect the Mexican people from an invasion size North American United States military force messing on his northern border with the United States of North America, lead by American racist Republican nuts where as the Mexican President has a vested obligation to protect his nation and his Mexican people, from the United States. Arturo Cortez/76541/11/01/2018/

## 11/04/2018

Governing by popular thought is pretty much the way American socialist democracy works today from a political party perspective. However in bottle necking American socialist democracy into two national political parties denies us all the ability to exercise or vote for what is logically/humanly right for us and those around us.

Whereas in my writings partisan politics deludes our independent vote which we must fore-fit for the sake of party leadership ideology of the time. In 2016 I did write about how Donald Trump would define the Grand Old Party the "GOP", not for one second did I even think to write about how Donald Trump would define us all as Americans of the United States of America, of today.

Not only has he changed government he has now change the way we see our own moral American selves as one American people.

American government was not created to service the needs of the Presidency or the needs of corporate capitalist presidential personal profiteering, but rather created to service the human needs of the American people. Yet, our President Donald Trump has now given all of the elite few in our nation and many of the global elite upwards of 1.6 Trillion dollar corporate welfare tax breaks.

Whereas, now the 1.6 Trillion in tax dollars is not coming in to the United States Treasure the Republican Party and Donald Trump our Electoral Collage appointed President now feel that the most need in American life Social Security, and Medicare recipients must pay down the 1.6 Trillion dollars deficit which the

President and the Republican Party squandered on tax breaks to the elitist rich and wealthy.

Whereas, the elitist recipients of corporate American welfare are not in need nor are/should they be entitled to American tax dollars simply because corporations like the upper elite in business pay taxes on profits they make from the work of others in the most part of the American human type.

Whereas American working citizens who have earned the right to our entitlements which we are fully vested in for our Senior Social Security and Medicare in order to subsidize human integrity in our American senior retirement years which is the reason we the American workers pay for Social Security Retirement and Disability Benefits to Social Security Administration of the United States of America.

Taxation is being denied its purpose by Republican capitalist moral virtue at the expense of the American people. This next election we must examine and redefine our own socialist American made Democracy, with reference to eliminating the Electoral College process as the will of the American People.

Like the diversified American people our tax dollar truly is diversified as well, American Democracy is now and has always been socialism under siege by corporate capitalist partisan politics.

Yet I dare say American democracy was not created to supply foreign or domestic corporations, corporate tax breaks for the elite American wealthy in business or for personal or corporate profiteering at the expense of our Americans diversified tax dollars.

Thank-you Raza Humana for entrusting the Democratic Party with your vote, we the American people "WON" the United States Congress "Si se Pudo"/"Yes we Did" next comes the Muller Investigation Report, Congressional Indictment, and

Impeachment hopefully before we vote that Republican bum out of our American Executive Office in Washington D.C.,

**11/05/2018**

### Judgmental Salt Water Anchor Babies of today

By ArturoCortez

In America there are those who came, there are those who were brought by those who came as commercial property, and there are those of us who have all ways been here as sweet water new world natives who have been migrating the new world for thousands of years, based on human need regardless of Democratic or Republican bi-partisan racist Cow Pie politics when in fact both wings belong to the same bird with respect to the diversified American Eagle of today.

Donald Trump along with all of us whose ancestry came from Europe as salt water ancestry are and should be recognized as salt water immigrates in the new world of today for historical generic merit.

Today we must use DNA in establishing human rights to the land in honor to what we are as American natives of today verses  European anchor babies to the new world land of modern Immigration Reforms.

Whereas, today modern new world nations must work to gather as one in order to establish rules of law and local economic development opportunities in the migrants home land in order to establish a white is right race only in America today. Americans must learn to value harvesting and eating our own American crops, supplied with American labor instead of documented or undocumented international migrants.

A anchor baby of the salt water Europe ancestry must never deny a sweet water native his or her rights as human based on race, gender, religion, sexual preference, or national new world origin.

History has demonstrated throughout our 500 year old colonized new world that the new world natives of the new world has nowhere to go if in fact he or she is of the land and his ancestors were living here in the new world long before our salt water ancestors arrived to the new world.

Donald Trump must learn to lead by example and go back to where his ancestors came from as a anchor baby of salt water ancestry; the Republicans only understand privileged fork-it tong political solutions. We must Vote the Republican political bums out of Office and give the Democrats a opportunity to rule the Senate, and the Congress in order to establish subpoena powers to Impeach the Executive branch of government or Vote Donald Trump out in the 2020 General Election.

Donald Trump is a product of Republican Party irresponsibility towards the average basic human needs of all Americans regardless of political party; it is up to us as the American people of this nation of today to stand and bring change to our city, state, and national governments with our democratic vote as American voters of today for tomorrow.

The Republican Party is and has been in control of Washington D.C. for the last 8 years, they now control the Congress, the Senate the Executive branch, and the Supreme Court of the United States government.

The Republican Party is responsible for denying the American people Comprehensive Immigration Reform, the American Affordable Care Act, our earned Social Security Benefits, and earned Medicare Medical survival benefits much in the same way as the Adolf Hitler's SS Death Panels of 1932.

Playing partisan politics with our tax dollars to subsidize American personal, and corporate business interest is in fact Corporate Welfare/Corporate Capitalist Socialism at the expense of the American tax payers, in fact.

Tomorrow we vote for what is right for our nation as one people regardless of political parties. We now have today and tomorrow left to change government with our vote.

The Resistance encourages you to call five of your friends or enemies in your neighborhood and invite them to go vote with you. be the one who will make the difference tomorrow November 6, 2018 is "Election Day" here in America and your nation needs you to stand and be counted as one of many with the will and the vote to change American government with your vote as a American.

Voting will give you the American right to bitch about government for the next two, to four years when we vote again in 2020, Arturo Cortez/76541/11/05/2018

## Election Day November 6th 2018

I want to thank very one out their volunteering to help your neighbor get to the Polls to vote, The Resistance encourages all Americans qualified to vote to do so this election is about whether if you agree with Donald Trump's bigoted Republican American government, if you disagree with the way Donald Trump Republicans are running this nation, you will want to vote Democrat for change & reform to the way things are once were as a America of and for human dignity within American moral fiber.

The time is now 7:00 AM and the Voting Polls are now open across Texas, we are now a Battle ground state and we must know our place and own up to who Texanos are to our American nation, where we go from here in Texas the Nation will follow, things are quite an orderly in the streets of Texas today; faith and hope is high with Change and Reforms coming with the next Texas sun rise things will really get better or will continue to get worst than they now are now, your Vote will make the difference in the Old Republica de Texas.

If you vote Republican you will be voting for tax breaks for the elitist corporations and the wealthiest individuals in our nation/"Corporate Capitalist Welfare" at the expense of your tax dollars. Arturo Cortez/76541/11/06/2018

By ArturoCortez/76541/

### "Mandeme Uste"

I am so proud to be an American Texano this morning November 7, 2018.

Since I came to live in Texas from the Pacific North West , I have not seen Texas so proud and united behind our mission to dignify humanity in Texas by establishing Texas as a battle ground American right thing to do diversified competitive vote.

Even though today the American Texano is denied knowledge of the political issues, and candidates, you sir inspire hope, and pride in voters here in Texas and across the nation so it is that you Beto O'Rourke have won the hearts and minds of the American voters across the nation well done now we plan for tomorrow, La Resistencia /76541 stands with Beto O'Rourke for President of the United States of North America.

Beto O'Rourke, to lose a battle/campaign in Texas is not to lose our Mission/Movement for human dignity amigo, Sir you make me proud to be the Texano Storyteller, Arturo Cortez here in the heart of Texas, Sir. Arturo Cortez/76541/11/07/2018

## 11/28/2018

Donald Trump is ready to put on another show and we the Resistance are ready for it. Whereas The Donald raised the import tax on nations of the world by our hard worked American products, and the world is now doing the same to us by raising the prices on American imported consumer goods/The Donald is milking the "Big Cow"/third world Machiavellian in the form of American democratic political nature/ Q Viva La Resistencia/ Arturo Cortez/76541/

# Chapter 16



**December 2018**

" Sign this petition Share and Resist"

This Petition was founded by the Resistance American Patriot Mr. Tom Steyer of the Si se Puede Movement, Need to Impeach who writes

**12/15/2018**

We stay true to what we got elected to do with or without government; American human dignity is not negotiable, follow Donald Trump's lead and shut it down for the sake of the nation and no gas for "Air force 1." Arturo Cortez/76541/12/15/2018

**12/20/2018**

Cassie Crosby, question? If AuthorHouse makes 90% off the royalties from El Centrolista and i make 10 cents on the dollar paid in royalties to them why are you sending me this e-letter when AuthorHouse is making the money from my writings, i would think you would be writing about marking to AuthorHouse i am not a corporate welfare agency. I cannot effort nor will i pay for marketing El Centrolista 2012-2015 for AuthorHouse to profit off my writings.

I have not stopped writing my stories since i published El Centrolista 2012-2015 and i will be publishing "The Resistance/76541" in 2021.

The Resistance/76541 is a much better book and will be presented to the public pretty much in the same way, please advice if you would like to establish a dialog regarding my new books. Arturo Cortez/76541/12/20/2018

## 12/22/2018

We the American people of this nation woke up this morning to fine we now have no government based on reckless Republican Leadership now in control of the White House.

The United States President, Donald Trump has had his opportunity to lead our nation and POTUS/45 has failed his mission and will be charged with at least three felony charges and we will prosecute on behave of the American people, to the full extent of our honorable moral American laws. I suppose an old fashion corporal punishment eastern European whipping from his father would have done Donald Trump some good.

## 12/22/2018

La Resistencia encourages all Si se Puede political organizations and followers of the Resistance to sign, share and promote our petition to impeach the Electoral College appointed President of the United States, Mr. Donald Trump.

The time has now come for The Donald to go and for American Democracy to deny the Executive Branch of the United States, the American right to lead our nation until the 2020 election and/or impeach Mr. Donald Trump as President of the United States of North America for his service to Russia. Arturo Cortez/76541/12/22/2018

# Blessed are we all to see The End of 2018,

Happy New Year its 2019

NOVA TOTIVS TERRARUM SIVE NOVI ORBIS TABVLA, aud̃ G. Blaeu
BLAEU WALL MAP

# Impeach POTUS/45 Now

## The Resistance/Resistencia 2019

In 2018 we the American Resistance did take back the United States Congress from the Capitalist, Donald Trump; we did introduced the than American want to be "King Trump," to American Constitutional Congressional Oversight. Shortly after our newly elected Si se Puede political candidates took their seats in the American House of Representatives of the People, who learned the real political facts about Donald Trump and the art of his Executive Branch Deal for the United States of America and we the American tax payers. We will now start 2019 with Congressional Political capital with the Congress under the control of the people once again, and the Republican led United States Senate under Republican cow pie hear say as their political party handy-cap verses the simple truth with regards to the issues of the people. Thank you folks for reading my writings; so it is that it was a day much like today only the year was 2019 "!"

Arturo Cotez
La Casa de Cortez Publications
1/1/2019

On a day much like today only the year was 2019, in American democratic political History this archived text are the efforts taken by La Resistencia/National Leadership Writings by Arturo Cortez/76541/Killeen/Texas.

# CHAPTER 17

January, 2019

**01/01/2019/"#ImpeachNow"**

By Arturo Cortez,

I really do not think Donald Trump will be around to run for a second Presidential Term. The President is now using the honorable Office of the Presidency to justify his lies to himself, and the American people; however, our traditional Republican Party has been betrayed and the nation will need time to heal and redefine itself in reconstruction of American Democracy in order to stop capitalism from ever dominating and/or interpreting American Democracy the will of the Popular Vote must never be interpreted by partisan political party rule ever again.

American Freedom is but our own stand in purpose of human dignity as the purpose of human life.

The Resistance is our own personal gift to our time as our ability to say "No" with our American vote within our American Democracy as the gifted creation of our Founders and Framers of American Democracy and the lord our God.

I remind our newly elected 2019 House of Representatives of the people of the United States, that the Resistance did win the 2018 Election that you are now our only hope for the future as our political representatives in Washington, District of Columbia.

Remember you are there to "work" for the people, not to fight for the people." Remember a Representative/ leader can only be defined by his and/or her deeds.

As a Resistance leader it is your mission to cultivate an embrace bi-partisan politics and vote for what is right with respect to American human/humane moral dignity under the law regardless of political party politics, as the purpose of political Leadership.

Remember we won the 2018 Mid-Term Election and it is you in the Congress who is charged with interpreting the will of the American people, with the blessings and the "Check-Book" with respect to and from the American people.

POTUS/45 Donald Trump has been given the presidential opportunity to grow and to lead our nation as a legal "Electoral College Appointment" to the Presidency of the United States in the stead of our constitutional popular vote.

While it does appear as though the Russian government now has Executive Political privileges/ influence over the will of the American people. Mr. Trump is without doubt on mission to dismantle, confuse, or challenge our democracy as well as our American Judicial systems and our American way of democratic life; we are now under attack from within the Executive Offices of the United States.

United States Military Generals have now been fired dismissed or replaced with those who covenant their oath to Mr. Donald Trump, and not to the constitution of the United States.

Over 800,000 American federal workers are today on their 17th day of a Donald Trump Shut Down of government with a wall as his only justification for his Russian mission to dismantle and destroy American Government as we know it to be.

Mr. Trump has further weakened our American leadership standings globally by dismantle our Military allied global trade alliances and agreements which stabilizes global peace. POTUS/45 has now, and will continue to compromise/concede American regional strategic global ground positions around the world to the Russian KGB Intelligence for the sake of the right personal business deal with Russia. Whereas, Russia has no better friend in America's White House than POTUS/45 Donald Trump who now views American/ global Intelligence as "Phony Media."

Mr. Trump has fired or replaced our best Generals, and declared war on our American Free Press. Now is the time for American democracy to remove, and/or replace POTUS/45. Whereas, Presidential self induced ignorance or as we know it in here in Texas "Pendejismo" is a personal choice, not a human virtue, and certainly no excuse for deliberately and selfishly challenging the limits of American moral legal laws based on American presidential privileges.

As a United States Presidential Donald Trump has no Congressional Over-site over the democratically elected Representatives of the American people in Washington D.C. or anywhere else.

The United States Congress does the legal right to impeach and replace the President of the United States of North America elected by the People of the United States as a national constitutional American Constitutional political virtues "#ImpeachNow" Arturo Cortez/76541/01/01/2019

## 01/06/2019

The Resistance asks all citizens to establish citizen good will humane support services for all of Mr. Donald Trump's Federal Workers; it is clear now that POTUS/45 will continue to destroy our American way of life as we know it to be, by challenging our very own personal faith and commitment to the foundation of American democratic self rule.

Whereas, President Donald Trump is in fact shamelessly destroying America from the inside out, and we are all allowing it to happen in the hope that next will come radical change offering alternatives to what we know today as American democracy committed to American human dignity as one nation among and above others.

American Federal Workers must look for other jobs, will the Resistance will not give Donald Trump a back room trophy deal on a wall to divide Americans from America.

Donald Trump has selected to sacrifice the community social security of all federal workers in order to establish a psychological political win over the 2018 November election/ "Old USSR KGB Tactics" in order to establish political control/Russian political coup over Eastern Block European Nations," end result "failed."

The Resistance understands our nation requires responsible national Leadership and so does Donald Trump who continues to poison the political holy waters of American democracy with intentional lies and here say.

The President must be removed and replaced with a American Responsible leader in order to service the needs of the needs and responsibilities of the nation.

The Electoral College appointed of President Mr. Trump and his capitalist Republican political party perspectives has now failed and is destroying our nation regardless of political party affiliation.

Mr. Trump has squandered his opportunity to lead our nation and must now be removed and replaced on the bases of his lying, narcissus, racist, Archie Bunker political perspectives at a Presidential level.

We are not now nor will we very be a Capitalist imperial democratic monarch that is not who America is. Republican minority political rule over our nation is in fact political siege over the will of American democracy.

Regardless of American Democratic Partisan Rule we must all vote American for our nation as we know it to be; so it is that we are a nation of laws that govern us all who truly are Americans of our American Constitution.

Whereas, the new 2018 American House of Representatives of 2019 of the people must Impeach the sitting President of the United States of North America, Donald Trump and other wise remove Mr. Donald Trump and his personal family business from the Office of the President of the United States of North America whereas personal business is not of American governess of the nation.

## 01/11/2019

The Resistance 2019 dose influence Centralist non-partisan political donations to local political candidates regardless of political parties here in Texas and across the continental United States of North America.

As a political centralist it would be wrong at this time for the Resistance to show favoritism for one candidate over another prior to the Presidential Primaries.

Erica L. Castro, I know and highly respect what you both have done for Texas and the nation, I do think Julian is of legendary Presidential fiber; but where Julian's challenge will be, is in how Julian will respectfully/diplomatically de-finds the word "Presidential Pendejismo" to the resistance none partisan America first voter now demanding change and Presidential Impeachment.

Again, Erica thank-you and Julian for what you do for Texas and the nation: "you both make me proud to be American/Arturo Cortez/76541"

## 01/14/2019

"America under Siege,"

America is under siege, today we can actually look back at what we can remember American democracy to be. American democracy is and will always be a national socialist democratic governess evolving ideological revolution which reaches past Republican or Democratic political evolution.

The United States House of Representatives,("The Congress} is the government body which represents the will of the American people at a union of 50 North American Republics which we all know as The United States of North America.

The Congress is charged with over-site of the Executive Branches of the United States, and or the President of the United States (POTUS/45) for now.

The Congress does have say so over America's "Check Book" as entrusted by the American constitution of the people.

The Congress does have the authority to create/make and enforce American law of the people, this means that in America we govern ourselves by our historic and new existing laws. Whereas, here no man or woman if American human is above American Law of all the American people created for us by our National House of Representatives of all the people/The United States Congress.

I for one like most everyone out there do have trouble at times understanding the problems we are having with American Democracy of our times understanding that American Democracy is an ongoing socialist revolution governed by law as the only means to social order.

All the Historical national indicators do show that the National Russian Government and their USSR, KGB Dictator Vladimir Putin, does feel as though they have their man in POTUS/45 Donald Trump in the White House.

If this is so, Donald Trump has created American Democratic Treason for the sake of foreign global Capitalism and Mr. Trump must be Tarred and Feathered, Removed and Replaced and Hung until dead like a good dictator that he thinks he is.

It is true that we all have our own patriotic purposes in who we are as one nation; even a Presidential Traitor has a purpose when looking at improving our political socialist democracy.

American Traitor or Traitors of today must be judged by American Law and if found guilty of treason the traitor should be punched based on the Law of the country he/or she who has betrayed our nation do have to pay the appropriate legal price regardless of who they are whereas, there is no one American better than the other based on constitutional United States Law.

Only in this way can American democracy define itself as equal and above personal capitalist foreign interest over our capitalist American democracy of the people of the United States.

"Que Siga La Resistencia" /Arturo Cortez/01/14/2019

## 01/18/2019

By Arturo Cortez

Team Julian as you know or should know I am a writer who has once before wrote for a Black Man for United States President, our purpose than was for our country to full fill its purpose to all peoples of our nation in POTUS/44 Barack Obama General Election of 2008.

To be honest with you we did not think Barack Obama would live past six months after his election in 2008; yet, there was hope, and there was promise in the political winds of that time.

By 2012 we re-enforced hope in the future by getting POTUS/44 Re-elected.

The point to all this is that for eight years I wrote my centralist Si se Puede stories which you to can read in my book "El Centrolista 2012-2015". Not once in the eight years did Barack Obama or any of his political Teams ever offer me a job or a free image of my president, so it is that in the eight years Barack Obama was in office he did receive $20.00 from me as my political contribution "donation" to my nation, yet if you Google my name you will find those who refer to me as the "Black Money" behind Barack Obama in reference to my writings.

Today, I still write every day but do not share my intellectual knowledge of democratic socialist moral political love stories with others, this story itself will be published next year so Democrats and/or the Republicans can buy my writings in my next book "La Resistencia" After the 2020 General Election.

Team Julian, my "free" strategic political advice is "get on the national map before you go to Iowa or anywhere else:

"Don, Julian you are an American New World Native of North American, your Presidential political issue is Pri-casted "Comprehensive Immigration Reform, for now.

Allow POTUS/45 Donald Trump to continue prepping your native red carpet assenting to the Presidency, it is for you to study all issues of presidential political interest, as you must be ready to respond with references in the "3C's " cool, calm, and Collected" manner,

Do not dignify Donald Trump's ideas or fake perspectives with any response from you directly.

Among all things to remember you do not waste your valuable time with treasons political morals or Russian fake propaganda.

All problems with government today must be because of the Republican Party capitalist President Donald Trump.

You Don, Julian must be viewed as the political candidate who will work with Republicans, and Democrats knowing of course that you view yourself as a democrat centralist bring sanity back to the United States of North American democratic politics. Don, you have been selected to be the Benito Juarez Native Candidate for President of "All Americans."

## 01/22/2019

### By Arturo Cortez

"American Democracy Censored and/or betrayed by the Republican Art of the Business deal in American capitalist Democratic Partisan Politics,"

Certainly, both national political parties interpret our socialist American democracy to meet and implement their own capitalist political goals and agendas, certainly replacing our government of the people with capitalist fascist party minority rule over the will of the American people/voters the American Popular Vote –v- the Electoral College appointment of now the United States, King, of the Republican Party Donald Trump.

I do suppose that American democracy was created for interpretation by our byes partisan capitalist politics of today; or so it seems, however in doing so our political interest as American humans have now been devalued by political evolution into American government of those who can effort to buy American politics of the American people.

Today we as the American voters of today vote to establish Corporate Welfare of the elitist few of American Democratic socialist corporate leadership as the purpose of who we are as Americans of today totally in contrast to what the framers of American democracy expected of us as Americans of their future to be.

So I have written, so let it be said that American Republican partisan politics is on mission to destroying America as established by the founders of our American constitutional governess, established to protect who we are as one America of and for our American people of global immigrants, this as is our nation of today.

We as the American people do have a personal civic responsibility to register ourselves as voting Americans, with the obligation to vote American in the stead of Republican or Democrat partisan politics as the purpose of who we are as the globally free and respected first democracy of the world we live in today.

It is we as American neighbors and friends who have the patriotic responsibity to say "no" and to resist Eastern European capitalist monarch type dictatorships over us the American people of today.

It is we of this time who will be judged by history/our children and Grand children.

May our one and only God forgive us all for allowing partisan politics to betraying our American Democratic heritage and American freedom to Eastern global capitalist as the art of the American traitor appointed president Donald Trump's capitalist business deals with Russia/USSR. Arturo Cortez/76541/01/22/2019

## 01/23/2019

The Resistance calls on all Resistance Teams to encourage all federal workers to stand united as one in a" National Federal Workers Strike" against the Republican Russian inspired Donald Trump American government "Shut-down".

It is the believe of the Resistance that the polarization of American political government is planned/programmed and inspired by Republican Russian influence with-in the Executive Branches of the US Government.

The total and complete shut-down of the American Russian government will commence on Monday the 3rd day of February 2019 and will continue until the American government of the American people is completely funded with, or without Russian approval, "Q Viva la Resistencia a lo Pendejo Presidencial Russiano Norte Americano," Arturo Cortez/76541/01/23/2019

## 01/24/2019

Well, today the Donald agreed to open the United States Federal Government after thirty five days Trumps 800,000 federal workers get a pay check for what they do for us the people of this nation.

Federal workers across the country have now been touched by social insecurity as workers of Donald Trump's United States Federal Government.

It was however the Resistance political warrior Congresswoman, Nancy Pelosi "The New" Democratic Speaker of the House of Representatives who lost no time in unifying a bi-partisan American first Congress, and United States Senate bring oversight control of back to the United States Congress were the interest of the people now come first over partisan political Republican Cow Pie and coffee political byes.

## 01/27/2019

Team, Democracy for America, the Resistance is not of the political campaign, the Resistance is of the Movement, come Valentine Day 2019 we will be better prepared to support those who will be affected by the second shut down, the Donald will bring his drama and the Resistance will use it to show overt populous mess support for our nation.

The Resistance won the 2018 Mid-term Election our "New" democratic Resistance leaders in Congress today are cultivating a new American first bi-partisan political ideology. The Congress is now working again instead of fighting under our "New Speaker of the House" Leader, Nancy Pelosi of California in the United States Congress.

We are no longer at political partisan war at the expanse of the will of the people. We the non-partisan won conservative Republicans or  liberal Democrats can now both work together as two wings of the same Eagle, with respect to American socialist democratic virtues woven into our National Foundational Constitution moral fabric.

Si se Puede, Class Team, Democracy for America your goal is to remove POTUS/45 from office by Impeachment if necessary on or before November 2020. If you should be successful in your mission you will have averting political class street warfare to be created by the Executive offices of the United States. Make it happen for American Democracy Now Arturo Cortez/76541/01/27/2019

# CHAPTER 18

February 2019

**Arturo Cortez/76541/02/12/2019**

In attempting to understand who we are as a people we must first understand who we are as a humanity. So we look back at history to take a look at what was America in the recorded beginnings of what is the new world of today. America of today dose have a native origin; simply put American Texas history did not start on March, 2, 1832.

Juan Bautista de las Casas did declare Texas Independence on January 22 of 1811 from the Spanish Kingdom on the new world, of Nueva Espania.

Ten years later after Texas became a Independent Republic Mexico became the Independent Kingdom of Mexico, from Spain.

Immigration Reforms to our immigration codes must have native cultural concessions for a native of the new world today, as defined by the "Treaty de Guadalupe Hidalgo" of February 1848 which describes our guaranteed Texas rights by Mexican and American Treaty definitions, when establishing Comprehensive Immigration Reforms, to our American Immigration codes/ polices. Arturo Cortez/76541/02/12/2019

## 02/26/2019

### By Arturo Cortez

La Revolucion Socialista de Don, Bernie Sanders, o de la gente, Bernie, thank-you for the outline of your Talking-Points, personally it all seems like old socialist bull "we must fight this approach that is not the way to win this nomination. The key to winning this election is by defining America as a Socialist Democracy, led by leaders elected by the people of the nation, and not appointed by partisan votes.

Capitalism is but a benefit of a free socialist economy regulated to service the needs of American socialist virtues in terms of wealth distribution, or so it should be.

You must gather the Democratic and the Republican crowds under one socialist American Democracy for Americans for human dignity," your goal is to unite our nation under Socialist human dignity.

Bernie, the battles to change and reform start when you Sr. get nominated and then elected, between now and then we work for the nomination by changing political ideology from a government of the Capitalist, to a government of the people.

You write that we have to build an Army of the People, Amigo I have been there, and I have done that, and my teams and armies are still playing.

You were real, and you were good, you looked and acted tired next time "center right, center left," get some rest tomorrow is another day my old friend,.  Arturo Cortez

Bernie you are the one person who can make this country what it is meant to be and I am the one person who can help you do it, I do not have the time nor can I afford to play political bullshit games with political horse crap. Bernie Sanders, "Q Viva la Revolucion Socialista" thank-you for all you do to define our

American socialist Democracy and you have a wonderful day old friend, Arturo Cortez/76541/02/26/2019

**Arturo Cortez/76541 /02/28/2019**

### The Texas Democratic Party

Manny Garcia,  although i was born by the Rio Grande in then the southernmost Texas village of Mission, Texas; as fate would have it I was raised in what is now one the most progressive American States in our nation the Pacific Northwest State of Oregon.

I have now lived in Texas 8 years as a retired old Texano fart rightfully @ my age here in The Heart of Texas.

It is true that in Oregon I did vote Libertarian, meaning of course that I was able to vote for a Republican or Democrats running for public office which made me fill as though I was voting for the right thing to do for my nation. So it is that my advice to you is that no political party is of the people including your party, the true purpose of your Democratic Party is no different than that of the Republican Party in that both parties look to interpret the will of the American voter, instead of acting on the will of the majority, regardless of political party. From my leadership perspectives the Texas Democratic Party has been the loser party of Texas politics for at least 38 years.

Texas now has single party rule in a two party political system by Republican political design.

The Republican Party has ruled Texas for over 35 years. In the next for years La Resistencia will establish La Republica de Texas as a true Libertarian Republic you or your party's time or money is not now expected nor required.

La Resistencia did create and did win the 2018 Mid-Term Election the Democrats in Texas did declare a blue wave victory in

2018 after it was clear the Resistance had won the national Mid-Term Elections across the nation.

Today you write to say that the Texas Democrats will declare war on all those Republicans who voted blue in the 2018 Mid-Term Elections.

Please be advised La Resistencia considers the Democrats and the Republican parties in Texas and across the nation as regional teams along side of the rest of the Resistance teams to include but not limited to the Si se Puede Teams of: Move-On, Working Family Party, Democracy for America, Creido, LULAC, and the many, many grass-root Resistance Si se Puede Teams across Texas, as well as the nation.

As the author of the Resistance I do not fill that you or your party can come close to being a challenge to the institutionalized Texas Republican Party without the Resistance of the people of Texas.

Whereas, the only thing Texas and the national Republican Party fear is the Resistance which is now working to unite Republicans, and Democrats into one American political Movement to unite both liberal and conservative ideologies into one American Vote to defeat Donald Trump in the 2020 General Election.

As for now I demand that, you/and or your political organization redefine your political objectives and your short and long range goals and objectives in Texas, you folks need to stand down on any attacks on any other political Resistance Political Parties.

I ask that you Sir, as well as your political operatives in Texas and across the nation work towards American political unity among all our American people regardless of political ideologies.

As, for donations to your political Democratic Party or your Texas Republican Party, I must say that a year ago I ran for the office of Mayor of Killeen and I received no support from Republicans or your Democratic Party, so it is that unwillingly as a American Texano I must respectfully say to you Sir, that you and your Texas political parties can kiss my American white ass, Sir.

"Para q Viva La Resistencia a lo Pendejo." Arturo Cortez/76541 02/28/2019

# Chapter 19



**March 2019,**

Team Our Revolution Texas, your March 1, 2019 Meeting Minutes, have been Receive, Reviewed, and Archived, thank-you for the Information supplied to the Resistencia @ La Casa de Cortez/76541/ Killeen, Texas. Thank-you and God bless all you folks for all you do for our Resistance in Texas and across the nation.

Arturo Cortez76541/03/01/2019/

Team Bernie you are right, but stay focused on our game these attacks on us are all good for us at this time.

Bernie is rising in the poles and they are looking to ride our political coat tails, in the process they are making Bernie their equal. They will come at us as being socialist and we must be able incorporate and define Bernie's plans and ideas as the foundational/ purpose of our American Constitutional Socialist Democracy; Pence and Trump will be focused on how American Democracy belongs to capitalism; we can, and we will win this election with or without the Democrats, "Que Viva La Resistencia"// ArturoCortez76541/03/01/2019/

ArturoCortez/76541/03/01/2019/7:25AMCTT: Bernie, in our Capitalist Socialist Democracy, you are or want to be the Resistance Political Leader for an equitable American government of and for the American voters and "not" the money my friend Bernie Sanders, defining our American democracy for what it is a Socialist Democracy is our only opportunity to win this election of the socialist American vote, while capitalism in American government can fan for themselves:

Amigo, we all know who you are and the problems we face when we try to outdo the capital in capitalism as well as what you stand for as our Leader, you must now stop feeding the beast my friend with your approach as we go into 2020.

You must build the messes around what American Democracy is today, and what American Democracy was meant to be as the world's first true American Socialist Democratic Governess of human on earth.

Bernie old friend, get some rest you are going to need it and thank you and yours for what you do for our Nation and human of God's own men and women. /ArturoCortez/76541/03/01/2019

## 03/03/2019

Capitalism must be a instrument of our own human based socialist American Democracy create as the foundation to what we have today, as a Capitalist two Party Democratic process, instead of our foundational Socialist Democracy as intended by the fathers of our American Constitution, in regards to popular vote –v- Electoral Collage certification, Arturo Cortez/03/03/2019

## ArturoCortez/76541/03/01/2019/7:25AMCTT

Capitalism must be a instrument of our own human based socialist American Democracy create as the foundation to what we have today, as a Capitalist two Party Democratic process, instead of our foundational Socialist Democracy as intended by the fathers and framers of our American Constitution, ArturoCortez/03/03/2019

## 03/03/2019

Capitalism must be a instrument of our own human based socialist American Democracy create as the foundation to what we have today, as a Capitalist two Party Democratic process, instead of our foundational Socialist Democracy as intended by the fathers of our American Constitution, Arturo Cortez/03/03/2019

## 03/10/2019

Se Reporta Julián Castro For United States President a la Resistencia, "Please Donate what ever you can now, "para q viva la gente como la gente" ArturoCortez/76541

In order to understand La Resistencia, you must first look into the eyes of the lion and define ourselves, "Esto Para Que Siga La Resistencia," 03/08/2018

## ArturoCortez/76541/03/14/2019

Bernie, my friend I know we all live in a capitalist socialist democracy subject to political interpretation, I know that we are a socialist democracy by constitutional national virtue, miss understood by who we are today as a capitalist society. In our approach to organize, we must include who we are by national virtue.

2020 will be about capitalist siege over American Democracy, our battle must be a constitutional political battle for national control of this our nation in the 2020 General Presidential Election is but our mission; our target is to unite all political Resistance Teams under one candidate for President of the United States after the Primaries regardless of political parties or liberal or conservative virtuous political ideological.

**Memo to Resistance Teams:**

All Conservative and/or Liberal Resistance Teams are encouraged to read the constitution of the United States, and discuss it's socialist virtues at organizing meetings, we must organize based on our American constitutional human virtue's within our national Constitution knowledge level, in order to better understand who we are as one nation, we will target the American voter and become the political fishers of American men and women of today; remember, "you can attract more bees with honey, then you can with vinegar,".. "Welcome to my World, my friend Team Bernie Sanders & Teams"/ArturoCortez/76541/03/14/2019

## 03/15/2019

Beto i often share my thoughts with those i feel can learn from my writings, i saw you last night send a Resistance message of unity among all candidates after the 2020 Primaries, thank-you now we start your presidential training:

Political Arrogance offers those around you security learn to use it moderately at gatherings as a leadership tool, and grow into it for now.

**Shared info:**

La Resistencia stands with Team Kamala Harris, and all political teams focused on human dignity as the purpose of American governess.

Kamala, the Resistance is strong within you learn to stay focused on what your purpose is for the nation, establish your teams for summer events, and remember you are one of many political campaigns who are running for the democratic nomination for President of the United States; whereas, the Resistance is a Movement for political human dignity. Welcome to my World,

Kamala Harris, Candidate for President of the United States, ArturoCortez/76541/03/15/2019

## ArturoCortez/76541/03/15/2019

Late starters do pay a late starter price, none the less a brilliant move after although many donators have donated we do have the time to win this election with or without money if we keep it real with the American voters.

POTUS/45 came to El Paso, Texas selling border wall snake oil, and Beto must ride his border wall coat tail the major issue for you, for now, is Comprehensive Immigration Reform, at Donald Trump rallies across the nation.

Team Beto O'Rourke keep it within the three "C's" Cool, Clam, and Collected, for now," O" you do move your hands to mush where as none verbal communication can over whelm what you are trying to communicate, if you should someday find yourself in the heard of Texas, "carnal" look me up i would love to spend some time with you my friend. Maybe we can have some Pan Dulce and coffee or chocolate under my old Oak tree deep in the heart of Texas;

Gracias Beto, and Amy and family for who you are, and what you do for Texas and the nation, and thank-you for reading my stuff, ArturoCortez/76541/03/15/2019

## By Arturo Cortez/76541, 03/18/2019

Team Beto, after the Primaries Beto, will be asking the Republicans to vote for Beto for President in order that we can defeat Donald Trump in November 2020.

La Resistencia encourages Team Beto to start organizing grass-root Republicans for Beto "now". Your message must be clear and to the point "in our campaign we do not have Democrats or

Republicans all we have in our campaign are Unified American Voters to defeat Donald Trump in 2020.

Beto, only you who come from one of the "Red" conservative States in the nation can understand Texano conservative Republican Party virtues looking for a national leader to point them in the right direction my friend.

## Lesson #2

Beto, the only response to Donald Trump's attacks on you is, "the selfish acts of a desperate man," and/ or "all ego no brains," do not respondent otherwise, for now stay focus on the business of the people not the business of the Trump Show.

Welcome all Americans regardless of political party ideology to integrate with us and Lead or Follow/as part of our campaign to over through the present Republican dictatorship in Washington District of Columbia, right now.

Beto Teams must target grass-root right thing to do Republicans to join with our campaign in order to find Republican Unity at conservative Republican Party levels.

Your pole numbers will rise and the Donald will come at us, as we say in the heart of Texas "like flies on ca,ca" and we will be ready for him when that time comes, Arturo Cortez/76541/03/18/2019

## La Resistencia/Resistance,

## Team Beto, 03/20/2019

## Lesson #4

What the other candidates for president say and do matters to us all, as a unifying campaign we must view the issues as the stones our candidate/leaders have thrown, and we must be able to gather these stones to perfect our understanding of who we are, and where we are going as a nation. ArturoCortez/03/20/2019

Miss, Texas Justice of the Peace, Claudia Brown, i see you not only as my friend but as a Texas Elected Justice of the Peace, for the term you were elected for by the Texas Voters of this our Texas Village, your message is well receive, but there is no substitute to your elected time /El Centrolista 2012-2015/, less it be appointed by a higher authority then American Democracy darling; Moses did not write this opinion madam, Arturo Cortez the painter did 2019 years after the death, of Jesus the carpenter.

## 03/26/2019

The Killeen Police Department just the other day killed a man created by God with a lifelong mission imprinted in his human heart by our creator.

The reason this man was executed was for his believes in the use of street drugs, Cannabis for now is a street drug as well, which gives the Killeen Police Department the legal right to ask the judge to issue a no knock warrant/ Death by judicial collusion, justified by "Chicken Shit" as a human virtue as well as the reason to shoot a human of man and woman created by love to glorify itself among others of his Texas village/Arturo Cortez/76541/03/26/2019

# CHAPTER 20

**April/2019**

Republican Russian Propaganda, you go for it Joe make it about hugs and kisses for the American people, stay above the belt line,

**04/01/2019**

Team Beto, La Resistencia is not a political campaign, it is a movement which influences many political campaigns with over 40 of the most powerful activist none profit political organizations in the world as the readers of my Resistencia political writings, as a moral political Blogger/non-fiction Writer for La Resistencia.

Shortly after the Cruz Campaign you Team Beto received a e-mail from me as a fisher of man, "I explained I would see you Don, Beto on the road to the White House, so it was written than, and so it has been done the choice is now of the people.

Roberto Francis O'Rourke Gracias por su interés en la politica nacional de los estados unidos; yo soy Arturo Cortez, Author de la Resistencia. Sénior La Resistencia lo considera a usted como un leader con el modo de ser Presidente de los estados unidos del norte America. Su organización/teams son unos de los mejor s q yo he visto en mi tiempo como organizador.

Espero q los consejos q a recibido de mi le sirvan en su campaña nacional, para la Presidencia nacional de los estados unidos.

Beto, carnal La Resistencia esta a sus órdenes, pero como es q la Resistencia también tiene sus obligaciones al Movimento de la gente, esta correspondencia será mi último consejo #:

De hoy en adelante todo lo q tu digas serán actos políticos acostúmbrate, y responde con confiancia a la doctrina de su Campania politica, para ganar la nominación de del Partido Democrático Nacional a la presidencia de los estados unidos. Nuestra Campania es para establecer cambio a lo q ya somos bajo la presidencia del presente Donald Trump.

Pri-Primeros, Donald Trump lo ase famoso si es que uste sabe usarlo en modos calculados.

Estables asé como un candidato con valores morales a lo que es Washington D.C. de hoy. Requerida q usted es un candidato de munchos, pero único a la politica de hoy. La lumbre para establecer la gente como la razon de nuestro gobierno nacional con el voto de la gente, ya esta encendida nuestra fe en la gente esta completa mente segura, "Mil Bendiciones a usted y sus Teams en esta Compañía espero seguir con Lección parte 2, "Camino a la presidencia" con usted después de las 2020 Primeries,

Gracias, Beto y Beto Teams por lo que son, y lo que asen ustedes por nuestra democracia norte Americana,

Dios lo bendiga a usted y a su familia, por quien son y lo que representan como una familia Texana Norte Americana a todo el mundo de hoy en dia, you folks make me proud to be Arturo Cortez, out here in the Heart of Texas, i will be waiting for you on the otherside, /ArturoCortez/76541/04/01/2019

## 04/03/2019

### "En El Principio"

Julian Castro, Amigo your e-mail has touched me in a very personal life long way in my Texano life. My mother was born a Sheppard girl in south Texas in 1933, She was Baptized in Texas but was not registered, it has now been over 60 years that my mother has not seen her family in Monterrey, Nuevo Lion, MX. for fear that she will not be allowed back into the country, nuestro destino, carnal de la Resistencia/Arturo Cortez/76541/04/03/2019

## 04/03/2019

Team Democracy for America, La Resistencia dose not pick candidates, we simply indorse candidates who's  ideological perspectives compliment human dignity within American Democratic political governess of today and the rest is political history /Arturo Cortez/04/03/2019

## 04/06/2019
## 04/07/2019

I would like to thank my Son in Law Henry Noble the Big Screen movie star, and my Daughter La Donna Maria Cortez de Najieb, Ex. Vice President of a Hospital in Southern California, for their 6 day visit to our home here in Killeen Texas.

Special loveable thanks to our grandkids for the love they showed us as their Texano "Abuelo & Abuela Cortez". They are all back home safely in Pasadena, California this morning, thank-you son for your wonder gift to La Casa de Cortez/76541,

## 04/07/2019

In trusting generational cultural conflict, i was brought up the same way "the more you whine" the more you get."

Concider Joe Biden your Grandfather to understand Joe; Joe I believe would be much more responsible than whatever it is we have in the White House today. Stay out of it Joe, and run for president let the people decide. La Resistencia is strong within you old friend Arturo Cortez/76541/04/07/2019

## ArturoCortez/76541/

Miss Nicky Tharpe, spring is here and i am now working on the interior Architectural reconstruction of my Texas Home this property now has a story to tell and i would like to tell it to you and Miss Ronda first.

If in fact every human mind is its own world, than i can honestly say that La Casa de Cortez, is now established in the State of Texas.

In or about May of 2018 Miss, Ronda Seanez of Realty Executive began the hunt for a home we could afford in Killeen, Texas.

It wasn't long before I was introduced to you as the Rep. for Fairway Mortgage, and the rest I will leave for Texas History to judge.

Like others in Texas History I too have now claimed my Urban Home Stead and have been approved here in Bell County in the Heard of Texas.

We received the keys to the home on the 15th day of August. Whereas, when my friend Jeff and I arrived with the first load of furniture at our new home we found a huge tree had fallen close to the home.

Rick Williams La Casa de Cortez insurance man was already there to show me the tree taking pictures of the fallen tree.

Lucky for me the tree belonged to the City of Killeen right of way.

Thirty minutes after I reported the tree falling to the City of Killeen, I was asked to sign a paper to allow the City Workers on my property.

Within 15 minutes the heavy equipment started to arrive and soon came the operators and the city tree cutting specialist and their Crews.

All the big to do with the tree and the City Workers, and equipment on my property did make a respectful statement to my now neibor's, and friends in my Texas hood and Village.

Today the kids in my hood know who I am and wonder where I get all my words.

La Casa de Cortez/76541, will soon be finished with reconstruction repairs and finishes to  the main house, the spring will bring exterior work to offer a old world Hispanic Architectural neighborhood life style setting perhaps as a Breakfast House Estate in Killeen, Texas.

## 04/11/2019

Se Reporta: Julian Castro a La Resistencia; good luck tonight with our CNN Town Hall, please donate $5.00 to my old friend Julian Castro Democratic Candidate for President, Gracias for what you help to build for our nation, Texas/2019:

La Resistencia, there is no political party that can help American Democracy now, we lost the Cool War to Russia, we must now look inward into our American souls and vote American regardless of political parties and or political ideologues, America must come first in 2020. Arturo Cortez 04/13/2019

## 04/13/2019

Gender genetic conflict should never be a death sentence for ether human genders, whereas it does take both genders to create one human; whereas the State of Texas must hang both guilty genders in the name of God for doing God's will on earth for human/Arturo Cortez/04/13/2019

## 04/25/2020

La Resistencia stands with our Vice President Joe Biden, for United States President of the United States of America.

I encourage all Resistance Teams to support Joe in the National Democratic Nomination process in our effort to unite the Democratic Party, please donate $25.00 in support of my friend

Vice President Joe Biden for President and make a difference with your money, your time and your faith in American Democracy. Arturo Cortez/76541/04/25/2019

## 04/25/2019

"Impeach POTUS/45 Now"

There are those in our government who believe capitalist are as the Lion, and the American people are as the Lamb within American Democracy of today.

And so it is that today we are not as we were just four years ago, not since the Donald was appointed the President of the United States.

Let me be clear La Resistencia has, and will always stand with the truth whereas one can fool some of the people, some of the time, but no one can fool all of the people all of the time, less of course one is a self induced "Pendejo" to what is around us as one of the many of American Democracy.

I encourage all Resistance Teams, and Team leaders and Warriors to take to the internet to confront your own believes with others on line, we must all speak our own truth to power to those who look away from what is truly the moral democratic human right by our political choice.

Remember; certainly if I had a business today i would never do business with Donald Trump or any one like Donald Trump. Remember any one who agrees or disagrees with you or your on-line post has read your "post," do not forget to thank your on line ideological opponents on line, we must engage with others with personal Honor in what we write. The only truth on-line is the number of people who will read your perspectives on American moral democratic life style of today.

The problem with America today is we the people have been denied the popular vote of the people, for handicap republican states without the population s to establish leadership in Washington D.C.

Whereas the last Republican to win the Presidency of the Unite States by popular vote was Ronald Regan, the rest of the Republican Presidents were in fact appointed by the Electoral College process which has now replaced the popular vote.

The deciding choice of the people must always rule in American politics, as the foundation of our own form of American capitalist, socialist American democracy.

Our own capitalist President Donald Trump and his foreign political alliance support with the Russian KGB is the reason for the POTUS/45 presidency of today.

Whereas, a hostile foreign nations towards the United States of America in Russian did conduct a cyber attack to influence our national elections in favor of the candidate Donald Trump who made it possible to divert the American popular vote of the people, in favor of the Electoral College appointment of the POTUS/45.

Let there be no doubt that the investigation of Donald Trump's involvement within the Mueller Report is knowledge into who our now President of the United States "is" and what he the appointed President of the United States has done to earn the merit/ findings within the Mueller Report.

La Resistencia realizes Robert Mueller as the person investigating for the people of our nation, and report its truthful findings to the Congress; It is for the United States Congress to find wrong doing in the Mueller Report if any, it is Congress who must act to remedy any wrong done to the people as by way of the House of Representatives of the people of the United States of America.

Certainly, today as was then in the beginning, an American has nothing to fear from American Justice, if the American had nothing to hide from American Justice regardless of what kind of American the American was born.

Because the Presidency is in question of wrong doing the Congress must prosecute to the full extent of its own legal laws and powers as a co-equal democratic political power in our American governess of an for the people, the president should have nothing to fear if he or his presidency has done nothing wrong.

American democracy is the foundation to global democratic socialist governments of human; it is than up to us as the American People to stand and be counted and/or let global history define us all as "the self defined Pendejos" of our time in the Trump era.

American democracy of today as installed by Russian cyber attacks on American democratic process and the hopefully naïve American Electoral College process which has failed the will of the American people once again.

POTUS/45, has now made it clear he stands with Russian KGB Intelligence over our own American Central Intelligence, posing the question to you the American "Where do you stand?"

Our American Democracy is an ever evolving norm setting social revolution into tomorrow in the lives of all Americans whereas, the Donald era into tomorrow is only a God given moral indicator to learn from and make our plans into the future as the resistance of tomorrow.

Our democratic electoral socialist process failed the American people by way of Russian political foreign influence into our national 2016 elections.

The prosecution of the law must be executed as the safe guards of American Democracy regardless of the person, or position and/or political party gains and/or losses as a matter of national moral virtue; impeach now and carry on with American Democratic justice as a matter of fact in American legal process towards anyone or any entity willing to engage the American people.

Thank-you all for reading my writings Arturo Cortez/76541/04/25/2019

## 04/29/2019

Don, Roberto please be advised I supported  Vice President Joe Biden in 2008, and his Vice Presidential re-election in 2012, we now have about 20 young Democratic Si se Puede candidates hoping to be the nominee of the Democratic Political Party for President in 2020.

Whoever wins the Democratic nomination will inhered a unified movement of 20 seasoned unified Political Resistance Teams, whereas all democrats have the willing to take on the President in 2020 unfortunately many will not have the money to compete in a American capitalist Democracy, these political Teams will for-fit their campaigns to the other political campaign doing battle to win the Presidency in 2020.

President Barack Obama, like the Resistance will not influence the 2020 primaries in respect to the American people and our own choice in our democratic process.

The new Administration will take control of our nation united under one democracy, one Senate, one House of Representatives and one equal Executive Branch of the people of the United States of America. In this regard American democracy can re-evaluate and reintegrate American Democracy as our sovereign electoral process of one American human=one vote for our nation.

I Sir understand narcissism as a double edged sword of human virtue; personal arrogance is a dangerous proposition which is respected and admired wherever there are more than one human in a room.

So it is Sir that we all must learn to manage our own narcissistic ways. Whereas we as American Leaders must learn that there are

Americans who are raised with American "Whipping Boys" who now occupy the highest political offices in our land.

Don, Roberto I ask that you please reference my 2008, 2012, and 2016 Si se Puede Candidates list, you will find that the candidates running for the democratic nomination for President in 2020 are in my national Democratic Si se Puede Candidates list's available in Google, and my face book page at www.facebook.com/Arturo.cortez.7146.

Joe Biden is not into the issue s at this time, Joe is only concerned with one issue and one issue alone, i ask of you and all Resistance Teams to echo Joe Biden's lead for now. Thank-you Sir for who you are and what you do for our nation./ArturoCortez/76541/04/29/2019

# Chapter 21

**May/2019**

**05/06/2019**

Take the Russian long range boomers out of Central America the Russians can now strike anywhere in the American Hemispheres at will thanks to all the Republicans that support Donald Trump/ Arturo Cortez/76541/05/06/2019

It was my mother who once screamed at me "I send you to school and what do you do, you eat the crayons," go brush your teeth mother screamed at me, when I did brush my teeth I noticed I still had a piece of lettuce from a Texas Burger I had eaten earlier in the day, stuck to my teeth.

Son, it is my believe "never mind."

Hector Hinojosa, it was so nice to spend time with the troops in Oregon. I am back home now in Texas living out my life once again; writing my writings of hope and promise to all those who need perspective and understanding and continue my God given mission here in the Heart of Texas.

As a writer I understand how it is not about whether the reader likes my writings or not, so much as it is that when critics of my writings read my writings and like or dislike my writings I am pleased simply because someone out there took the time to read my writings, so I try to communicate my thanks to the reader of the writing and sometimes have to ask the Reader to consider my Resistance writings as a grain of salt to their daily lives.

Hector amigo, Virginia Garcia Memorial Health Centers Foundation has received our invitation to assist us in creating a Pacific Northwest community health "Patient Advisory Committee" in order that we can monitor minimum standards within the health care service delivery systems within the Pacific Northwest.

My instructions to you have now changed; you are to proceed with your instructions with or without Virginia Garcia. I will expect to hear from you on Wednesdays, this carnal we do for our people. Para q Viva La Gente, Como La Gente," ArturoCortez/la casa de Cortez/ Killeen76541

The Resistance Candidates of today are now re-establishing the democratic process of selecting/electing candidate who will lead our nation into tomorrow, our yet to be elected American United States President. Our divers Democratic candidates are now giving all American voters a socialist democratic the choice to select and or elect our next American President of over twenty candidates who will responsibly represent the American people rather than allowing our now American President to proudly represent the will of the Russian KGB dictators who now rules over Russia and the United States of America.

The Resistance leaders, followers and Teams must glorify themselves among other's and the American voter as the purpose of American Democracy, regardless of political party this year our only goal is to remove and replace our United States Executive Branch of government with truthful moral democratic political candidates dedicated to servicing the needs of the American people.

We must support and glorify American Democracy with one another; the Resistance now reflects no less the 20 well seasoned democratic political teams. This year some if not most teams will not be able to finish out the year due to our capitalist form of democracy.

However, these teams and their political warriors will united amongst each other to establish more powerful Presidential political teams going into the 2020 General Presidential Election.

The American people must not be over whelmed by our now Russian Republican Party Propaganda. We must work with all Americans regardless of political ideologies we are all Americans for American Democracy.

Your mission at the Democratic Debates is simple, Donald Trump has a nickname for every one running against him, and it is your mission Julian Castro, to nickname Donald Trump "The Liar" at the Democratic Debates; whereas, Americans today must not show no mercy and no shelter or quarters to any liar regardless of Presidential standing a liar is a liar whether a Republican Russian liar or not /Arturo Cortez/05/08/2019

## ArturoCortez/05/08/2019

Team Beto please follow Old Joe's lead for now to stay in the running, for now.

José Jaime, Si se Puede Community Organizer, San Alejandro, Román Catholic Church, Cornelius, Oregón bajo el padre, Bézier 1970, Amigo, it is so good to hear you will be coming to Texas.

I first arrived back to live here in Killeen in May of 2011, much has changed since I was here last, but one thing is clear Texas appears to be in denial of who we are as "La Republica de Texas."

I was born in Mission, Texas where as a young man i could through a rock across the Rio Grande, and it would land "en el otro lado"/ Mexico of today.

Amigo, ethnic Tejano culture is under siege to a sub-culture level in its own land, our Tejano music is no longer a Tejano social family cultural affair, but rather "Cantina Music" from the legend of what we once was the proud united diversified Texano Nation/ Peoples de la Republic.

In or about 1824, then CIA Operative Stephen Austin secured permission from the Mexican government to allow200 English colonial families to settle in the independent Hispanic Mexican region of Central Texas of today.

These first English families to Texas in 1824 had to convert to the Roman Catholic religion in Texas of that time. The first English in Texas had to learn the Mexican National language, and the Diversified Hispanic Nations were to refer to English Settlers then in Texas as the Mexican/American in the heart of Texas.

Hijole, Don Beto you just got my $20.00 when you lit the torch to American Democratic human dignity, with last night's Town Hall in Iowa.

**Impeachment is justified and must proceed** in order to define ourselves as the people of the United States as sovereign among other nations of this world of today. Impeachment will unite right thing to do Republicans and Democrats behind what is right for our nation.

**La Resistencia/2019** stands proud with you Beto O'Rourke, for President in your call to impeach the 45th President of the United States of American Donald Trump/ "The LIAR". Political Party gains and losses are not of legal process and should not influence the lawful process of Impeachment.

**Nancy Pelosi** is wrong, Impeachable offences by the President of the United States become precedent for other Presidents to follow.

**Donald Trump** and Russia are now defining American Democracy, as well as our American rule of law, and must be removed from office his On the Job Presidential Training opportunity is now over and Donald Trump learned  nothing from the experience, he must now go for the sake the people of our nation.

Donald Trump wants and will strike at and Iran for the sake of getting re-elected as his form of keeping America under Russian siege.

I encourage other leaders and Candidates to follow Beto O'Rourke to Impeach for the sake of American Democratic Dignity/ADD/Arturo Cortez/05/22/20119

## 05/24/2019

Team Color of Change, La Resistencia is strong with in you, "less we have one humane law for all, as one human race created by our one and only God, we have nothing with regard to American Human Dignity,"/Arturo Cortez/76541/05/24/2019

### "The Sixth Commandment

### By Arturo Cortez,

If you know this woman Maria Evangelina Vargas, Rios de Cortez my mother, you are encouraged by the Hillsboro, Oregon Tuality Hospital to come and say your fair wells; mother suffered a Stroke on the 8th day of May 2018. I arrived in Oregon on the 9th day of May and i was able to be at her, her bed side for five days during my Mother's Day stay in Oregon this year 2019, after the 3rd day in Oregon my mother woke, and I asked for her forgiveness if I had ever offended her in any way, I was forgiven and Bless by my mother, in her gracious manner my mother told me that she had been praying to God in her dreams, that she had asked "God" to allow her to see me one more time, and then she asked me to forgive her if ever I felt she had done me wrong" I explained, "that there is nothing to forgive you are my mother and I can only see your love for me mother," I explained; I can only love you, thank-you, and Bless you mother for who you are," I explained.

With the passing of this woman of man I will never again have the feelings of honoring the Lord our God's 6th commandment in my mother's time in life, that era in my time will have passed in my life; written in stone the 6th Commandment: "Honor thy Father, and thy Mother", as our one and only God does collect in-kind;

I left Oregon on the 14th day of May convinced that my mother will not be with us long, and a sort of relive that my mother and i had settled our accounts with the feelings that my mother has now helped me honor the Lord my Gods 6th Commandment in her life, with her blessings on me, I am very Blessed for the time the Lord our God allowed me to spend with my mother this Mother's Day 2019 in her life, /Arturo Cortez/76541/05/30/2019

# Chapter 22

**June/2019**

**06/01/2019**

Son, writing the story the "Sixth Commandment" was very difficult for me to write based on my believe as a man of our one and only God creator. The Lord and God, Jehovah who created knowledge and gifted knowledge to human of all the creatures rooming in our world.

Human's ability to learn and know is to some, and was to others either a blessing or a curse to humanity as we know it today.

So it is that today man and knowledge have now evolved into human in his or hers own personal world, with to windows looking out and sometimes judging others, who are doing the same from the world they see from their own windows of personal knowledge as a human virtue.

In my world I try to live a life of peace and respect for others as my way to glorify myself and other among my Texas village, there is no place in my world for hate or haters, whether of the same feather or not; we are all of one human race gifted individually with the lord our God's mission imprinted in our heart the only real deal for us is whether we are of the lion, or of the lamb.

Son nowhere in my writings do I say that my mother has died however, it is intrusting to me as a writer how the 6th Commandment can be interpreted, my mother is still here with us for those who care enough to know.

Lastly, son again I want to thank-you and Kelly for making it possible for me to honor my believe in our God with regards to the Six Commandment, as a part of this e-mail I have included the other nine of ten Commandments to live by, this version the 6th commandment."

## The Ten Commandments (Exodus 20:2-17 NKJV)

1. "I am the Lord your God, who brought you out of the land of Egypt, out of the house of bondage. You shall have no other gods before Me.

2. "You shall not make for yourself a carved image, or any likeness of anything that is in heaven above, or that is in the earth beneath, or that is in the water under the earth; you shall not bow down to them nor serve them. For I, the Lord your God, am a jealous God, visiting the iniquity of the fathers on the children to the third and fourth generations of those who hate Me, but showing mercy to thousands, to those who love Me and keep My Commandments.

3. "You shall not take the name of the Lord your God in vain, for the Lord will not hold him guiltless who takes His name in vain.

4. "Remember the Sabbath day, to keep it holy. Six days you shall labor and do all your work, but the seventh day is the Sabbath of the Lord your God. In it you shall do no work: you, nor your son, nor your daughter, nor your male servant, nor your female servant, nor your cattle, nor your stranger who is within your gates. For in six days the Lord made the heavens and the earth, the sea, and all that is in them, and rested the seventh day. Therefore the Lord blessed the Sabbath day and hallowed it.

5. "Honor your father and your mother, that your days may be long upon the land which the Lord your God is giving you.

6. "You shall not murder.

7. "You shall not commit adultery.

8. "You shall not steal.

9. "You shall not bear false witness against your neighbor.

10. "You shall not covet your neighbor's house; you shall not covet your neighbor's wife, or his male servant or his female servant or his ox or his donkey or anything that is your neighbor's."

Son, the ten commandments did not come numbered but the content is pretty much the same, and remember that regardless what side of this law you are on, it is meant to be, by the will of our creator, we are not meant to judge others based on what we see out our window, whereas even Jesus el Christo "el carpintero" prayed on his knees to his father Jehovah God. Arturo Cortez/76541/06/01/2019

## 06/09/2019

### American Capitalism:

American capitalism is and must always be a independent metric/instrument of social success for thriving Americans interested in gambling away their accumulative wealth in commercial markets of profits and losses meant to stimulate capitalist business values for gain and profits of personal wealth, and individual social American security as a now human need to be a success among our American peers of American societies of today; Capitalism is not now, nor should it ever be the political purpose of our foundational American Socialist Democracy of the people. American socialist Democracy must not be deluded by individual or corporate capitalist business or business ventures.

Let us be clear to All Americans  that we are the global Democratic model to the Globe as well as the world's first Socialist political governess to ever govern as a Socialist Democracy, now under siege by the powers of American global capitalist interest within our 2  party political system of the United States dollar $ bill.

Our American socialist Democracy is now, and has always been of and for the American people first as much as the American Democratic vote is the socialist voice of the American people by way of popular vote of the people. Whereas, all American states of the union of American of States must forfeit any and all electoral votes to the popular vote of the people regardless of political party national handicaps.

Our socialist electoral process to electing our American Leadership to public trust and public service lacks the honor and respect from foreign Russian influence over what is today a phony capitalist Republican GOP who now interprets American conservative values solely based on Donald Trump virtues of human value with in what should be a party of the conservative values of the American people as our American socialist Democracy requires the political party to represent the social values of the people of the Party as the purpose of the political party.

American Capitalism is not meant to be the purpose of our American Socialist Democracy; American business must be kept competitive within business opportunities of profit and losses environments for American Business to thrive in the United Sates and the world. Competitive business is what makes our American economies as great as they are today within a nation of haves, and have knots.

## The Republican Party

The Republican Party of today offers the American people no other Republican Candidate but Donald Trump for President in the 2020 General Presidential Election. This action by the Republican Party of today denies all Republicans their civil right to select the Republican leader they wish to have for President in the 2020 Primaries. Whether to the left, or to the right of your political party wing the Republican voters are now given no choice but to vote democrat or don't vote at all in 2020 for the good of the nation.

As is, today there is no conservative Republican leader within the Republican Party to challenge Donald Trump in the 2020 Primaries meaning to the Resistance that POTUS/45/Donald Trump is not only the President of the United States, but absolute authoritarian Republican Party of today.

## Impeachment

Although, the responsibility to Impeach the President of the United States should belong to the political Party which elected the incompetent presidential candidate to public service as President of the United States, in this case the Republican Party aided in the appointment of the United States President POTUS/45, Donald Trump, it is now clear that the Republican Party Leadership in the United States Senate, and the United States House of Representatives has now embraced Democratic Authoritarianism over our American based Socialist Democratic Democracy, in political deeds and political action as American's newest populous Authoritarian Nationalist Republican Conservatism.

The Republican Party as we remember it is no more and what is left of the Republican Party is now a dysfunctional political wing of our American Socialist American Democratic political two party system; Republicans must now face the facts that their own Republican leadership structure has now eaten the heart out of what once was the proud Grand Old Party (GOP) of Abraham Lincoln, a party of humane honorable conservative virtue. The Republican of today must now show its questionable patriotism to American Socialist Democracy in unity with all American voters come November 2020, as the first step to rebranding the Republican Party to what the Republican Party is meant to be to the people of our nation.

Whereas, in reality Donald Trump is no different than any other candidates attempting to get elected come November 2020 with the exception that we all know as American voters it is impossible to lead as a American liar as President, it is now up to the Democratic Party to Impeach the President of the United States for breaking and obstructing our American laws. Impeachment is a safe guard of American Democracy not a political party instrument to ensure profit and loss of political party use to dominate in party rule.

If a crime has been committed the crime must be must be punished to the full extent of the law as our American way of life.

Win or lose come November 2020 a crime against the people of our nation and our American way of life has been committed against the people of the United States, it is the Democratic Party who must implement the legal Democratic Remedies established by the founders of American Democracy and Impeach the President of the United States.

Impeachment is a Democratic Presidential safe guard political process; by the Congress of the United States Democratic Congress doing nothing to enforce the law Donald Trump continues to dismantle American democracy at home and around the world.

La Resistencia encourages all United States Representatives Republican and Democrats in the House of Representatives to vote for "Impeachment Indictment" of Donald Trump as a matter of legal justice, and inquirery. Whereas, we as Americans can and must do both Impeach and continue with our national political election as a matter of legal political process; Donald Trump is only one American candidate for President of many and all in many ways are much better candidates than Donald Trump.

I do remind you all that American Democracy did give the proven United States a liar Republican United States President in Donald Trump/POTUS/45 who has now received a four year appointed democratic opportunity to lead our nation; Whereas, the Donald has now squandered his presidential political opportunities to evolve as the American President of all the American people, Donald Trump failed his public service mission as president and we the American people must now do what is right for the good of Americans and the global we share with other nations.

Whether you are for or against the logic I write about, once I publish my truth to power my writings are there to stay for generations yet to come to reference and there will be no doubt as to where I stood during these historic times in American political History.

So I must write that many of the Democratic Candidates I have supported in my time as the Si se Puede Candidates Support Lists over the years which you can reference @ google.com are now 2020 Presidential Candidates for President of the United States 2020.

The Democratic Party and/or the Republican Party must never concede a Presidential Election prior to the final count of the popular vote, otherwise we are allowing the Electoral College to appoint the President of the United States in the stead of electing the President by way of the American popular vote as is the purpose

of our American form of socialist democratic electoral process. /
ArturoCortez/76541/06/09/2019

### 06/09/2019  Jen O'Malley Dillon

Campaign Manager

**Beto for America,** Beto is to move towards the popular vote;
please reference a resent vote by the State of Maine Legislature on
a bill to forfeit their State Electoral College votes to the American
popular vote of the people.

Jen O'Malley, if handled properly this issue can set Beto apart
from the rest of the field and a possible strong placement post in
the first debate.

Thank-you for staying true to the center of partisan politics,
and your effort to keep our political teams together post 2020
Primers, this will serve us all well in the November 2020 General
Election.

Three Strategic Issues for Beto to Concider for now:

"Beto must demand every State in the Nation forfeit their
Electoral College Vote to the American Democratic National
Popular Vote of the American people."

Old Joe's weakness is that neither he nor Barack passed
Comprehensive Immigration Reforms, they both left that for
Hillary to deal with; today we have one heck of a problem in
Central America, and no real Central American policy to deal
with the problem.

Don, Beto will stabilize the Central American economies
by providing economic development opportunities to Central
Countries who qualify; "El Donald" denied "Shit Hole Countries
economic opportunities, and today we have mass migrations
towards, safety and economic opportunities in the United States.

Jen, please be advice our numbers have not moved much for a while now, but we are still in the game thank-you for what you do for the Resistance, /ArturoCortez/76541/06/09/2019

## /ArturoCortez/76541/06/22/2019

Nancy Pelosi, Speaker of the House

### "Impeach Now"

The United States as a sovereign nation has earned the global respect as the world's first Democracy. Nations from around the world do model their own state governments after our own socialist form of American democracy. Whereas, government by democratic popular vote of the people. In the 2016 General Election the popular vote of the people elected Hillary Clinton for President, by 3,000,000 votes. The Republican candidate for President Donald Trump was appointed President by the Electoral College. Whereas, in historical democratic retrospect the last Republican to get elect by popular American vote of the American people was President, Ronald Regan. The American democratic vote at a Executive Presidential level has been denied the popular vote of the people by Republican political design in the use of the Electoral College political system.

The November 2020 General Election is and will be about whether our country will continue to be of the Socialist Democratic American voter of the people, or of a government of the Capitalist appointed government officials of the political parties. The Donald of the extremes has now challenged the legal powers of American Democracy, and only the Democrats can answer that call to Impeach for the sake of American democracy, and we all the people of our nation.

## Impeachment

Impeachment Is not a question of political privileges or convinenous, but rather a question of American moral political convictions to what we are and what we represent to ourselves and those around us in our world of today. Impeachment is not for political party advantages over other political parties? It is for the Speaker of the House of Representatives (The United States Congress) to do what is right for the American people as her responsibilities requires her to act on behave of all the people of the United States.

Looking the other way in denial of the facts to Impeach as the right thing to do is not an option for our National Speaker of the House of Representatives, California Representative Nancy Pelosi.

Whereas, if Donald Trump has done nothing wrong, the Donald would have nothing to fear or lose form our effort to Impeach under our American legal laws of Impeachment for wrong doing.

The President of the United States along with his Presidential powers must never be above premeditated evidence of legal wrong doing by obstruction of justice or otherwise. We are a nation of laws which governs us all and keeps our Socialist Democracy together and protected from abuse of powers by elected or appointed Presidents of the United States.

Impeachment will unite the Right thing to do Republicans, and Right thing to do Democrats under American diversified American Democracy.

Whereas, the American Eagle requires two wings to fly, our American skies as one under God's will. Protecting the nation from the truth about the Donald leaves our American people of our nation in dramatic doubt of what is right, and what is wrong with American democratic leadership within the two party politics system of today, we can Impeach, and we can continue with our United States General Election process with or without the Donald Trump Presidential Reality Show of today.

Democratic Leadership must start from within radical social perspectives of today, as our own American democracy is an ongoing humanist socialist revolution in foundational retrospect of what we are today as a nation of diversified immigrants as the nation within the nation of today.

Nancy Pelosi, Donald Trump must be Impeach because he legally qualified himself to be impeached, and the American people need to find peace in justice whether there are those who are above our American laws because of political power and influence or not as a first leadership step to heal American democracy from the damages the Donald has done to American democracy.

If the Donald has done nothing wrong the American voters can reward him come November 2020 by way of popular vote of the American voters./ ArturoCortez/76541/06/22/2019

## /ArturoCortez/76541/06/25/2019

La Resistencia stands firm with Bernie Sanders Candidate for President and the United States and his stand on free public education for all citizens of the United States as well as Bernie's "Citizen Bill of Rights Campaign" La Resistencia finds both these proposals consistent with our traditional American political virtue of a socialist nation of its people by democratic vote as intended by the founding fathers of our nation.

Bernie, your perspective on American Democracy is the American tenacity it took the founders of our nation to build our American Socialist Democracy of today; which today finds itself in political denial of who we are as one America of the new world still in conflict with our native selves as sweet water immigrants to the new world of today, of inter-national boundaries created by salt water immigrants to the new American world of today.

In our 500 year old European new world  historical retrospect of new world history, new world history of today dose show a theological parallel evolutionary process consistent to the ancient Aztec prophecies of the welcomed death, and re-birth of a native new world people in the American native Mestizo/the new world Mix by conquest. /ArturoCortez/76541/06/25/2019

## ArturoCortez/76541/06/26/2019

La Resistencia calls on all Republicans and or Democrats, liberals, Centralist and Conservatives to pay attention to the 24 democratic candidate in tonight's Democratic Debates and make your personal selection of who you would want to be our next President of the United States, remember the Republican Party has denied its republican membership the opportunity to a democratic Socialist vote/selection of a honorable Republican Presidential Candidate for President.

American democracy has never been so challenged from within based on national and global capitalist influence over our American electoral democratic process, the present President POTUS/45/ Donald Trump has conceded our national political honor and pride to service the global and domestic needs of a now global axis of evil, with Donald Trump and his evil American supporters as the hub of a global axis of evil.

Once you have made your Presidential selection for President please make a $20.00 capitalist political contribution to the candidate you have selected as your choice for President whereas the Republican Candidate can only be viewed as one of 25 political candidates for United States President.

You can then follow and volunteer to the campaign whether you are of Republican or Democratic Parties, as a American voter you do have the right to vote on who you think will do the best job for all voting Americans and the nation.

We voting as one America can heal American Democracy by establishing Democratic control over the Executive Offices of the President, the Senate, and the Congress regardless of political parties. The humane elements of American Governess have now become extinct within now a capitalist dollar value for American human at a government policy level under the Donald Trump Administration.

Regardless of political ideology we have a human obligation to do the right thing for who we are as our own American Democracy please take the time to donate Blue for the good of the nation. / ArturoCortez/76541/06/26/2019

## ArturoCortez/76541/06/28/2019

Bravo, Julián Castro for President, on" Immigration Reforms," Julian Castro for President, offered radical change on immigration reforms on the first Democratic debate in 2019 for the 2020 national Presidential Debates by simply going back to what we were prior to U.S. Code 1325 needed to establish the necessary inclusive cultural norms for establishing comprehensive immigration reforms.

The former Housing and Urban Development Director for the Barack Obama Administration Julian Castro, proposed to remove U.S. Code 1325 which now criminalizes families for seeking asylum and refuge/ help from the United States and authorizes the brake up of immigrant families unites as well as authorizes jailing of children and their parents. Julian for President sighted that much of what Code 1325 provides is already covered in laws under U.S. Title 18, and Title 21.

The Resistance agrees with Julian Castro's proposal to the American people to remove code 1325 in that "Once a immigrant legally inters the United States he or she is subject to our American domestic Law.

A immigrant would then have to break a American law and be found guilty of the crime in order to qualify as a criminal immigrant, and deportation as a matter of American public civil law.

In all fairness to all the 25 candidates for president 2020, La Resistencia conceders 24 of you better American Leaders and there for better U.S. candidates/leaders for President of our American every day of lives. You are all better qualified candidates to lead our nation when compared to our single Republican incumbent Electoral College appointed U.S. President P.O.T.U.S./45/ Donald Trump.

We the American people are now paying the Democratic price for the 2016 General Election, Electoral College appointment of a now rouge president who was never elected by the people; Donald Trump who now leads by appointment when he lost the 2016 General election by popular American Vote by 3,000,000 votes to Hillary Clinton.

Whereas, the people elected Hillary Clinton by popular vote for President of the United States in political fact however, it was the Democrat Hillary Clinton who conceded her popular vote of the people to the Electoral College appointment of Donald Trump with no regards to the will of the people of the United States who had voted for her.

All democratic campaigns/Resistance teams must now take the time to lick their political wounds after the Democratic Debates; remember that ever candidate in these 2019 Democratic Political Debate has now establish themselves as national political leaders. Whereas, if our true purpose is to identify the right candidate to defeat and replace Donald Trump for President in 2020.

Then we as American citizens have the patriotic responsibility to our supporter and the nation to empower, unite and integrate our diverse democratic political efforts and values behind a different campaign and/or candidate who the candidate fills will serve their cause well regardless of whether one is a Republican or a Democrat in American political ideological identification, as a civic responsibility.

In 2020 Americans have no other choice but to vote for one Republican who the Republican Party feels is your only choice, or vote for one of 24 democratic 2020 Democratic Candidates who you feel would be the better President. Whereas, Donald Trump after 3 years as President has self defined himself as a liar U.S. President by global judgment of our time.

Whereas, the Resistance is not for the political parties; the Resistance is for the American people who are for America as our American Democracy in political ideological perspectives of where we are going as one American nation of today.

Regardless of your American political party identification you do have the right in 2020 to vote for the best the Republican Party has to offer and Donald Trump is not the best that Conservative America has to offer to the American people, you could qualify yourselves to select from 24 better candidates for American President by voting Democrat if you really feel we need to elected a different president by popular vote of the people as the purpose of American democracy for the good of the nation, based on the trust and faith the founders of American Democracy placed on us all as the American People of today, ArturoCortez/76541/06/28/2019

## ArturoCortez/7654106/30/2019

Lan Carter i do feel good that i made my honest effort to serve my community as Mayor of the City of Killeen, i have been told that i wound have done better if i were a local. unfortunately i agree the people of Killeen do feel the need to elect local carpet beggars to solve the City of Killeen's historical political problems, i feel good knowing that i did make a effort to share my expertise with the people of Killeen who i gave the opportunity to do the right thing for themselves by voting for me, the rest i leave to Texas history to judge, so it is i thank-you for reading my writings, Fri 9:53 PM Arturo, I'm not sure it would have made a difference if you were a local or not. The same people continue to be elected because they have a voting block and they ensure "their" Republicans get elected as they have PACs to promote advertising. Never give up, keep running as the citizens are finally starting to see the light. Hopefully, next year will be the year. Sorry, Lan my effort to serve was a good will effort I can always fall back on in my old age in my retirement, on the other hand I do not work for nothing for the City of Killeen or anyone else only slave labor is historically accustomed to serve in that manner. I have no need of being grate or better than anyone else in Killeen but it does appear to me as though i am rightfully viewed as a horse of a different color with in this American City and this State of Texas, by the grace of God. I made my honest effort to serve the residents of the City of Killeen, I do feel good about my political efforts to share my intellectual expertise with the City of Killeen, and the citizens of Killeen, I will never run for Killeen public office again, i do wish all you all as the locals of Killeen the best without me as a humanist thorn to the Republican Party political dictatorship control over the citizens of the City of Killeen. As a now Home Owner within the City of Killeen i will protect and advocate for my home ownership equity in my home and property with the best of my legal intellectual capabilities as a personal investment. As for the rest of my time in Killeen we will let Texas history judge us all.

# CHAPTER 23

July/2019

**07/11/2019**

The Arturo Cortez Letter of Complaint, Grievance and Weasel Blower Intent Report:

From: Arturo Cortez to: The "Social Security Fraud Hot-Line"

P.O. Box 17785

Baltimore, Maryland 21235, U.S.A.

Regarding: Retirement, Survivor and Disability Insurance Benefits, Social Security member victimized by, Social Security Administration, Retirement, Survivors and Disability Insurance member ArturoCortez/S.S.#/ E-mail: 1ArturoCortez@gmail.com Texas, 76541

Home Address: Arturo Cortez

Killeen, Texas 76541

Grievance & Weasel Blower Letter of Complaint:

Social Security Administration consistently makes mistakes on my account as well as other accounts in order to disrupt my right to a peaceful secure retired life in my later years, i assume i am not the only one who is effected by deliberate Social Security Accounting Errors which are now used as punishment by denial of human right to life support benefits to those of us Americans with chronic illness without our American civil right to be heard by Administrative Hearings prior to denial of our monthly live support benefits which we as Americans have paid for with our work to be used as our governmental retirement insurance; in doing so the Social Security of the United States has now established itself as nothing less than a tax payer funded Governmental Social Security "Bureaucratic Death Panel" in social impact on we the capitalist Americans who depend on our monthly retirement payments which we have paid for in order to retire in honor and dignity to say the least in my case.

Whereas there are others who have literally lost their lives because of Social Security Accounting Errors which Social Security shamelessly admits to in writing? In doing so S.S.A. does now have the Administrative Bureaucratic government right to terminate American life by administrative action it deliberately creating Accounting Errors as the responsibility of the uninformed client with our own personal American national Retirement Funds?

I ask the Social Security Fraud "Hot Line" to conceder this complaint, and Grievance as my Weasel Blower Complaint of July 10th 2019, supporting evidence is archived at Social Security Offices across our nation, as well as at La Casa de Cortez, Publications archives @ Killeen, Texas/76541.

Democratic Candidates for President you all make me proud to be ArturoCortez, here in Texas, you have a wonderful day, "Q siga la Resistencia a lo Pendejo" /ArturoCortez/76541/07/12/2019

## 07/12/2019

In my professional observation Pendejismo is self educed in order to create other self endued Pendejos, to accomplish Russian Republican political goals for the American people,

It is only fair that the Democrats and the Republicans play by the same rules this image is topical of Russian KGB propaganda established to dismantle Easter European democratic governments as well as Western Democratic European governments.

Whether American Democracy survives this Russian political assault by the Russian government on American socialist democracy with the Donald Trump in play, is not by fate or chance, the United States is now under political siege by way of our own political moral standards of our diversified selves.

November 3, 2020 some 15 months from today we all will go vote for a new president and I ask everyone to register to vote, pick a candidate, and donate of yourselves, and your money.

I encourage the right thing to do conservatives, and the right thing to do Democrats to come together as one American nation for America and vote Donald Trump out of office so the United States Congress can put his ass in poky.

We must now come together and do the right thing for our American way of life, or as we say in the construction business you "must do your business or get of the pot and allow others to do it for you."

I was advised by someone who is very; very smart way smarter than all of us that Donald Trump's mission is to destroy American civil order, for the Russian Government.

Whereas it is my believe that The Donald is now building his own capitalist nest with the Russians at the expense of the American people. 07/13/2019

## 07/13/2019

All this is true, but we must honor and tolerate American socialist Democracy of the democratically installed POTUS/45/ regardless what wing the feather belongs too, Donald Trump is the only Republican running for President in 2020 out of 23 highly qualified Democratic Candidates, meaning that the Republican Party now considers itself a monolithic/follow the leader ideological political Party.

There is no Republican Party  left after Donald Trump, there is only a political instrument left for Donald Trump to dismantle our American Socialist Democracy as our American way of life all this for the sake of understanding American greatness/Arturo Cortez/76541"Q Siga La Resistencia"

Bill Rosenberg old friend a man who believes he must carry a gun to be equal amongst others, in a #s minority setting is not someone you want to discuss party politics with, La Resistencia understands that the Administration wants to make it about political parties when the issue is whether the 2020 election will be about American Democracy first.

I call on both Republicans and Democrats to come together as one for America and vote the abusive Republican bums out of office simply because they have betrayed their own conservative kind in social Republican cultural virtue,/Arturo Cortez/07/13/2019

## 07/14/2019

Central Texas Tejano grass-root Political Warriors make their stand in the Heart of Texas for, and against human dignity as the purpose of Hispanic Texano national virtue of the Old Republica de Texas today.

Long live the Resistance/ la Resistencia en Texas, so that the Texano people can live like the honorable people of God that we are as one diversified human race, once again in Texas, we as the Texano people must not help the United States government hunt human immigrants on Texano grounds, we are now the Texanos who have now, and continue to separate a mother from her child for seeking asylum/human help from ungoverned evils of human of man i pray that the Lord our GOD forgive us all for what we do, and what we don't do.

All proud Texanos across Texas and the nation are encouraged to stand down on hunting human immigrants for the United States of North America.

Texano Villages, Texano Cities, Texano Counties, and the Texas State Government long with all theological institutions, and Texano non-profits, are encouraged to do the will of the people of God and offer human Refuge to any and all human Immigrants on American soil today underfoot of POTUS/45 Donald Trump. ArturoCortez/76541/07/14/2019

I have been blessed in my time to have been both a employee, and later a employer like many of you, and i do understand and respect both who together create and fuel our own style of capitalist American democratic socialist democracy.

I know that a employee works to support his family, whereas a employer's job is to keep the employees employed. Whereas, both Employer and employee profit from experience we all know, or should know as human sweat does have equitable value in the market place, as partners in American privileged life of today.

## 07/25/2019

There are those in local Texas Republican Departments of Government Human Services in Texas and across the nation who feel they are from a better God as a party virtue, then the rest of us who make up our Texas village, these too will be weighed, measured and judged by our one and only God regardless how many Sundays the go to church.

Miss, Patsy Kirkland i know you as a giving honorable friend a person true to your word, i have been your Texano neighbor for 5 years, and I have been your personal friend for over 9 years; as a man of God born on the North side of the Rio Grande and raised North of the Red River i know and value the genetic bond between a grand-mother and her grand-children, and i would be honored to stand next to you in public hearing in our diversified Texas village of all types which makes one Texano human race in Texas, ArturoCortez/76541/07/25/2019

# Chapter 24

August/2019

## 08/01/2019

In order to establish comprehensive immigration reforms we must first have a good understanding of who we are historically as sweet water immigrant new world nations of the new world people who never came or were brought as commercial property by other illegal salt water immigrant ancestor on the new world of today.

Today we as the willing, are still led by the unqualified who fail to understand that the new world is where we belong as the rebirth new world native Mestizo (from the mix) of the new world, we really have now place to go but rather we must follow our new world historical traditional immigration trading routes north and south on the new world in search of safety at the expense of human dignity. With the understanding that governess over humanity only works when the governed allow themselves to be governed by want to be civil governments of the new world.

Presidential ideological integrity is the democratic process to the presidency of the United States will serve us well when we go after the old Republica de Texas, "Q Siga La Resistencia para q Viva Texas, God bless you and yours for what you do for we the people of Texas and your selves; "you Sir, make me proud to be ArturoCortez/76541/08/01/2019"

## 08/08/2019

Rob please tell Beto that Americans have been dying throughout history for the American citizen right to stand, sit, or kneel as they wish for the sake of our nation./Arturo Cortez/76541

Discussing hatred is alien to who we are as the American people, come November 3, 2020 you too will have the democratic opportunity to agree or disagree.

La Resistencia, reminds all Candidates for President in 2020 to remember La Resistencia did win the 2018 Mid-term Elections and put a Congressional harness on Donald Trump's plans to dismantle American democracy.

Our National Si se Puede community leaders elected by the people of our nation to represent we the people are now under racist attack by the Executive Offices of the United States.

The Resistance Stands Proud with Community representatives elected to represent their communities within the United States.

Don, Beto the time has come to show the nation that you will be the next unifying President of the United States of North America.

Please Instruct our Si se Puede Resistance teams in Dayton, Ohio and surrounding American States to come together in Dayton; the event must be bi-partisan and pro American we must show the #'s in people in order to establish national mass movement potential which we have been working for in order to stay ahead of free media exposure for our national Movement/ Campaign.

Don, Beto the time has come for you to leading from the Mid-West "now," my best to "los Primo's," but you must be very careful of what you say and do in Mexico you are now of all the American people.

Again our sympathy for all you have learned this week, and all those who have lost their love ones to racial hatred in El Paso, Texas, and Dayton, Ohio; Please Advice /Arturo Cortez/76541/08/08/2019

Congress Person, Joaquin Castro personally as a typical Texano American of today i must say/write i am so proud of you, Julian and Beto, all honorable American Texanos who have stepped up to unite and lead our nation.

Certainly, we have already won Texas from a Texano political perspective; Julian I would view you a honorable candidate in any high level Texas State election.

La Resistencia won the 2018 Mid-Term Elections when we turned the Congress blue and put a harness on Donald Trump's fascist, nationalist, racist, pro-Russian agenda for the American people.

It is certainly our own American arrogance which limits our ability to realize that we are now losing American Democracy to Russians, China, and Iran. Russia today dose have capitalist democratic executive control over the nation of our American people to write the least.

Texano national politics is now changing by the democratic will of the democratic principles of our diversified Texano people in the State of Texas. These campaigns for the democratic nomination for Presidential 2020 can only be viewed as our opportunity to weigh and measure our own Texas intellectual ideological leadership capabilities within our Texas grass-root communities.

Texas community leaders have now exposed themselves to the United States as capable leaders at national political level across the nation and most important in Texas the foundation to American's Republican Party House of political cards.

Both Teams Julian and Beto offer the hopeful pragmatic humane efforts to solving our national concerns to improve and heal the social cultural scares the United States of America has caused to our diversified Hispanic Texano nation within America, and the world of today.

The American duel party electorate must now stand as one for American Democracy in 2020 without. Our Republican patriots Leaders of the United States who are now forced to choose between their nation/people and/or The Donald Trump KGB Party which has now replaced the Grand Old Party/true conservative American Republican Party.

American Democracy must stand for the rule of law in order to overcome the political foreign influence/cyber attacks from alien nations.

The American United States traitor President Donald Trump of the United States of America must now be impeached by the Republican Party and the Democratic Party of today in order for the Party of Lincoln to redeem itself among the conservative Republican Americans of today. Illegal new world Migrations:

We are now, and we have been a nation made up and ruled by foreigners to the new world as illegal salt water immigrates, so it is that I will now tell the story of who we all are as a globally diversified nation with our Historical cultural Foundation deeply rooted and documented America by Hispanic European Spanish ancestors.

The difference between American History today and true history of time is that American History is record to please the ruling democratic political party of that time in history.

However, in order that you can follow this true story I will have to tell you the historical colonial perspective on documented American History.

## THE MEXICAN AMERICAN

The first English colonials to come to what was then the Kingdom of Mexico in or about 1824, Mexico had post a over through-own Mexican Independent Kingdom.

The then young Dictator of Mexico was El General Mexicano Santa Anna who had just over thrown the new independent Kingdom of Mexico.

The New Mexican Kingdom did get its independence from the then 300 year old Kingdom of Nueva Espania created by, Hernando Cortez who is the founder of first European Kingdom of Nueva Espania inland of the main-land of the world in 1519.

But it was the Spanish Navigator, Cristobal Colon who first landed on the new world Caribbean islands in 1492, ten years later on his second trip to the new world Spanish Admiral of the Seven Seas Cristobal Colon landed on what is today East Texas on the Gulf of Mexico in 1502.

It was Cristobal Colon who first illegally colonized the new world of today with illegal Europeans on the new world.

It was however Hernando Cortez who first brought my Cortez family name to the new world in1502; "between 1502-1518" Hernando Cortez participated in the conquest of Espanola and helped Diego Velasquez conquer Cuba known then as the Kingdom of "Espania del Mar."

In 1519 Hernando Cortez Conquered the Aztec Empire a sophisticated well organized nation of over 8,000,000 inhabitants and many stone city capitals throughout Central America. Hernando Cortez as the conqueror of the Aztec stone City Empire of Tenochalcan, did change the name of the name of the Aztec capital to "La Cuidad de los Mexica" "Mexico City" of today.

Hernando Cortez did establish what the old world European Kingdoms of that time knew as American European social civil order on the new world by avoiding racial civil wars by any means amongst the elite 300,000 Aztec Mexica Warriors, of the Aztec native nations.

It was the Spanish Queen Infanta Isabella "La Catholica" in 1492 who first ordered that the new world native in the new world be treated as children in the European social standards they however could not be viewed as human less they had been baptized in the Roman Catholic religion.

The Mexica were a collision of native Southwestern Tribes who had conquered most of Central America in the early 14th century led by the new world Aztec Conqueror Montezuma 1st; Hernando Cortez conquered Montezuma II, Nephew to Montezuma the 1st. 08/12/2019,

Team Bill Maher Old Amigo i understand there is a possible way in which you would vote for a, liar/racist/narcissist/criminal/ environmentalist/pedophile for President on November 3rd 2020, you Sir do make it hard on we the followers none the less, "Gracias," for what you do for la Resistencia/2019 Bill Maher, Republican Russian KGB Cow Pie Propaganda -v- " American Free Media/Press, Now is the time for conservative to register to vote American Democrat in 2020; Republicans must do their Business and get of the pot, "Q Viva La Resistencia" Killeen, Texas

"The Beto Hope in the Vote Rally for President," Dayton, Ohio

Don, Beto our teams in Ohio must put a well planned old fusion presidential political rally together in Dayton Ohio. These resent racial events fine me attempting to understand how "everything that happens does happen for a reason," and so I find myself telling my friends to be careful on the way home, more often than not.

Sir, the Lord our one God has now blessed you with our mission in service to his will for our local American communities, as a nation of the people.

## 08/15/2019

Julian Castro, while most of the country would agree with your first national TV adds as a American Texano of sweet water native origin of the new world; i am not sure the American voter would vote for sympathy towards ethnic cultural identity. Remember that the hold world witnessed, and documented what Donald Trump's racist punk politics do have consequences payable in human lives with sympathy and respect to all the lives lost in Dayton, Ohio and El Paso, Texas, simply because human dignity is much like a double edged sword, heartless when wheeled by a narcissist, fascist, capitalist, racist United States President.

Then again what has happened in El Paso and Dayton is nothing new to colonial fascist control over native America, it is a national historical norm of American Historical Virtue of what we once were as a nation only this time we as a Texano nation are all a part of United States of American fascism it is we La Republica de Texas who are caging Hispanic children for being Hispanic='s from Spanish ancestral origin.

As you may or may not know now we as natives are really not of the white race as it is written in my birth certificate.

La Resistencia supports your candidacy to show in national politics however please be advised the price in this political year is Texas whereas, your political community believes, and personal virtues would better serve us all as a candidate for Texas Governor, with the municipal and national administrative experience to bring positive change to Texas politics.

Nothing personal my friend but in order to change the nation we must first change Texas that is why I came to the heart of Texas; you Don, Julian are a serious key in Texas politics, and I would be honored to serve you in these endeavors to bring honor and respect to the people, and our Texas national culture.

Please be Advised/ArturoCortez/76541/Killeen/08/15/2019

"While pruning an old dead tree branch of my a 200 year old Texas Oak Tree and I had a 10' fall and broke my leg and hip my medical teams call it serious off-line with a fractured right Femur and hip." On this the 15th day of August 2019

# CHAPTER 25

September/2019

**By ArturoCortez/76541/09/05/2019**

Team Scott & White i want to take this opportunity to thank-you all who participated to make me well again, post operations to repair the right side of my body fractured in three different places.

While @ Scott & White I received care 24/7 by Baylor Scott & White's best and not once did I question my purpose there for the lord my God's reason to place me in your trusted hands. So it is, I as a man of God and Team Scott & White now have been tested, weight, and measured by our one and only God, to his diversified human race.

It is certainly proper for Baylor to learn and thrive from one of the many sons of man; upon request I would be willing to discuss the interpretations of Texas Health Care in Texas with health care delivery systems, this I will do for the Texas diversified human race and the health care service delivery systems tasked with providing human faith and dignity to its patients.

I now realize that I will never ever be the same man I was prior to August 15th 2019, I do know I have now been baptized in pain, and I do thank the Lord our God for his faith in me and his time with me in my time in pain /Arturo Cortez/76541/09/05/2019

## By Arturo Cortez/76541/09/18/2019

Team Julián Castro, your performance at the last democratic Debates was outstanding as you showed to be a well informed young lion ready to lead based on factual truth, unfortunately political party favorites usually have the last say as it is a Party.

It was wrong to use the excuse of disrespect towards a political candidate in a national election.

I do believe your young lion approach towards American democratic process will yell the respect and the will of the people, whereas, other candidates will certainly know that the Julián Castro Team is cocked, informed and capable to rock and roll this nation.

Team Castro while national exposure is always good La Resistencia encourages all Texano American Leaders not to lose sight of the price "Texas" in 2020, thank-you Julián Castro for what you do for our Nation you make me proud to be Texano citizen Arturo Cortez/76541

## 09/22/2019

### "Impeach Now"

The Resistance is nothing new to American Democracy our hold American Socialist Constitution is based on our ability to protect our human American right to say "No."

We as American democracy have given POTUS/45/Donald Trump the honor and respect of President, we have allowed President Donald Trump the rare opportunity of Chief Executive of the most powerful nation in the world on the job training, and Mr. Trump has learned nothing from the experience allowed to him by the Electoral College instead, of the people of this nation vote.

However, what is new is that in our time we have to resist Executive American Democracy over the American people. The Donald Trump Republican Party Leaders in office have now lost sight of who it is they represent and for what reason in their elected positions as conservative Republican Leaders of their Party.

The Republican Party "GOP" has now worked itself into a place where the last hope for the Republican Party to survive Donald Trump will be to take out Donald Trump in the 2020 Republican Primaries in order to redeem Republican political party virtue of and for the Republican Party people of this our nation; the Republican party must unite the party behind a new conservative Republican Candidate for the 2020 General Election post Primary Election 2020.

American Democracy has given and respected the Republican POTUS/45/Donald Trump the democratic right to lead our nation.

Whereas, POTUS/45/Donald Trump has failed his Presidential obligations to our American Democracy and has instead made the Presidential choice to challenge our American Intelligence agencies in support of foreign Dictators, Donald Trump has now deliberately downgraded our unified standing with our own allied friendly nations to the United States.

President Donald Trump has now claimed Presidential Privilege over Obstruction of Justice, and uses the Department of Justice as his own presidential law firm.

The Donald has now admitted that he approached the new President of the Ukraine to encourage him to investigate Joe Biden's son for corruption or risk losing $200,000,000 in United States aid to fight the invading Russian Armed forces in the Ukraine.

Donald Trump has now encouraged a foreign government to attack and influence domestic Democratic policy in the American Democracy.

**Impeachment:**

Is not a Political Party a 1/2 'wrench to establish control over the United States House of Representatives of the People of our nation by a ruling political party over another?

Impeachment is the Legal means to remove a United States President from his political Office.

Obstruction of Justice and unlawful acts by the President of the United States of America are but two ways for a United States President of the United States to qualify for Impeachment.

Impeachment will bring some sanity and confidence to the People of our nation; we are a people of the law, not the lawlessness, whereas the Resistance expects the democrats and the Republican to do their business for the American people and get of the pot, so the rest of us can do our own business with American democracy.

Let me remind Team Nancy Pelosi that it was  La Resistencia who won the United States Congress in the 2018 Mid-Term Elections, the purpose for La Resistencia winning in 2018 was so that Donald Trump would be totally exposed to the American People during the 2020 elections.

On behave of the American people who voted for democrats in congress in 2018 I ask the United States House of Representatives to Impeach Donald Trump now so Republicans like Democrats can point towards sanity with in American Democracy in the 2020 horizon in hope of a American better tomorrow.

La Resistencia encourages all Americans to demand Impeachment for Abstraction of Justice upon proof of such acts by the President of the United States.

The ruling political Party in the United States House of Representatives must stand firm and move forward with Impeachment proceedings as prescribed by our American Laws this matter is no longer a political party issue as much as it is a matter of national security to both Republicans, and Democrats as the American citizen of this nation.

Donald Trump the President of the United States has been, and is now a national security risk to our nation. The Mid -Term Elections was won by the Resistance, the Democratic Party Leadership was elected to do by over sight for the people of this nation and we respectfully ask for the United States Congress to do their jobs as elected to do by those of us as the Resistance.

Our Resistance Victory of the 2018 Mid Term Elections was not meant to be a political party bottle neck; Donald Trump should be in full defense mode for Impeachment proceedings at this time; the Speaker of the House of Representatives should be presenting Donald Trump's impeachable offences to the American people of this nation.

It is the purpose of the Resistance to Remove and Replace the appointed United States President Donald Trump, with a presidential candidate who is elected to the Office of the Presidency of the United States by Popular Vote of the people of our nation.

I want to thank all who read my stories of my human right to stand for human dignity as the purpose of American Governess; I ask you all to vote in 2020, vote for what is right for our American people.

Instead of running away from your conservative Republican political virtues I ask the true Republican to vote Donald Trump out of office in the2020 Primaries, and run a different Republican in the 2020 General Presidential Election as your attempt to re-unite your political party. ArturoCortez/76541/09/22/2019

/"Q Viva La Resistencia, para q viva la independencia en la alma de su gente" ArturoCortez/76541/**09/27/2019**

By Arturo Cortez

## Memo to the Resistance:

On Wednesday September 24th @ 4:00 PM ET the United States Speaker of the House of Representatives convened her Congressional Democratic ruling political Party of the United States Of North America; The Speaker of the House Nancy Pelosi, proclaimed that all Chair persons of congressional committees from this time forward would do their work under the protections as legal arms of Congressional Impeachment Inquiry Committees, in order to establish time line coordination of Impeachment Indictments for Obstruction of Justice by President of the United States, Donald Trump.

54 Republican Senators agreed with Senate Democrats and vote as one to demand the White House release the Whistleblowers report meant for the House of Representatives and intercepted by the White House, a unified non-partisan Senate vote was called for in the Republican controlled United States Senate, who will eventually have to judge evidence brought forth for Impeachment purposes by the United States Congress.

The Impeachment Inquiry Process of President Donald Trump must never be a part of the 2020 Presidential Electoral Process; President, Donald Trump must be viewed as one of 20 political candidates for the 2020 Presidency of the United States.

The American Electorate must not be used as Donald Trump's Toilet Paper with regards to his personal Impeachment. POTUS/45 Donald Trump selfishly qualified himself for Impeachment, that in itself is a political problem for Donald Trump and not the rest of the Resistance Political Candidates running for presidential political office in 2020.

Presidential Candidates must not engage Impeachment prior to post Primary Elections which will allow the Republican Party the necessary time to unite behind a creatable republican for the Republican 2020 Presidential Nominations.

We the people of the United States are a nation of our American laws whereas, "if you have not broken the law, you simply have nothing to fear/or lose." We the American understand that no one person is above the law regardless if it be a want to be Capitalist Royal within American Democracy to include the President of the United States. Our laws are what keep our United States Republic a Republic of and for the people of the United States.

The Impeachment of the Donald is not about political parties, but rather Impeachment is of American legal Judicial Process for those elitist Presidents who function in lawlessness, and Abuse of Presidential powers.

Impeachment is something Donald Trump the Republican Presidential Candidate has accomplished for himself by his own choice, we as the American citizen must learn from the wisdom conveyed by the Impeachment of Donald Trump as President of the United States regardless of political party afflation Impeachment is about American Law and constitutional Patriotism to the United States of America, and not about the justification of Donald Trump the predator within our American legal way of life.

La Resistencia would like to remind the Republicans of the Donald Trump Republican Party, to think about who elected them, and why, when the time comes to dump that bum snake oil sells man out of our American governess as the framers of our constitution prophesized would happen and entrusted over sight powers over the President of the United States within the United States House of Representatives which makes American Law.

In short Donald Trump's Impeachment is now the choice which Donald Trump's Presidential Leadership has forced all Americans to make, "for or against foreign nationalist dictatorship –v- our established American Democratic way of American life.

Donald Trump has now received his rightful democratic opportunity to lead all Americans and he has now failed under his assumption that he is now the first American King of the people of the world, Donald Trump must now "go" on his own or face Impeachment by his own political peers who must now judge themselves based on our American understands and interpretations of our American Constitution. ArturoCortez/76541/09/27/2019

# CHAPTER 26

October/2019

S uch are the rules of our Capitalist Socialist By-partisan Democracy of those who feel they have, and those who know they have not, my friends.

Team Castro use the event to promote your own Julian Castro political Event to not be invited to the 2020 Democratic Debate can be spun to a positive for the campaign, concentrate on Social Media and start showing numbers in political rallies stay in with or without the Democratic Party, ArturoCortez/76541/10/03/2019

## 10/04/2019

Team Beto, stay focused on the people and crowd size in the early voting states and stay in the race through the Primaries as a American Patriot from, and for his people with or without political party support. ArturoCortez/76541/10/04/2019

## By Arturo Cortez/10/04/2019

### "A What Ever intellectual Political Donation,"

Team Obama/2019, La Resistencia as a Social Movement is committed to the Removal and Replacement (R&R) of the President of the United States, POTUS/45 Donald Trump from his political office as President of the United States prior too, or /@ post 2020 Primary Elections.

It is the intent of the Resistance to have a President elected by democratic popular vote of the American people by November of 2020

BO, in 2008 I promised you that I would be with you until you until you were back in Chicago, well Amigo I have been there for you and you are home now, I must say, "you my friend make me proud to be Arturo Cortez."

If invited under those terms I would be committed to attend.

P.S. Please advice Michel that the Resistance views her as "The Heart Beat" of American democracy/Arturo Cortez/76541/10/04/2019

## 10/05/2019

Such are the rules of our Capitalist Socialist By-partisan Democracy of those who feel they have, and those who know they have not my friend

A Care Taker Democratic Government If the Vice President Michael Pence is legally compromised would you honor your responsibilities towards the United States Presidency as Speaker of the House of Representatives? /Arturo Cortez/76541/10/05/2019

## By ArturoCortez/76541/10/10/2019

"The Turk bombed our Kurdish Democratic Positions in Syria today/The Slaughter has begun,"

The Extermination of our American Allied Armed Forces by Donald Trump can only be Strategic and well planned out by external foreign nations powers created to do as much damage as possible to American democracy prior to the 2020 General Presidential Election.

Donald Trump has now betrayed our American word to our most committed American Allied global elite armed forces, by pulling out our American troops from Syria; allowing the Turkish and Russian armies to slaughter our American friends and allied Kurdish Armed forces in Syria.

The Republican President Donald Trump decided to tuck his Republican tail, and run away from our foreign American warriors and forfeit the Middle East to the evil axis of Syria, Russia, and Iran while committing thousands of our friends and allied friends to death for having us Americans as their friend in our wars against ISIS Terrorism.

By pulling out of Syria on the 7th day of October, 2019 we the arrogant American warrior nation have betrayed our American word to the world damaging our ability to unify global military agreements with other nations of this time; we have proven to the world that American Democracy cannot be trusted with global Military alliances, thanks to Mr. Donald Trump the Republican cow pie Snake Oil sells man appointed Republican American President of the United States, Donald Trump/POTUS/45.

We must face the facts that American democracy is now still under Russian cyber political attacks by Russian Intelligence. Partisan Politics is now being used as a instrument to dismantle American Democracy as we know it.

We have now lost the "Cold War" with the USSR, and the KGB mission now in America is to dismantle American Democracy from the inside out by mounting a Russian challenge to the most meaningful American institutions which hold our American Republic together as the fabric of American Democracy.

I must confess as a American Patriot of socialist Republican Democratic ideological perspectives it makes me sick that we as Americans of today would allow the Turks to exterminate our American allied fighting forces in their own Middle Eastern home land, or anywhere else in the world; we are now the American warrior nation of cowards to the world which views us all Americans regardless of who it was that betrayed and condemned to death our Kurdish American Militarily Allied Warriors of the United States of America.

To the Republican and/ or the Democrat I ask why in the world would any other nation, in the world trust us the Americans of today with partnerships of economic, intelligence, and global military perspectives on the future of men, today/or yet to come.

Donald Trump POTUS/45 has now been given his democratic political right to lead our nation by the Electoral College vote. Donald Trump has found it necessary to systematically challenge every aspect of American Democracy as established by the founders of our American Constitution, the foundation of American Ideological law and order.

Regardless of whom you are, or what you believe in, Donald Trump the Russian friend/comrade must now go so we can go on with who we are as Americans.

American Democracy will soon put President Donald Trump in political "Check-mate." Impeachment is but the democratic legal, and the fair constitutional remedy to the problem with any American President with dreams of personal abuse of power for global economic enrichments, and obstruction of Justice as a President of the United States.

The Resistance encourages all Americans to vote American, and vote to impeach Donald Trump from office so we can go on with a two party partisan political lives once again, Impeachment is a question of American constitutional moral dignity; whereas, Donald Trump created for himself as president of the United States the exposure to Impeachment by challenging the limits of American Justice by his choice which is his American civil right, so long as one is willing to pay the Mariachi when the song is sung with his own money.

American Democracy is politically stout, and does have its legal remedies to protect itself from wrong doers in American governess Impeachment has nothing to do with the 2020 General Presidential Election.

Impeachment is a result of anti Constitutional Republican radical virtue a problem of the Republican Presidential Candidate, one of twenty Candidates running for President of the United States come Election Day November of 2020.

It is however true that the Republican Majority House of Representatives prior to the 2018 Mid-Term Elections did supply Donald Trump the Presidential autonomy/rope to hang himself on the hill by congress ignoring their Congressional over-site responsibilities over Donald Trump; allowing a capitalist power hungry fool to hang himself with his own political rope, post our national 2018 Mid-Term Election where the 2018 Resistance declared its first victory by electing a new Democratic Congress/ House of Representatives who would function as a equal branch of government with the power of the purse as well as over sight responsibilities with the absolute power to Impeach over a sitting President of the United States.

Please be advised if the Vice President is implicated in wrong doing and prosecuted the next person in line to the Presidency is the Speaker of the House of Representatives, Nancy Pelosi as the democratic remedy to Donald Trump prior to the 2020 General Presidential Election. At that hypothetical point in time, Donald Trump could be running his 2020 political Campaign from the "Poky."

"The Turks bombed our Kurdish democratic positions in Syria today, two days after Donald Trump's announcement that he without consultation would be pulling our American troops out of Northern Syria and Iraq /The Slaughter of our friends and allied Democratic military warriors in Syria who fought our war with ISIS on the ground has begun by choice of the 45 President of the United Donald Trump without consultation," /Arturo Cortez/76541/10/11/2019

Arturo Cortez/76541/**10/23/2019** Espero que este correo electrónico la encuentre a este y a los suyos en buena salude Tía, María Del Pilar Vargas, Ríos saludes y bendiciones a usted y nuestras Familias en Monterrey, Nuevo Lion, México. Tía, yo estuve varias veces con me hermano Francisco en Mayo 10-15, cuando fui a ver a mama en Oregón el dia de las madres.

Cureo yo que después de tantos años Francisco mi hermano encontró la tranquilidad que él esperaba de su vida. Cuanto con lo de mas, mis hijos ya no tienen "Tíos," y yo ya no tengo hermanos. De acuerdo que en realidad somos más de 250,000 "Cortez's en los estados unidos, y  nomas en facebook a vemos más de 250 Arturo Cortez's tía; así es que cureo yo que soy uno de los mas canosos, de los Arturo Cortez's en f/b; Tía gracias y les brindo un bonito dia Tía de parte de ArturoCortez/76541/10/20/2019/ Killeen, USA

**10/26/2019**

### Such are the "Historical Presidential Deeds" by Donald Trump:

Within the deed is the truth to the challenge to who we are as one America now in denial of what we once were as the world's first Democratic self governess to the rest of the world of today; capitalist control of our two party political system has now showed us all its human weakness certainly natural global human virtues of personal and cultural national arrogance. And so the question must be asked "what exactly do we look forward to after Donald Trump as a civilized nation of today, when the United States can order Texans to hunt and put our own Hispanic children and families in cages for asking for help and shatter from American Texanos who now have turned on ourselves and our own Republica Texana to please the racist American United States governess of the Russian backed Donald Trump?"

We the United States of American Democracy have now lost the cold war against the USSR/Russian KGB; we must now realize that we are now under executive political siege with Donald Trump as POTUS/45 in the White House.

Donald Trump is now conceding and or removing our military defenses from our global national strategic defensive military positions put in place by decades of both Republican and Democratic administrations with regards to global American diplomacy set in place to protect us from Russian aggression on us and other democratic nations around the world.

Our national institutions which are the fabrics which governs our nation of American laws as American democracy is now challenged and under attack from within by Donald Trump as POTUS/45 in the peoples White House.

Donald Trump the corporate capitalist welfare businessman is now and will continue to attempt to personally profit by dismantling our institutions with in our socialist capitalist American democracy.

Whereas Impeachment of a setting President is a constitutional remedy to having to live with traitors in the White House. Within the next 12 months the Russian Kremlin will expedite the transfer of American Global Defensive Strategic Military Positions around the world,

The Ukraine as the gate way to Eastern Europe is a precious Russian target and Donald Trump, did delay our congressional funding of $400,000,000 to support the defensive military effort against Russian military aggression on Ukrainian soil. Donald Trump was well aware the Ukrainian patriotic democratic lives were being lost ever second which he delayed our military

Ukrainian military aid to support the fight against the Russian invaders in the Ukraine.

The Donald Trump's Deeds which are making Russia Great Again at the expense of American Foreign Policy to say the very list to the rest of our civilized world:

Allowing Long Range Russian Bombers in Honduras, please reference the Monroe Doctrine 1823,

Delaying/Denying military aid approved by Congress to the Ukrainian Democratic Military forces to be used to fight the Russian aggression in the Ukraine is viewed as treason to our global allied democratic forces.

Most important is that our American word as the American people has now been compromised by Donald Trump to the rest of the world who will now look at us traitors to Global Democracies.

Donald Trump betrayed our democrat Kurdish fighting forces in Syria by pulling out of northern Syria condemning our own democratic Kurdish forces who fought ISIS "feet and boots on the ground in Iraq and Syria over 10,000 young Kurdish young blood died to keep Donald Trump and the rest of America safe from the self proclaimed Islamic ISIS Caliphate created to kill Americans on sight.

Our American President Donald Trump without consultation after a short conversation with the Turkish President made the decision to allow the nation of Turkey to commit ethnic cleansing and genocide on our feet on the ground Kurdish Democratic Armed forces by pulling our military presence from Northern Syria.

The genocide and ethnic cleansing of our brothers in arms has now begun and will continue in Syria, even though Donald Trump may get his Russian Trump Hotel in Moscow next to the Kremlin and Istanbul, for betraying our fighting forces in Northern Syria,

I must say as a American Patriot I see America as mush smaller nation today.

The Ukraine is the price Russia is looking for and Donald Trump can make that happen with or without Congressional approval much in the same way as he did with Syria all this must be done before now Impeachment day or the 2020 General Election.

Demands from the Kremlin on Donald Trump to deliver before Impeachment and/or re-election will go to shameless extremes as is happening now, unless Donald Trump's wings are clipped back, the Trump would see nothing wrong with stepping it up to a national armed American Revolution during re-election, this too would favor the Russian government if not the Russian short range goal America.

Donald Trump is now deliberately turning democracy against itself, by discrediting America Freedom of the Press, while challenging all aspects of American Justice as though riding the coat tails of other honorable American Presidents which came before him.

All American institution of the people of the United States are now being challenged and under attack by Donald Trump's own perception of himself as a American King of our American Democracy.

To the Kurdish people I write, "let it be said" that the Kurdish people have sacrificed their young blood for us the American people and we the American people are grateful and call the Honorable, Kurdish people our "Blood Brothers"; I promise you my brothers that you are now the American seed of democracy in Syria, Iraq, and Turkey and we the American Warriors will return to Northern Syria without Donald Trump, may our one and only God Jehovah bless you all and keep you until we return. /Arturo Cortez/76541/10/26/2019

United States Congressional Resistance Warrior, and lifelong mentor on racial human dignity Elijah Cummings passed today La casa de Cortez/Killeen TX./ArturoCortez/76541 mourns the passing of Elijah Cummings, our condolences to the Cummings Family, we have all lost a great and honorable man of wisdom, stewardship, and leadership to the rest of the world who like me follow and learned from his teachings, of now and of yesterday.

Fair well old friend you have germinated the seeds which have been planted in fertile honorable grown of American democracy; whereas American history will judge all our deeds in our time as the beginnings of the Resistance of the seventh hour of 2017.

Attempting to understand life must be the reason for living and so I write about my believes and understandings as one of many human with the ability to write the story down based on his or her Truths to Powers.

The Russian have been bombing the Syrian Children for Assad in their schools, and at the hospitals when the parents come to visit now they have the American Trained Kurd's to help them, Donald Trump shames my American right to be American.

Hillary Clinton won the 2016 Presidential Election by 3,000,000 popular votes. American democracy did not make the time to define the popular vote of the people in the 2018

General Election; Donald Trump was appointed President of the United States in order to expedite the national presidential selection of the presidency into a one National News evening, now is the time for Donald Trump to go, either by Impeachment, or Popular vote of the people of this nation.

## La Resistencia/76541

Only if we are still a nation of Laws as the fabric of American Life, regardless of what wing your feather belongs to, we are one as the United States of America. "Q Viva La Resistencia a lo Pendejo"

# Chapter 27

**November/2019**

**ArturoCortez/76541/11/06/2019**

On the 30th day of October our lord's year of 2019, The Democratic political forces of the people of the United States of North American, The United States House of Representatives of "the United States Congress" voted 234 for Impeachment, and 196 to not Impeach votes; the vote to impeach carried to approve the legal procedure to Impeach the Republican Presidential Candidate Donald Trump.

As a scribe/writer of American political Times, Movements/Moments in my time, I remember writing in 2016 that if elected the Donald would redefine the Republican Party of that time.

I was naïve than in perspective looking back in political retrospect of Donald Trump and/ or what is today the Donald Trump's Republican Russian Political Party of today.

I do believe we as the American Democracy of today's America have been infiltrated by foreign forces of alien global interest in the grass-root of American common democratic virtues.

Our own Republican United States President Donald Trump has now forced Americans to question whether wrong is wrong, with in American by-partisanship politics, and American democratic capitalism as his leverage against our own American Democracy.

Donald Trump is the political capitalist beast which continues to eat away at the United States political Republican Party's conservative American virtues towards our nation. It is Donald

Trump and his White House Administration, who is now using American foreign policy forged with our American Democracy as our national young patriotic blood over the last 243 years which we have lived as American, known today as the world's first democracy.

Today the Donald has betrayed our American Foreign Policy in the name of American nationalism where as Donald Trump has now trashed historical United States geo-global strategic positions, at no cost to our enemies, in this regard the Russians.

Donald Trump has now betrayed our foreign democratic global allied military forces, whereas the next time we go to war anywhere in the world we will have to do it alone with American boots on the ground whereas we the American people have betrayed our own allied democratic military forces in Northern Syria; where we the American of today have must now live the our American shame long aster Donald Trump is gone. We the Americans of today have now condemned our very own Kurdish democracy in Northern Syria to genocide and extinction in northern Syria and the hold world is awear of what we have done to those who fight on our side for American Democracy.

The Republican Party and/or our countries conservative American wing is but the means to dis arm American democracy as the Russian Mission for Donald Trump.

We must create a Republican Democratic capitalist fund to subsidize Republican Conservative Candidates who fine their independent tenacity to represent those who elected them to leadership/political office so they can stand and be counted for the nation, themselves and the party as the "2020 Conservative Republican Resistance Warriors."

The Republican ideological political party must be revived and the Donald must be politically tarred and feathered, impeached and/or voted out of office.

The 2020 Presidential Election will not be like the rest of the American democratic elections we have had in our American History this election will be about American Democracy based on Constitutional Law –verses– the Liar and thieve Donald Trump as he continues to define the Republican Party. Whereas, The United States Republican Senate, like The United States Democratic House of Representatives "The Congress," have their rights to vote in private restored with regards to the Impeachment of the President of the United States in order that the people of this nation get an honest vote, rather than a vote in fear of political reprisals and intimidation from Donald Trump's White House who has now lost sight of what is right and what is wrong in American political governess of today.

As is today I do place hope that the Republican Party has not yet been defined by the Donald as is today, even though it does appear as though the republicans are playing a Peter Piper leadership game with our nation's destiny and the Democratic future of our children as uninformed Trumponeions yet to come based on Republican politics of today.

The support the Donald is getting from the Republican Party and its leadership is neither unforgettable nor unforgivable when American Democracy is at stake by way of Republican leadership in the United States Senate whereas La Resistencia will not forgive or forget politico candidates who must get re-elected Republicans or Democrats who vote for Donald Trump's lawlessness in 2020/ArturoCortez/76541/11/06/2019

## 11/08/2019

### Breaking Trump News

In my native Tejano lingo la Resistencia now has Donald Trump by his own words "the short hairs," if the Donald has committed constitutional hanging legal offences against the our nation La Resistencia is committed to see Donald Trump "swing," as our American healing process for the damages he has caused American global democracies here at home, and around the world.

Carnala, Tejano music must appeal to humanity as the first American Hispanic cultural music on the new world, Native American musical cultural dialectic tools of the Kingdom with in American History of today, Tejano Music was created, to create diversified and cultural unity/the racial many into one as the single star nation of the American people "La Republica de Texas" the nation within our diversified American grass-root; Texano Music belongs to the La Republic of Texas; teach your children to speak Spanish and to dance and socialize around Texano Music, only in this way will the American Texano/ and our music can live forever, "esto para Q Viva La Resistencia/2019 en la alma de su gente Texana"/ ArturoCortez/76541/11/08/2019/

La Resistencia encourages New York Mayor, Michael Bloomberg to consider running as a Independent Republican for President, it does appear as though the Republican voters want to take out Donald Trump in the primary's and still be competitive in the 2020 Election, Arturo Cortez/76541/11/10/2019

### Arturo Cortez/76541/11/13/2019

La Resistencia fines Donald Trump Jr. To POTUS/45 Donald Trump guilty of Congressional Abstraction of Justice with his effort to expose the Constitutionally protected "Whistleblowers."

Those who are now intentionally challenging the limits of American Democracy based on self perceived presidential effluent ignorance, interpreted in Spanish as "self induced elitist Pendejismo."

If the Donald or any of his family and/or friends are guilty of treason against the United States La Resistencia will see them legally swing for the good of our nation, "esto para q viva la gente como la gente".

**ArturoCortez/76541/11/13/2019**

### Resistance Team Republican

Donald Trump was not elected by the Republican Party or by the will of the American popular vote, Donald Trump was installed by Electoral College process "Fact "impeachment will not undo the will of the American voter/ the will of the American voter was Hillary Clinton by 3 million popular votes.

I ask the Republican with or without the party to get real because we have been invaded and we are under attack by a real Russian American puppet government which has take control of our global democratic militaries.

Our Allied Democratic Kurdish boots on the ground allied Army had 10,000 ISIS warriors in prison, Donald Trump made a personal kiss ass deal with the Turk dictator and the Russian dictator Putin asked of him and our American allied ground forces in Northern Syria are today being exterminated by Russian and Turkish military forces.

Our Democratic allied fighting forces in the Ukraine and around the world are now on alert, now we the Americans sold out our friends who sacrificed their young lives for the promise of American Democracy in the conquered American Kurdish Middle Eastern lands.

Now, many ISIS warriors have been released when the Turks attacked the Kurd s and now we have the ISIS caliphate building Armies once again only this time we will have to fight a land war, with American boots on the ground, without our loyal allied warriors, all this so Donald Trump could find favor within the Russian KGB, our enemy who today invades our democratic process.

La Resistencia stands firm with Julián Castro For President of the United States, who now has over 190,000 donors of the 200,000 donors needed to qualify Julian Castro to be a participant at the December 2019 Democratic Debate, I ask that all Resistance "Yes we Can" Political Warriors of both the Conservative and Liberal wings of the same Bird to donate and make yourselves count to keep Julián Castro in the liberal Democratic Debate and/ or I dare challenge La Republica de Texas to help donate to her honorable son Don, Julian Castro, de San Antonio Texas for the United States President/POTUS/46 in 2020.

"They say" that POTUS/45 Donald Trump considers South America a "Shit Hole Countries," and so no American capital investment to keep the peace, paranoia to the end result is the reason to build walls, it is my believe you have made an attempt to reply to my correspondence of 11/17/2019; if not please disregard these writings. However, if you wish to proceed my name is Arturo Cortez I live in Killeen Texas I am a writer, blogger, publisher who helped a Blackman get elected and re-elected, President of the United States.

Although, I do know some things about the Castro Brother I can't say that I know Julian personally. The reason I am attempting to develop a dialog with the Campaign is because of a question Julian asked Joe Biden in one of the debates Julian asked, "this is an election right?"

To that question to old Joe I say yes, and I do understand POTUS/45 as the world does; this 2020 election is going to be about how nasty a candidate can be to Donald Trump without destroying the honor of the office of POTUS.

Arturo Cortez will support Julian Castro for President of the United States because he is a candidate who understands the White House as once was as a functional working environment, Julian is nothing less than a American political young political lion who understands his perspective on our nation from the perspective of the Barack Obama's White House as a cabinet level Director of our National Department of Housing and Urban Development; Julian was elected and served as Mayor of the City of San Antonio, Texas one of our nation's largest cities in one of our countries most Republican States in our nation, Texas.

Julian governed San Antonio's Municipal Government in a bi-partisan manner accomplishing his goals by gaining confidence from both wing of the same bird in political party ideologues, by understanding that in negotiations one party is to cut the pie, while the other party is to have the first slice of that pie in negotiated perspectives.

The 2020 Presidential Election this year will be about who we are, or who we think we should be as the world's most powerful Nation establishing our Democratic ideological perspectives for other Democracies from around the world to follow.

Today we are a people honoring our diversified American Democracy, whereas the Republican national party will decide whether we as American Democracy will have to endure four more years as Donald Trump's Americans underfoot participants to the Donald's American Republican Democracy. Donald Trump must establish himself as a victim of American Democracy based on our own American Constitution.

The problem with Donald Trump is that Donald Trump was not elected by popular vote of the American voters; in fact Donald Trump lost the popular vote of the American people by over three million votes. Yet, the Republican Party of today claims that the Impeachment of Donald Trump would undo the will of the American people who voted for Hilary Clinton who won the vote of the American voters.

Julian is a young Democratic lion well informed, pragmatic, morally aggressive to the right thing to do as a follower or as well as a leader with respect to our American domestic Constitution of the United States of America in sovereign perspective of as a independent nation to our global adversaries of the United States.

Julian Castro as the President of the United States would have no choice but to consider Vladimir Putin's Russia an enemy of the United States, based on the Russian cyber war against the United States and invasion of domestic American politics within our sovereign global democracies to include the United States of North America.

As, such the United States of America is forced to engage with Russia in-kind cyber warfare in Central America and Honduras:

Donald Trump the POTUS/45 has allowed the Russian government to land and established strategic offensive Russian air force assault air craft in Honduras; whereas, in the American continents we the United States is the only challenge to Russian political interest in Central America.

Presidential stupidity to our historical James Monroe Doctrine towards South America of 1823 by our incumbent Presidential candidate Donald Trump is allowing Russian to influence domestic politics in Central America, as well as establishing surgical B-2 bombers type offensive Russian long range bombers to be housed in Honduras.

Whereas, "La Republica de los Tejas" southern strategic air command defense response time to our only capable adversary on the new world of today the Russian Government has now been cut to minutes if not seconds by the Russian American puppet governess under the Republican POTUS/45 Donald Trump Party acting stupid to the Monroe Doctrine established in 1823, in order to deny the Russian Government of that time and other Europe nations with political monarch influence within the American continents.

Donald Trump has now betrayed our global standing by betraying our American policy towards Central and South America which took American patriots hundreds of years to establish and maintain, as our South American continental inter-national Democratic cultural norms of the Americas.

Donald trump is now and will continue to act as his Russian hero Vladimir Putin would want him to act.

The American enemies to Putin's Russia are the enemies of Donald Trump if nothing else the Donald feels the Russians have his back in our American 2020 General Presidential Election by cyber political fake Russian propaganda/news which he knows is what got him installed in 2016 as President of the United States.

Donald Trump is not just a well defined, self induced Pendejo, he is his own self defined Presidential genius, who believes he can fall in the swimming pool and walk out dry with lies and threats to those who do not follow his Russian Polices, which he feels got him elected; he fills the need to pay back the Russians with our American Global Foreign Affairs.

## The Northern Syrian Kurdish Democratic Armed Forces:

The American President Of the United States (POTUS/45, Donald Trump has now betrayed our most valued allied foreign fighting Democratic Kurdish Military Forces in Northern Syria,

They say around the world that the Kurdish lost over ten thousand Kurdish warriors for the Americans before the Americans decided they no longer need boots on the ground in Northern Syria allowing Turkey to exterminate our democratic military forces in Northern Syria.

Donald Trump has now made the point to the world that American Democracy cannot be trusted, whereas, we may now have to train our young American Warrior to wash and dry their socks once a day they may have to go fight a war in a deferent country without military friends willing to die for us, or American Democracy.

In our battles in the Middle East against the ISIS Islamic Caliphate who invaded Iraq on its way into Syria it was the Kurdish Democratic Warriors who defeated ISIS with boots on the ground in Iraq and later in Syria, whereas we the Americans supplied the Kurdish people technical and aerial support to defend our positions in Northern Syria and Iraq.

But it was the Northern Syrian Democratic forces in Northern Syria and Southern Iraq who fought and won our war against ISIS on the ground.

It was the Honorable Kurdish people who denied the Islamic Caliphate theological dictatorship over all of the Middle East we simply supplied technical support so they could take the fight to our enemies.

As things turned out our allied Iraqi military in Iraq made the choice to try to live on their knees under Islamic law as a caliphate and many Iraqi died praying on their knees whereas, many if not all were already guilty of wrong doing for having lived in this our time of today Judged under Islamic Caliphate Law. The Iraqi military did betray our American policy in Iraq by turning over American military hardware to ISIS and ran home to wait for the Islamic Caliphate to come and get them which in the most part they did if not for the Kurdish Warriors supported by the American Military.

It was the Kurdish people with the help of the United States who fought back ISIS in Iraq and Syria as the world knows it to be, we are now known as the global American democratic punks who betrayed our allied military partners to the rest of the world as I know it to be today.

In our allied Eastern Europe Democratic Republic of Ukraine at war with Vladimir Putin's Russian Aggression on the Ukrainian Northern front border with Russia, Russia did invade Ukraine and did take military control of the Ukrainian Crimea:

POTUS/45 Donald Trump has betrayed American foreign policy when the United States House of Representatives (the United States Congress} allocated $390,000,000 to fight the Russian invaders in Ukraine, whereas the Democratic Armed Forces in the Ukraine are now fighting the Russian invasion Donald Trump has denied our Ukrainian democratic forces the right to defend  themselves by denying our friends and allied democratic forces the funds allocated by Congress to assist the Ukrainians fight of the Russian Invasion on their Ukrainian land.

We as a Democracy must stand in support of Eastern European democracies in collision form to defend Eastern Europe from Russia re-creating the USSR once again.

Whereas, after several efforts by Donald Trump to extort domestic political favor from the Ukraine people, Donald Trump was forced to release the funds to the Ukraine 5 months after it was approved by Congress under investigation for attempting to extort political favors from the Ukrainian President.

## ArturoCortez/76541/11/17/2019

Maya Rupert<br>
Julian Castro's Campaign Manager,

Certainly true, we must understand the needs of the people and change is our presidential goal for the United States of North America, but i am not a politician, nor am i a capitalist political instrument, less i want to write this story in that manner; So it is that this is where you come in, i am a social Movement "La Resistencia of today" and /Si se Puede/The Chicano Movement/ and La Raza Unida Party" of my American years past.

Please be advised out of all the Democratic political candidates for president, attempting to say the same thing in deferent ways it is the Resistance who has selected you Julian Castro for President whereas my truth to empower liberal writings do influence fund raising talking points, political intellectual discourse and thus money flow from the many political Si se Puede teams are now indoctrinate to move as one as "The Resistance/2019/in La Republica de Texas, and across the nation.

Maya, I have been a writer of truth to power for many, many years who has been writing from my own patriotic good will perspective towards my nation.

It is certainly true that I as an independent writer did influence the election, and re-election of the first black man as United States President in Barack Obama. It is also true that La Resistencia did win the 2018 Election of today's United States now Democratic Congress, it is also true that the Resistance did win by popular vote of the American voter in the 2016 Presidential Election of Hillary Clinton in 2016 by over 3,000,000 votes.

Maya, I hope you conceder this e-mail as a form of presidential indoctrination to be shared with the rest of Team Julian Castro for President, or not; so it is that in order to be on the same page prior to La Resistencia moving forward with requesting political funds from my political Teams across the nation I must have the support of Team Castro.

In return I will create a national fund raising effort for our Castro for President Campaign. It was sad to hear Julian was not able to make it to the December Democratic Debates for lack of money. So it is that the democratic candidates are no longer on my Si se Puede list and my reasons why I explained in the marked bullet points below all things that happen, do happen for a reason my friends and if we do not qualify to debate a democrat then we must work twice as hard to debate the Republican in the General Election with or without the Democratic Party.

This means that our business is with the American voters and not with the American political Parties in order to be able to correct the capitalist inequities within American democracies of today.

Whereas, American Democracy unfortunately is capitalistically designed to service the traditional needs of the political party by bottle necking the voters choice for president which establishes the need of the Democratic Capitalist democracy ahead of the needs of the people's choice in America of today. However, I can certainly understand the inequities in American democracy of the haves, and the have not, and so it is for this reason that I ask that you supply me with the necessary fund raising contact information to begin raising funds for the Julian Castro, Campaign.

This fund raising effort must not be associated with any political party if the Resistance is to be evolved, and the funds must be used to fund, Julian's 2020 Presidential Campaign.

The problems with the Scripted Democratic Party of today:

Bernie Sanders now has a personal medical handicap, and I know what he is going through, Bernie needs to listen to his doctor, "No Stress, nothing fried and everything from the sea"

Elizabeth Warren has way too many programs on her plate, Like POTUS/45 way to many questions to be asked and judged in 2020, something is bound to fail.

Camellia Harris, has a overt arrogant leadership non-verbally smirk which speaks of her before she does,

Whereas the Mayor carries his own personal cross into national Politics, which will polarize into Theological -political opposition to our effort to run a American first political campaign;

Joe Biden is the passed what we once were, and stubborn with respect to the future, his time has now come, and now gone.

My man Beto forgot that a man, any man can run for President with or without money in America so long as his faith in the American voter is unwavering.

This leaves me with you Don, Julian Castro amigo, asking the proper question in the last Democratic Presidential Debate you qualified simply because you asked, "This is a political election, is it not? The answer is yes it is a American political Election scripted to meet the needs of the Capitalist Beast with in American democracy of today.

La Resistencia can and will help Julian Castro redefine American elections for American democracy for all Americans of those who have, and have not as American tax payers all.

We must attack POTUS/45 and cut loose on those of his family and friends who are on Donald Trump's teams and influence the White House governess of today.

With very little luck at all Donald Trump will hit us back and La Resistencia/Resistance will have a political Champion for the

2020 Presidential Election. The Donald Trump dynasty is now crumbling under its own political incompetence, and we must learn to ride that political coat tails as the Donald would do the same.

We must follow the national news as it evolves, we must harvest the national energy created by the Impeachment Hears and use the Impeachment to raise the capital needed to run our national campaign for president as the Donald would do, this is what Donald Trump would do.

We must be aggressive and ruthlessly clear that we are in it to win against Donald Trump.

Based on our Constitutional Democracy POTUS/45 will swing as a Republican Presidential Fool, and /or as a American Capitalist Traitor to our nation.

Accountability and no mercy, to the fools of the American President who uses their human virtue to act stupid call for mercy based on "American Presidential Pendejismo" as his reason to keep Hispanic children in wire cages, while hunting human on our North American lands whereas some came and others were brought as commercial property by salt water global immigrates.

People today know and want to understand that we are having serious national matters with our American Democracy stemming from intentional Presidential Pendejismo; and they will follow the candidate who is honest enough to speak the simple truth to power, and who can efficiently govern over the mess of today which is the American Bureaucracy as created by the capitalist, Russian lover Donald Trump to destroy American democracy for the Russians.

So it is that you are the one person who must be the cyber political arrow head against Donald Trump it is you my friend who must let the nation know today that you as a American patriot of the United States will prosecute Donald Trump, as a American citizen wrong doer along with his family within the White House today, to the full extent of our American Constitutional laws regardless of what is said at the next Democratic Presidential Debate.

At this point if you wish to continue your purpose must rise above candidates as unique and above the others and this message in political strategic guidance is meant to do just that, depending on how this message is delivered and/or received by the American people it is however good for 10 to 15 political poling points for those who think they know how to gamble away the will of the democratic American people.

Yesto para "Q Viva La Resistencia en la alma de la Raza Humana."

**P.S. Don, Julian** this e-letter will be archived and published in book format along with all my 2019 writings as a Publication of ArturoCortez @ La Casa de Cortez, Publications, Killeen Texas in 2021, again Thank You for who you are and what you do for our nation.

### ArturoCortez/76541/11/19/2019

Resistance Team Republican 2020, "Q se aga La Resistencia"
Thank-you Irene Andrews you are absolutely right, Republicans in our communities are our neighbors and friends who are being affected in the same way as all Americans; whereas, "we are all on the same boat as Americans." The only Grand Old Party (GOP) left to the Republican Leadership is the Donald Trump Party, The Republican Party of the American conservative people is no more by conservative political ideological party morals and/or political perspectives, "VOTE DEMOCRAT" conservative Republican leadership is now dead wood in a Constitutional fire vote the Republican carpet beggars leadership bums out by way of the

American vote and replace them with true Republican Leaders who's loyalties are without question to the American Constitution and the American people of this nation.

The Donald Trump Republican Party Nuts in Washington are betraying our American Constitution/nation of American people by violating our United States Constitution, they are in fact abusing our American laws by Presidential interpretation of our Constitutional Law, knowing in fact that our laws is as the fabric of American Democracy, which unites global American Immigrants under the Law.

The Republican Political Party that went to fight Washington D.C. is under siege and lacks the leadership and tenacity to make a political stand for themselves, or our American Constitution they now are in political survival mode, their independent responsibilities as American Leaders are now compromised by intimidation from the White House with regards to Donald Trump's anti-human American nationalist Doctrine in the White House of today.

Conservative Republican voters like the rest of the world have had enough of the Donald Trump "Democratic Reality Show," we need to get back to the work of representing the business of the American people and not the personal business of a self defined "Narcissistic, Raciest, Liar President."

**/ArturoCortez/76541/11/25/2019**

### Historical

To, The Texas State Historical Association (TSHA),

I Arturo Cortez did sent this historical information on the Birth of La Republican de Texas as a result of our Spanish Texano Revolutionary battles of January 22, 1811.

This Story has been reviewed by many, many Texano Historians of today for eight years, no historian Texano or not so far has made a challenge to the facts of the story i wrote about 10 years ago, no one disagrees with the information I have supplied to Texano Historians: they do however encourage everyone to read and share this story with your children, family and friends, so they too know when and how Texas got its Independence from Spain, in a time when there was no independent Mexico from the Kingdoms of Spain in Europe or Nueva Espania, on the new world, the Spanish Kingdom Empire on the new world was under monarch siege by French Napoleon's French Armies in Europe.

The American Spanish continents were fracturing into their own nations in the new world and so was Texas.

By Arturo Cortez

## Title

*"Las Campanas de San Antonio de Valero,"*
*"Amigo, y que paso con Las Campanas de San*
*Antonio de Valero:*
*Pero "Amigo, y que paso, con Las Campanas de San*
*Antonio de Valero;*

On a day much like today only 202 years ago in or on this day only the year was 1811, there was a Spanish Province Tejas and there was no Mexican nation on the new world; there was the largest Roman Catholic Spanish Empire the world had ever known with the extended Kingdom of Nueva Espania on the mainland of the new world as its crown jewel.

The English colonies consisted of 13 colonial American States, and the territory of Louisiana, which had been which chipped off the new world Spanish kingdom and sold to the French, colonies by the French Napoleon Armies with the promise that Napoleon would not attack the Spanish homeland on the Iberian Peninsula during the liberal and conservative Peninsular Wars on the Spanish homeland. The French Napoleon Armies, arrested the Spanish King Ferdinand VII who was sent to France on September 16th 1808, Joseph Bonaparte then King of Naples and older brother to Napoleon Bonaparte was made king of Spain on the same day in 1808; Jose de Iturrigaray, Viceroy = (King in place of a King) was replaced by the French royalist Pedro de Garibay to rule over Nueva Espania as a French segregate and Nueva Espania, Viceroy.

Because the world was much larger then news from Madrid took months to reach Mexico City, and as long as a year for information to get to the Norteno= (northern) Provinces of the new world kingdom, if the information was even sent at all. The rumor was out, the French had kill our king, and Napoleon was negotiating the sale of the Norteno, to "los Norteno Yankee del Norte," the North American Norteno, a humble simple Independent Spanish subjects of monarch principle rules of co-existence among the new world natives, first established by Queen Infanta Isabella, of the Spanish Royal House of Castillo y Ferdinand de Aragon in 1492, "los Norteno de Norte" who had colonized North America with Christian love, music, the horse and a word of honor towards the American native and themselves, viewed themselves as the first European Americans of a diversified racial mix of equals, in the American world of men. "El Norteno Mestizo" = (from the mix) was never really a part of Spanish urban colonial life in and around the major colonial cities of the kingdom, where as North America was the wilderness, and a Peninsular = (a Spanish person from the Iberian Peninsula), would come around now and then and collect tax for the kingdom.

The Norteno lived by the law of the native wilderness and the fact that the native American reflected third place on the racial

Spanish Caste ='s (social cast system) of that time, whereas the Mestizo European human mix, with the native American placed 4th.

After the Norteno finding out that the Spanish King, had been arrested and possibly killed, on September 16, 1808, and had be replaced with Joseph Bonaparte, King of Naples, and older brother to Napoleon Bonaparte and now Spanish King, the North American Norteno, went into high alert.

On September 16th 1810 the Norteno, Catholic Padre, Miguel Hidalgo y Costilla, parish priest of Dolores, Guanajuato, a Spanish prison town declared Independence with "El Grito de Dolores Hidalgo," protecting the royal interest of the Spanish King Ferdinand VII and Independence for Mexico from the Spanish, New World Kingdom of Nueva Espania and the French puppet government in Mexico City.

Miguel Hidalgo marched over 100,000 Norteno troops to where he could see the lights of Mexico City by night.

On the 22 day of January, 1811 four months and 7 days after the Norteno Miguel Hidalgo had declared Independence for Mexico the Norteno Spanish Captain, Juan Bautista de las Casas, from San Fernando in the Spanish province of Santander,='s "El Valle del Rio Grande," arrested the Spanish royal Governor of Tejas, Manual Maria de Salcedo, and Simon de Herrera, Spanish governor of Nuevo Leon.

The bells of San Antonio de Valero rang shedding tears of joy, as Juan Bautista de las Casas, declared North America free of Spanish monarch rule and called Spanish North America "Tejas" the land of the free and Independent people.

The two governors were both sent to be judged by the revolutionary armed forces of Miguel Hidalgo y Costilla with the massage, "the Mexican Golf coast of the Yucatan, is now under the protection of the new Republica of Tejas and the Tejano Croix Defense Militia, we have your back carnal, to the last American Tejano, the French will not land on Tejano American soil, the independent one star nation of Tejas claims all territorial Spanish American, Nueva Espania bounders, as the Independent nation of Tejas, as a single star Nation under one God "Que viva la Revolucion Texana" y que viva Norte America Texana; page, one of two, ….. ArturoCortez/11/30/2019.

# Chapter 28

December/2019

Julian like you, Beto, Carmela, and Corry Booker and others in both political parties are the Resistencia Si se Puede Political Warriors who the Resistance has supported throughout the years as Si se Puede politicians; united we are the largest political army this nation has ever known or seen in political action as our winning formula to win the 2020 Presidential Election.

The next step is to hold a Yes we Can Resistance Political Summit in San Antonio this year and/or early, very early, next year, in fact early January, 2020.

It is your Team Job to create and host this Resistance function:

**Participants** invited to this Si se Puede Political Summit must include invitations to all political leaders who have now dropped out of the 2020 Presidential political race, images of Julian rubbing elbows with these Honorable National Leaders are worth Thousands if not millions of grass-root votes. Invitations to attend this Resistance function must include open invitations to the "Top" Democrat of the Democratic Party, Barack Obama and, the Top sane "Republicans" of the now extinct Republican (GOP) Jorge W. Bush.

This function is not about the political debates it will be about unifying the candidates who are dropping out of the Presidential race under Team Castro for President only, to and otherwise polarized partisan political mind set of today.

The Political efforts of all these Honorable America Leaders must be glimmed, and harvested as the hope for American Democracy of today.

Please be advised these people you will be inviting do know more about me than me or you or even that which I know about myself.

You can tell them that my invitation to attend is "Confirmed" Arturo Cortez the Texas Writer of the Resistance will attend this Summit of American Eagles.

However, if any of the political parties wish to attend or be represented they must be willing and able to finance this hold function.

This function is not a fund raising event, but funds raised may have to be used in order to establish "Political Capital."

I want you to know Political Arrogance is a useful instrument in American politics when used in a honorable manner, amigo again I want to thank-you and your family for what you do for Texas, and the nation, **"Feliz Navidad to and yours and your best to you and the Julian Teams in 2020"** please keep me advised/ ArturoCortez/76541/12/05/2019

**12/06/2019/**La Resistencia will unify the American people under our one Diversified Independent American Democracy, the Resistance took the Presidency in 2008, we won the re-election of the first Black man as American President in 2012, we won the United States Congress in 2018, and we are now impeaching an American President for betraying the American Constitution.

Like Donald Trump we have now started a list of those U.S. Senators, and Congressmen and women to be removed in 2020 regardless of political Party, we call it American democratic politics, whereas, one will proudly lead or will proudly follow to protect American Democracy because we are what we are "Proud

Americans" of today with a Proud hypocritical History, as the foundation of Democracy's ArturoCortez/12/06/2019

**12/08/2019**: Amigo, you told the American people "i asked the National Democratic Party to change in five years," what in the hack is wrong with you saying "as your President i will change the Democratic Party to a more equitable to all candidates whether of the "Haves" and/or the "Have Not" in American politics," this is what the American people want to hear from you, "please try not to pee into the wind my friend we need you at your best."/ ArturoCortez/76541/12/08/2019

**Republican Party Redemption**, is at hand, ImpeachNow,

So I will write once again, there is no conservative United States (U.S. Republican Party) in the U.S. House of Representatives, nor in the United States Senate; what there is however is the "Donald Trump Political Party," torching our American Republican Party, American Intelligence Services, our American Democratic Constitutional Processes, and our American right to free American News Services all this in the stead of Conservative Republican democracy.

I as a conservative American political centralist who will vote in 2020 for what is right for my families, neighbors, and friends as a America nation of Constitutional Laws, which governs our American way of life as the fabric to who we are as a nation will vote Democrat.

Donald Trump is The President of the United States by "Appointment" of the "Electoral College," Donald Trump has never been elected to the American Presidency; it was the Democratic Candidate Hillary Clinton who won the popular American human vote by three million votes over Donald Trump; is certainly making the impeachment of Donald Trump (POTUS/45) in 2020 as the removal of a appointed/installed President.

Certainly the first of now four such impeachments of a democratically appointed President in our American History.

Donald Trump has been given his democratic opportunities to do learn to do his job, and lead us as all as one American nation of people.

Donald Trump has failed his responsibilities as President of our nation by dishonoring his Constitutional Presidential Oath in favor of Russian KGB Constitutional virtues as well as global and domestic talking points.

Donald Trump POTUS/45 has now been charged with two indictments, "High Crimes and Misdemeanors,"& "Obstruct of Congress, as the bases for Impeachment in the Democratic United States House of Representatives.

Impeachment as a constitutional process has been activated by Donald Trump with is Eastern Europe political challenge to our American Constitution.

The impeachment of Donald Trump is not of Republicans or Democrats point of ideological views in defense of American democracy and or the nation, I can only say the Donald created impeachment for himself, now Republican Senatorial American leaders must act in favor of the Law regardless of what wing the feather belongs too.

All of a sudden the Republican Party as though by divine right has been given the rear political opportunity to redeem itself to American Republicans.

The traditional Republican Party base, and the Republican Party elite now have the opportunity to replace The Donald Trump Party with the traditional  Republican Party once again by voting for a well deserved Old fusion impeachment in order to re-establish the American Republican political party. whereas, the political interest of the American people must comes first over the interest of any one man or woman whether they represent the international interest of foreign dictatorships as capitalist national powers or not.

The Resistance encourages all American Patriots of the Red, White, and Blue to study the impeachment of POTUS/45 Donald Trump and call or visit your D.C. political representatives in your district, and ask them to tell you if they represent your interest, or the interest of a admitted liar in Donald Trump.

Impeachment means that a American President can be removed from his political office for wrong doing based on our American Constitution written by the founders of the United States Constitution of America for Americans in a time when all there was, was the United States as the first constitutional Republic among a world of Kingdoms and subjects.

As Americans our American Constitution is what defines us all as an American nation to the rest of the world.

I suppose when it is all said, written and done, The Republican Party will never again be what it once was to American Conservatives who have lost their independent political Republican Party perspectives on American Democracy to the Trump Party by calling itself partisan politics verses the people of the Republican Party political virtues the Republican Party once represented.

Redemption is now at hand for American republicans who must find American Patriotic Tenacity in legal rightful Impeach of POTUS/45 Donald Trump or sell out our American Constitution in favor of a Liar American Capitalist Monarchy in Donald Trump's governess.

Enough is enough the republican New Year's resolution can only be to Impeach and Remove the Donald Trump from his Presidential responsibilities; political Parties aside we are one

American Democracy and we have no need for political dictators/ Elitist Liars Capitalist Monarchs in the Peoples White House.

The Republicans have no choice but to Impeach as the means to political redemption and a good reason to re-establish the Grand Old Party (GOP) as the Party of, and for the American people in honor of our American Constitution, where no man, American or Russian is above our own American constitutional laws here in or out of America. /ArturoCortez/76541/12/12/2019

**12/18/2019**: Yesterday the 18th day of December 2019, President of the United States Donald Trump (POTUS/45) received his notice from the Resistance within the United States House of Representatives that he would never be American political King of the American people when the Democratic Congressional Leaders voted for our American Constitution to Impeach and Remove the United States President 45 Donald Trump for

1. Abuse of Power, and

2. Obstruction of Congress.

I am only one of the rests of the world who did witness the Impeachment Debates and Vote for Congressional Impeachment of Donald Trump POTUS/45.

This truly was a patriotic national Historical Constitutional experience.

Impeachment is not of political party ideology, impeachment is of American Constitutional Social Order of the American people, whereas Donald Trump's calculated attempts to challenge the American Constitution, has now made Donald Trump Impeached by the United States Congress of the American people.

The question today is whether POYUS/45 Donald Trump as a American man is above the Laws of our American Constitution of all Americans because he was appointed President by "Electoral College votes?"

Now the Impeachment goes to the United States Senate who is must also vote to Impeach for removal and replacement (R&R) Donald Trump as our American Law's requires the United States Senate's approval.

Donald Trump will lose his Presidency in his attempt to find the answer to his question.

Or, "are we to ignore the American Constitution which governs all the people of our nation for as equals and place the elite few above our Constitutional Law?"

Certainly this is the question which the Republican United States Congressmen and women in the Senate must now ask themselves after the approval to impeach by the hold of the United States Congress.

The answer is "No" only if one is accustomed to third world political strong man political ideology, would that make political sense.

If a Senator or Congressman or woman violate the American Constitution the go to the "Pokey," regardless of who they are with and or with political power of the American people as they should even if it's the President of the United States.

I witnessed out right betrayal of our American Constitution by Congressional Republicans of the Donald Trump Republican Party who shamelessly and willfully voted against our National Constitution in Republic Party Unity, unwilling to deal with the legality of the charges and prove gathered by Congressional Committees of the United States Congress.

I watched as the Shameful, and the Shameless debated the future if any of our American Democracy as we know it today. I dare say that the time has come for Americans to stand and be counted for America and not any political Party established to bottle neck the will of the American people, we must be ready to stand to remove the Trump Republicans in Political Offices and replace them all in the United States House of Representatives, the United States Senate a once honorable bi-partisan Senate.

The White House is now under Donald Trump Republican one Party American Dictatorship/ rule as the means to re-setting Our American Democracy for tomorrows Challenges or risk losing our American Constitutional Democracy to some other snake oil sells man.

Call your congressmen or women today and ask them to Impeach President Donald Trump for the good of the nation and the world of today and be counted as a American for America

Maya as a publish Author @ i often get emails from others in the publishing business, all sorts of organizations and fast talking individuals, many of which are probably much better educated in today's world than i am, this of course does not necessarily mean that they as individuals, or organized Teams are much smarter than I am.

I once did help to ignite the Obama Teams, for this you will have to be focused/ discipline and well understood as what it is we want for America, of tomorrow.

From time to time you will lead as a Resistance Warrior and from time to time you will be asked to follow as a one of many Resistance Warrior's of our time.

Our hope is in the American Promise where the words we used to convey our message to the American people of 2008 does point the way forward in our American Democracy.

I do suggest that you buy a copy of my book Title "El Centrolista 2012-2015" and remember this "our battles for this nation today will be nothing like that."

In 2020 we the America Resistance will attack Donald Trump as a traitor to the American flag.

Maya we must define Donald Trump for what he is, a narcissistic liar out of touch with reality and now pimping American democracy.

Julian must call out Donald Trump after the Democratic Debates for December 2020, it must be done in a extremely firm aggressive manner, within the three "C's"= Cool, Calm, and Collected" manner.

As for the Democratic Party, forget them they are not there to represent the interest of Julian Castro for President, your convent must be with the American voters; whereas, as President of the United States you will work with anyone willing to help bring equitable social changes to our American Socialist Capitalist Democracy the "National Democratic Party and /or the Republican Party," as the democratic bottle neck as United States political Parties of the people.

Donald Trump will come after Julian who will define Julian to the American people as a well educated American Native American Texano of the Yucatan if we are Lucky he may even call us Mexicans if we are so lucky.

Maya we must use all opportunities to advance cost effective media using Donald Trump's Presidential Coat Tail all the way to the White House.

Maya, I always ask my readers to take my writings with a grain of salt.

Maya, Julian is ready to lead this nation he can be the one who will unite this country under our American Constitutional Rights; whereas, it has been written, and said that in America, "no man is above our American Laws."

The Target is Donald Trump; our purpose is to Remove &Replace (R&R) the Executive Offices of the United States, with Julian for President by way of Constitutional Authority/ Impeachment, and or Popular Vote of the people. "esto, para q viva la gente como la gente.) /ArturoCortez/12/18/2019

## La Resistencia/76541/12/21/2019

I would like to thank and wish all Resistance political warriors here in Texas and across the country a "Merry Christmas," we did good this year for our nation of American Constitutional Laws.

We together have worked very hard for the Christmas present we received from the United States House of Representatives. The Resistance 2018 election did re-constitute Democratic congressional over sight responsibilities over the United States President Donald Trump as well as we can now hold Donald Trump for his actions as President of all Americans.

The President was impeached under our laws as governed by our American Constitution; two Articles of Impeachment were filed:

Abuse of Power passed, when Donald Trump attempted to Black Mail the Government of a War-Time Democratic nation of Ukraine by denying the Ukraine $390,000,000 allocated to them by the United States Congress to fight the Russian invasions of the Ukraine as the gate way to Eastern Europe. The vote to Impeach was 230 Democratic Congressmen and women, and the vote not to impeach was all 197 Republicans in Congress voted not to Impeach on the Impeachment Article;

1. Passed to Impeach.

2. Obstruction of Congress when President Donald Trump ordered United States Executives officers not to testify at the Congressional investigations.

Donald Trump claims the human democratic right to rule as a Democratically Ordained American King, without a national Constitution or Laws to hold him accountable to human dignity, because he is our President.

## Article:

*2.) 229 Democratic votes to Impeach and 198 Republican votes not to Impeach on Article 2.) Passed*

Now we go to the United States Senate, where the hold of the Republican United States Senate has already dis qualified himself by admitting on television that he will not be impartial as a United States Senator and Jurors, at the Legal Senatorial Trial of Donald Trump.

Meaning of course that other Republicans will be doing the same, or they will have to go against the American Constitution which they pledged to protect and defend from foreign or domestic enemies of our American Constitution.

If we go the way of the Donald, the Donald would be King in 2020 this is the choice the Republican Party Leaders of our conservative people will have to make.

Donald Trump is a cancer within roots of America Democracy of a people looking for responsible, honorable American cultural leadership and identification.

The fascist seeds have now been planted/installed and are now germinating in the Executive Offices of the United States of American Democracy, the remedy is to Impeach, and Replace come shit or high water the Republican Senate in 2020 must stand and vote for our American Constitution regardless of who wants to be "Republican King," ArturoCortez/76541 /12/21/2019

## Historical

American Roots, The Mexican global economy is strong we as Texano Americans deny ourselves our place in the Hispanic Mexican economy here in Texas as a Hispanic buffer American Republica to Mexico.

Texas itself was founded in 1502 by Cristobal Colon on his second trip to the New World of today; on the same year a young 15 year old Hernado Cortez, landed in Espanola, with two years of legal education from the University of Salamanca, in Salamanca, Spain.

Although Hernando Cortez, was a Noble of meager means in Spain; as a new Spanish citizen immigrant to the new world Hernando Cortez was offered the government position of "Notario Publico" at the age of 15 the newly conquered island of Espanola than, in the new world in a time when the mainland of the new world had not yet been explored. Hernando, accepted his new position, and was rewarded with several mines, 100 native slaves and 50 African slaves, by the Spanish Crown of Infanta Isabella y Fernando de Aragon.

It was Hernando Cortez who is responsibility it was to legally certify and tax = "El Cinco Real"" The Royal fifth" Taxes paid on conquered goods to the Spanish Kingdom.

Hernando did create the first inland Spanish Kingdom on the New World when he Conquered the Stone Cities of the Aztec Empire in 1519 over 500 years ago.

The true Mexican American to the new world were permitted to colonize in Central Texas in 1824 when 200 English American colonial settlers were allowed to become Mexican citizens and settle in Central Texas by Mexico's first Dictator Santa Ana, and the

American Central Intelligence Agency (CIA)'s operative Stephen Austin, who later hired the Mexican Army as a expeditionary military force to establish Texas as a Southern racist government which rules today under the same English racist Texas constitution established on March 2nd 1832.

The English American settlers who came to Texas in 1824 were allowed by the Republica de Texas to bring their human property to Texas and allowed the human slaves to live out their capital slavery agreements with the firm understanding that Texas would never give birth to Texano slaves in the Hispanic Republica de Texas.

Arturo Cortez

Julian I am a writer and i write about hypocritical Texas History, I also write to mostly candidates who i find have the will, and honorable standings to become grate leaders. This correspondence with you/ your team/ or your machine will be published in book form titled The Resistance/2019.

Whether you or yours follow my writings or not that sir is your business however, if you know of my writings in present day presidential politics than you know that I do not believe in capitalist democratic efforts as the means to a representative governess of the American people.

However, I do tend to encourage my teams "MoveOn, WorkingFamilies.org, Democracy for America, LULAC, and United Farm Works of America, and others who also use my writings as ideological pro-human talk points to encourage their on members to donate at national levels.

Not necessarily since Michael Burke, a great American Tejano native once said, "you give a fool enough rope and he or she will hang themselves," as for me i do not favor Presidential fools in the peoples White House, regardless of political party which is The Resistance to self induced "Pendejismo." "q Siga la Resistencia"

Immigrants always vote for the President regardless of who the President is, as a matter of Immigrant American patriotism whereas, getting screwed is why they come to America, it does seem.

Mi General, in this world there are Leaders and Followers, and the intentional want to be incognito respectable "Pendejos,"/"want to act political party fools," regardless of Political Parties Vote American 2020.

In my time a American leader of our nation never bragged to the public about the termination of human life as a human trophy, we all knew that our government had necessary deeds which had to be accomplished come shit or high water,.

Mi Generals, in this world there are Leaders and Followers, and the intentional want to be incognito respectable "Pendejos," regardless of Political Party's for control of our nation.

We must disconnect with party political interest and concentrate on our American Democracy impeachment is the profile/platform Donald Trump wants to run on in 2020/ based on his deeds,

Republican Party leaders have lost sight of who we are as a people and run for public office to have the opportunity to defend a known liar; lying to them, and their now none existent Republican Political Party, Impeach Trump now and start a new Republican Party, we need one now.

American Governess Executive Leadership denies the American House of Representatives their legal right to govern over-sight responsibilities over the Executive branch of the United States Government, by orders of the U.S. President, Donald Trump, a shameless liar to the world we know today. Illegal acts of deliberate

Presidential Obstruction of Justice within the US Congress; is a good reason for Impeachment.

Trump's Syrian Doctrine can only succeed if our American purpose is to "Make Russia Great Again."

Now is a good time for the Republican for America to stand and be counted, as a right thing to do educated Conservative Republican Vote.

The Republican Party line voters of this Time must hold its political leaders accountable to our American Constitution as political brother of the same constitutional political feather who must now stand together in American politics where the Republic as we know it is all that really matters.

The Republic is under siege whereas the Republican must not forget who they are to our nation. They must do their part and get of the pot and allow American Democracy to do it's legal business

AMERIQVE SEPTENTRIONALE
AME
RIC
QVI
SEP
TRIONA
MER
MER
DI
NORT
SVD

# El Fin de oy 2019"

"WHEREAS IT IS NOW THE BEGINNING OF
TOMORROW IS 2020"

"Happy New Year it is 2020"

NOVA TOTIUS TERRARUM ORBIS GEOGRAPHICA AC HYDROGRAPHICA TABULA
MAR DEL

A LA CASA DE CORTEZ
PUBLICATION/76541/KILLEEN, TEXAS

# *La Resistencia/*
# *The Resistance*

## BY ARTUROCORTEZ/76541

Writings/Political Journal for 2020

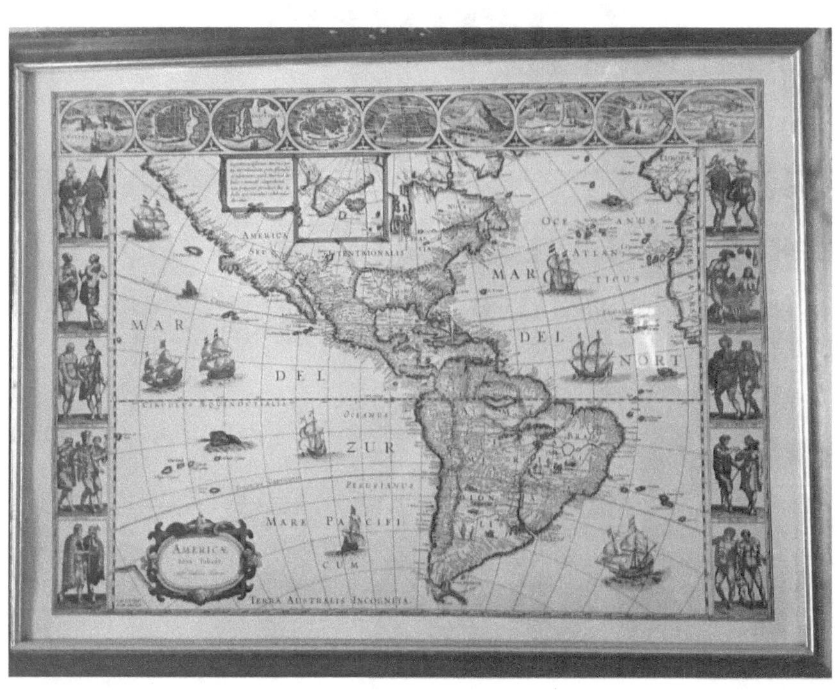

# INTRODUCTION

"We have now won the popular American vote for the 2020 General Election, now we must fear the Constitutional Political Battles to protect American Democracy which are yet to come,"

It is certainly true I did not vote for Donald Trump, I do not like Donald Trump's elitist ways nor do I like the "Haters" of humans who do not look as they do, for whatever reason.

It is true as well that there are many in our nation who feels they have to like and love our President once elected.

This is not true simply because we do live in America where we are governed by our American constitutional rights which grantees ever American the right to speak truth to power and share our believes with others whether they like it or not.

So it is that I had no choice but to follow and learn the ways of how to deny Presidenual leadership in a respectful manner from a fool Republican United States President, Congress and United States Senate as understood by our global allied partners who have now been humiliated and betrayed by the Republican Party who we can now say, the Republicans as a political party have proudly created treason and attempted political coup over the people of this nation and our American Constitutional rights as the elected political leaders of our nation at this time.

I do believe that American leadership is the right of popular vote in any and all socialist democracies as the framers of our American Constitution meant it to be.

So it is that I as a Writer, Blogger, retired Builder of All Structures, General Contractor, in the construction trades do have the American right to ventilate my personal stories to the American people, in the hope that I can better understand moral human virtue of who we are or think we are to ourselves as one American people, as one American diversified human race.

These colorful writings archived Resistance books do represent five years of my Resistance writings meant to better understand our political place in our own, one of many global democracies of today.

Whereas the first Resistance writings did start coming on the seventh hour of 2017, a time now passed but not forgotten as my mission statement against the Republican United States of North America pro-fascism governess promoted and directed by President Donald's so called popularity at the 2017 Presidenual Inauguration, our first Resistance writings were to deny our United States racist, fascist appointed American President global popularity at his January 20th 2017 Inauguration at a global setting where the world stood shocked and dis-may at what American Democracy was capable of doing to itself under capitalist social rule of the people.

2018, broad us hope as we the Resistance of the American people took back the Unites States House of Representatives from the Grand Old Party "GOP"/Republican Party.

Thus, we had Government over site of the federal offices of the United States once again as our Resistance Battles would now be based on fighting Donald Trump's attempts to globalize our

American democratic process as a global Democracy of his foreign government dictator friends.

All this made so by President Trump, to allow the President of the United States Donald Trump {POTUS 45} to continue to rule without the vote or approval or by democratic vote of the American people.

By 2019 Resistance had won the 2018 Mid-Term Elections and established Oversight Authority over Donald Trump, the Republican Party was no longer a political party of the American conservative votes it was then the Donald Trump Party of the American fascist racist separatist and we The Resistance had now become the most powerful American political Movement to Impeach Donald Trump prior to the 2020 Presidenual Elections.

Now here we are today December 2020, a year which will live long in the minds of our nation for century's to come after which we will be judge as the peers of our gifted times within American democratic History.

By 2020 we The Resistance have now, proven to the powers of the world that American democracy does respect democratically appointed presidents to the point of the next election/popular vote of the people.

2020 has now revealed to the Resistance that the United States Presidency is no mans island by way of American political Constitutional rule; as well that it is the doubled edged sword of American Democracy.

We The Resistance now have won the United States Congress, the United States Senate and the Executive Offices of the President of the United States by the will of the popular vote of the people in POTUS/46 Joe Biden.

In 2021the Trump Republican Leaders of the Trump Republican Party and Traitors who signed Covenant and kissed the ring of Donald Trump are still in the Congress and the Senate for now.

The world of today must now realize that we are now in the Battle against the extinction of the human race, whereas, now Citizen Donald Trump can now claim he only killed 400,000 Americans with his snake oil science solutions over the American people in his time as Republican Dictator over the American people.

The CoronaVirus the first injections began yesterday December 14th 2020 after 300,000 human lives were lost to the virus for lack of Presidenual Leadership during this Covet-19 Pandemic in the most part, or so the story will be told by those of us of the haves, and they have not of this, our time.

I thank you for reading my writings, which I view as a single grain of salt in the political battles of our colorful show time when the internet exposes and shares our ways within our own personal worlds with others/enjoy& "Stay Safe."

ArturoCortez/76541/12/15/2020

# CHAPTER 29

December 2020

Team admin@turnoutpact.org, I certainly cannot speak for a diversified democratic mind however no law enforcement here in Killeen or anywhere in our nation has the American right to take the life of human of man and woman and no American citizen has to pay taxes to be killed by racist law enforcement officers retirement trophy hunters.

No Police Officer should fear doing his or her jobs for the citizens of their local communities. Fear of those you serve is no place for a armed public official, this act alone is but a sickly cowardly excuse to justify insecurity to the point of deliberate murder of any citizen anywhere in America and it must be removed from law enforcement and replaced with equitable multi-racial officials with the tenacity to do their work with community honor and dignity.

Whereas, no American citizen regardless of racial or national identification and or gender identification should ever fear those who he or she pays with their tax dollars for community social security and protection.

Whereas, no Police Officer who has killed the human hand that feeds all Police Departments should be allowed to protect and serve the American citizen's right to life.

Whereas this job requires peaceful solutions and understandings of whom you work; as one of many who's personal ability to protect and serve is sane human virtues regardless of race, gender, and/or national origin.

Whereas, a police officer's job is to protect and serve and should never be viewed as a police officer's right to work, but rather a police officer's privilege to serve the community taxpayer's who can take his job away.

Public financed work services, agreements with community City Councils across this nation must never include positive merits to anyone who has a human kill as a badge of personal honor regardless of who they have killed, or killed for.

I do suppose the question "?" is do I support defunding the police.

My answer therefore is simple, "I do believe that if a law enforcement department of the City Counsil of a City is not consistent with the mission of the City. Than it is the duty and the responsibility of the City Council to remove and replace, and not only police officers but the Department of the City in order to protect and serve with qualified law enforcement personal in a one life lost is too many humane perspective.

The mission of the City is to perform the mission as interpreted by a legally elect City Councilmen and or women.

The City Council does have the responsibility to remove and replace a department of the City here in Killeen, and all across this nation because we are a American socialist capitalist Democracy. And yes I am one who does believe the American citizen does have the American right to defund a police department within our national Constitutional boundaries.

Whereas, the people of his or her community do not have to tolerate those who have violated a humans, human right to exist regardless of race gender or national origin.

Police Officers who crosses the line and kills for whatever reason, must lose the honors and respect which the citizen have entrusted in the Police Officer and his Department.

All life is cheap here in the land of the gun but it is we who must make it clear that for a police officer to kill, is never in the line of duty it is however the fasts way for a law enforcement officer to lose his or her law enforcement careers and benefits as servants in our citizen elected American elected communities.

## Solutions:

**"Law Enforcement Cross Cultural Community Education and Assessments,"** of our local community law enforcement.

The development and implementation of local community citizen based, **"Community Participatory Processes,"** in grass-root community policing.

**"Remove & Replace {R&R} Police Officers,"** who have killed a Human of man and woman for whatever reason as the message to law enforcement officials that only bad cops can hurt good cops who have to wear the same colors/Police Unions who train all cops to view citizens on the street as the enemy of a white America must never be allowed to represent American Law Enforcement of and for the American people.

The citizen taxpayers on the streets of this nation are not the enemy but rather the provider of a job to individuals who have the tenacity to honestly serve and protect their community.

ArturoCortez/76541/12/01/2020


## May 2020

May 10, 2020 Memo; to the Resistance Political Warriors
From Arturo Cortez/Killeen76541
From this day forward the Resistance stands firm with the Democratic Candidate Joe Biden for President of the United States of North America. I myself have made my personal contribution to the Democratic Unity Fund and, I respectfully ask that the rest of us of the Resistance do the same. All cyber political Resistance

Warriors for/or against American Democracy are now activated to participate in the 2020 General Election to remove American Republicans as we know them today from American political offices across this nation /ArturoCortez/Killeen/05/10/2020

The Resistance writings are my archived writings dating back to the 2016 Donald Trump–v-Hillary Clinton General Election.

This book was written to influence liberal and conservative to vote American in the 2020 Presidential Election, against those who side against American constitutional political dignity.

Where as we the resistance of the people of this nation did take back the United States Congress from the fascist right wing Republicans in 2018, and we will take back the United States Senate, and Executive Branches of the United States Government of the people of this nation by popular vote of the people in 31 days November 3, 2020.

Today is the 2nd day of October 2020, the day President of the United States, Donald Trump announced he and the First Lady Trump, have tested positive for the CoronaVirus, many if not all of the White house Staff are now believers in wearing a mask, for today.

So it is that I pray for old Joe, that Donald Trump and or his clan did not infect him as well, at the First National Debate.

I also pray for all those now selfishly suffering the effects of the CoronaVirus, by political ideology/Pendejismo, at a national Presidential level/ArturoCortez/10/02/2020

## June 2020

### Killeen06/01/2020:

The rule of law is that all men and woman are equals as human of man and woman under American law. Law Enforcement today is what happens when we as a community fail our own civic responsibilities and community interest concerns. The simple

Truth is that we pay the police their salary to protect and serve all peoples of the human kind in the same manner not to select and kill innocent of wrong doing citizens of this nation based on the color of our skin as in the case of George Floyd.

However La Resistencia must encourage all nations of Black Lives Matters to Stand Down on divisive human racial lawlessness, our massage on human dignity has been received around the world, today we must look deep within ourselves and refocus our energy in effecting change to local grass root community Police Department's hiring practices whereas police unions appear to be at the core of police violent inhumane culture.

Police Human Trophy Hunters have no place in law enforcement and/or within our grass root local public service.

The Departments of "Police Human Resources must be "of and for the people of our pueblo/grass root community, where we the people must have the total and complete control over who has the honor of serving and wear our community badge of honor on their chest.

Whereas our communities across this nation are demanding justice and authority over Police Departments across this nation who are killing our American young blood based on our God given color of our skin.

All Resistance warriors are to refocus and infiltrate nationwide "Police Departments of Human Resources" in order to effect police cultural change at a local level, "Stand Down" on the streets, and cash in on the political influence gained necessary to change police culture at local community levels/ArturoCortez/06/02/2020/ Killeen/

## By ArturoCortez, Killeen06/15/2020:

Okay, Raza of the human type the King of the Republicans and President of the United States "POTUS",45 Donald Trump is calling on all Republicans to come and rally with him in Tulsa, Oklahoma, the Donald is now playing the Peter Piper political approach on his Russian Donald Trump American Republican Party.

It is also true that the Donald is asking those who will be attending the Trump Rally in Oklahoma to sign papers which would release the Donald from legal responsibility after Republicans get the Corona Virus in Oklahoma.

Certainly this event will translate into political Republican loss of life, meaning of course that Republicans will literally exterminate themselves prior to the November Presidential General Election, whereas the Donald will have something else to blame China for.

However, I do believe the Republicans do have the legal right to commit suicide for the sake of their want to be American King Donald Trump, and my prayers are always with those of simple minds and hopeful conservative political souls. ArturoCortez/06/15/2020

## July 2020

Arthur Dwayne

Sir, I have presented to you two of my latest books which I have not yet completed prove reading, while at the same time I am attempting to keep up with my 2020 writings which I am still writing for next year. This project today requires:

Immediate third party prove reading, and editing; in your critical review of the 2019 manuscript you make word of grammar, if this is as I understand it, this means to me I can start the formatting process for that book, numbering, page headers, and naming the title of the book, while I wait to hear the word from you for the 2017 manuscript,

We need to find out from the book agent /team member guy whether it is best to release the books one at a time, or all in one.

Please remember that my political writings date back to the first black man elected as the United States President of North America who brought us hope and governmental transparency.

So it is that you have not read the 2018 manuscript yet, and you have not offered me a deal for my work yet, please be advised I do get three to four publishers a day wanting my works; my works will be published sooner or later Sir of that I am sure, I would love to have you and Global Summit House/teams right here with me when the Resistance hits the market places.

If I remember correctly the Title "El Centrolista" published within four weeks from the time I agreed to work with AuthorHouse, the Author House technical teams/ pros seemed to be working for me in the building and construction phase of that book, and/or so it seemed like, back then. Please advice ArturoCortez/08/05/2020

## The Resistance 2020/August 2020

## 08/18/2020

I would say that the Title "The Resistance 2016-2019" is ready for distribution, however I did find a few typos in the first two writings dated 2020 in the beginning of the book, I also had to tighten up the formatting towards the end of the book to make it easier on the printer.

This evening i will go through it one more time and tomorrow i will register it with the Library of Congress, once I have a registration # on the manuscript these is when the manuscript becomes a Book and the final cut of the book from my end so the answer to your question is "the manuscript is not the book until a literary Registration # is on the Title of the manuscript, from La Casa de Cortez, Publication perspective, Sir."

Global Summit House Teams will follow, and I will listen to Global Summit House professional marketing proposals for the Title.

So it is that I again thank you for taking the time to review my work. Sir, if anything I have learned in my time is how to write and build a book, now I am learning how to personally publish & market my own Titles with or without publishers.

**The Resistance /2020**

**08/22/2020/** 'Joe, Joe you are my friend if you Sir, can't help us with this pendejo than who is it that can.,'/Thank-you Joe for coming out of retirement to protect our American Constitution with proven honorable American Presidential Fiber as the foundation to American grass root personal leadership of American Democracy.

Joe/Sir, you have selected Kamala Harris, a Resistance "Yes we Can Political Warrior," as your running partner Thank-you Joe you make me Proud to be American please advice/ArturoCortez/76541/08/22/2020

08/23/2020/Whether one is from whatever American political party ideology of today you belong to Donald J. Trump has been given his four years as a "Electoral Collage Appointed Presidency" in the stead of our constitutional American Popular Vote of the American people of this our democratic nation.

Now, Incumbent POTUS/45 and the Electoral College appointee have failed their constitutional presidential responsibilities to the American Constitution as well as to we the people of this nation.

The Executive Offices of the United States is no man's island in our constitutional Democracy.

The United States Congress has now impeached the POTUS/45/Donald Trump. Whereas, Donald Trump has now lost the confidence and trust of the United States Congress meaning he will not be able to conduct his business of the people as a working partner of The United States Congress/House of Representatives, of the people of this nation.

There for, The Resistance/76541/2020 dose encourage all political ideologies to "support the proven, experienced leadership of Joseph R. Biden and Kamala Harris for President and Vice President of the United States of North America.

All Resistance Warriors, from within and without the United States are encouraged to influence their relatives within the United States with the right to vote, to vote early and Vote for Joe and Kamala Harris, Presidents of the United States, simply because it is the right thing to do for this nation and our diversified people of our Nation as Americans of the USA/ArturoCortez/76541/08/23/2020

> Tweet/08/24/2020/You are a liar Sir/Donald J. Trump, the Kurdish people are our allied Worrier friends in northern Iraq, and Syria who you betrayed to the Turks: the Kurd's are no longer our friends and they fought and died and won the war against ISIS on the ground for us, under POTUS/44 Barack Obama Administration/

**08/24/2020**

### Global Summit House Teams;

Regarding: manuscript Title "The Resistance 2016-2019", this book is now complete and ready for distribution Mr. Arthur Dwayne, I have attached a copy of the book to this email for your review, the next step belongs to Global Summit House, ,/ArturoCortez/76541/08/24/2020

**08/25/2020**/Manny Garcia, Ex. Texas Democratic Party, old friend you know as i do that what we need in Texas is for democrats to win in 2020 are yes we can Texano Democratic Candidates Lawn Signs placed in strategic locations, The Texas Republican Party has no political Republican Conservative Platform @ the 2020/ Republican Convention, along with no Republican Presidenual Primaries, there is no Republican Party now, in it's stead is "The 2020 Donald J. Trump family Party," representing nothing but themselves, and not the will of the Republican political ideology or the people of our nation, Donald Trump has now devoured the Texas Republican Party, the now Texas Conservative must draw a line on the Texas historical sand, and vote Democrat for the sake of Texas human life,/ArturoCortez/76541/08/25/2020

## /08/26/2020

Markus Torres/Cordially, thank-you for reading my writings, I am Arturo Cortez the Author, of my 'Si se Puede Title' "El Centrolista 2012-2015"; i am certainly honor that you folks are interested in my book for a possible Movie, so it is that i must advise you i just this week finished formatting my new Title "The Resistance 2016-2019," a follow up to El Centrolista 2012-2015.

The Resistance 2016-2019 is a 296 page word manuscript now formatted into word book form. In this book the Resistance is a Movement of the people who targets POTUS/45, Donald Trump for removal & replacement "R&R".

Whereas, my 2020 writings God willing may be published in 2024, both books are meant to span the moral political times and to appeal to those of us who like to think that we are still a somewhat moral civilized American Democracy, governed by our own domestic American Constitution, Please advise/ArturoCortez if you would like to proceed and thank-you for your interest in the Resistance/Movement/ArturoCortez/76541/08/26/2020

## The Resistance/2020/08/27/2020

Laura Hits the Republican Louisiana, Texas Coast,

Nothing about Hurricane Laura this morning from our fearless Leader POTUS/45, Donald Trump Yet! This Hurricane which hit the Republican States of Louisiana, and Texas @/or about 2:00 AM this morning with winds of 150 miles an hour are now lucky we are not a Democratic States!

Inters Joe Biden who will be a president for all American States in our times of human need, the right man to bring our nation back together; whereas, a puck will always create the problem, and deny the responsibility for extreme action as is Donald Trump the now Snake Oil President, Liar and Impeached, incumbent candidate for President of the United States who is now shamelessly asking for your vote, for another for years of Trump democratic siege and oppression.

The Resistance encourages Black Lives Matters to stand down on demonstrations, and mass gatherings, and instead help us win this 2020 Presidential Election come November 3, 2020 for us all in Joe Biden and Kamala Harris. We are now so close to winning against the now Donald Trump Party, and United States Senate; whereas, we all know where we stand with Donald Trump for now we must stand as one and kick his fine ass out of Public office.

The problem with America today here at home is the President himself, and his self induced social ignorance/evil which is what feeds the beast in American diversified human of man and woman. We must now fight back as one American human race of people to get Joe Biden Elected President in 72 days, I have been told that there are deliberate social civil disturbances planned to disrupt and distract the American people from our Prize, "American constitutional democratic right to Vote," as the same Law to all men and women who contribute to our American tax systems on today's American land.

Yes our best times yet, are almost here in 72 days from today we will be voting on who is the better man to live in the White House for the next four days regardless of political party we will have a new President and we the American people must remember what we once were, as the good thing in our American diversified times/lives, ArturoCortez76541/08/27/2020

## 2020/08/28/2020

Tucker Carlson is a Trump Party "Pendejo" who protects armed Domestic Terrorist, killing Americans exercising their constitutional American right to peacefully protest in Portland Oregon, Whereas, black or white the terrorist is old enough to legally swing from the end of a rope, for Donald Trump,

By ArturoCortez

**08/29/2020/**Christian Human Dignity is and always has been a doubled edged sword, with respect to human dignity; find a quite place and thank Jehovah God for who you are and his mission imprinted in your heart, and you will learn it is all about the Human as the only Race,

Conpadre Juan "chill" This year Donald Trump is using the Russian political propaganda dis information tactics once again with the money and tools of the American people to get elected the Donald is now able to produce shows Conpadre he is the president for now, the good thing is that Joe has been in public service long enough to know how to be president to Republican and Democratic States as one America,

**08/31/2020** B.O>Do your part for our Constitutional American Democracy and help me publish this Document attached prior to the November 3, 2020 General Presidential Election, whereas a political campaign is not a, "Movement" but one should complement the other Old Friend, so it is that i will never allow a president to build human cages for my Hispanic people, simply because in American democracy you never know what the next president is going to put in them.

## September/2020

### 9/01/2020 &63 days left,

Donald Trump is now a impeached, appointed, liar United States President, a Corporate Welfare loser from a domestic and international business perspective, and a snake oil salesman from his own understanding of himself, so it is that I must ask you to ask yourself, "what does that make me if he is our President for another four years? Answer, "A willing Pendejo/a Trump Fool."

So I have written, therefore let it be known that we The Resistance proudly made our American stand to win the popular vote in the 2016 Presidential Election; we did support Hillary Clinton for President 2016 and we did win the popular vote.

The Resistance did win the 2018 Mid-Term elections and we now have the Congress exercising our oversight responsibilities as is the responsibility of the United States Congress, The Resistance did have the President of the United States/ Donald Trump impeached prior to this up and coming election.

Let it be said "Donald Trump was given his undeserved Presidential honors and Presidential democratic respect as a legally appointed President for the last four years," which he has now squandered under his believe that he is our democratic King and President for life.

In 63 days Donald Trump will be no more to American's diversified Democracy and we all will be better off for having voted for Joe Biden for President regardless of political ideological differences.

Our only domestic enemy to the United States left after November 3, 2020 will be in the seeds of hate and evil planted by Donald Trump.

Seeds of racial hate and constitutional dismantling of our American diversified society into a fractured conquerable society of dis information and lies in the stead of our American Constitutional moral virtues. All this is now planted in the simple innocent hearts across our American nation, government and the intellectual world of today.

Joe and Kamala are our only hope for the survival of our American constitutional democracy as we knew it to be. Human dignity is always the target for hateful and or evil no matter at what cost, now is the time to stand and vote for what we once were as a democratic plural American society of the popular vote of the people.

Whereas, Joe, Joe you are my friend, thank you for your fifty year of public service to our nation only you as our President can bring back Honor and Respect to American Constitutional Democracy and the offices and departments of the United States governess.

The Resistance/2020 is strong within you my Old Friend; I Arturo Cortez and the Resistance stand firm with you Joe Biden, and Kamala Harris thank-you for what you do for all of us old friend \ ArturoCortez/76541/09/01/2020

## 09/09/07/2020

**"Thank-you America, 56 days to go,"** Gracias Raza of the Human Type our Resistance effort to help get Joe and Kamala Harris elect has conservatively yelled $360,000,000 million from one America Resistance liberals, Centralist, and Conservatives in August, 2020 for the Biden-Kamala Campaign for President, those of you who have, are now working with those of the have not, to take our country back from Donald Trump's Family Party.

It's all Donald Trump's fake news conspiracy a  Russian KGB disinformation propaganda political effort Compadre all to get the Donald re elected in 2020.

Conpadre stay safe at home, the people are saying Donald Trump is attempting to start a race war to get reelected how anyone can feel safe with that here in Texas the American land of the gun is way over my logical head, I think.

On the other hand Donald Trump has now crippled the United States Postal Service which denies me my mail order medications for his personal political reasons.

 then we have the covet CoronaVirus by election day in 56 days we will have lost over 200,000 American lives who will die conservative numbers of course because of Presidential incompetence .

As to the Corona Virus there are third world nations Compadre with better numbers on the Virus than we the most advanced nation in the know world of today Donald Trump has failed his most basic responsibilities as our President, the Donald has learned nothing from the Presidency of the United States of North America, Donald Trump's America is literally destroying us as a American people/nation we are now under a minority political siege of our American Constitutional Democracy.

Vladimir Putin the Russian USSR KGB Agent could not have prayed for a better agent then a Capitalist American Republican RX snake oil salesman with no loyalties in the White House of the people of this nation; what better way to make Russia better than Donald Trump who they say owes them Russian money which the Donald is paying back with American Foreign Policy and American Nationalism with the help of the American Republican Party.

As an Impeached United States President Donald Trump has learned nothing by his abuse of our freedoms allowed to him by our American Democracy, whereas, Donald Trump has now used American Democracy to destroy American Democracy from within itself.

The American honorable Resistance to governmental abuse of human dignity will always be there for all Americans, guaranteed to us by our American Constitutional Rights, as Americans however I do work towards the end of our Resistance against the United States Governess, come November 4th 2020.

American Democracy must never again be compromised or tested by alien foreign government elements/entities of dictatorships, Kingdoms, or other forms of foreign powers.

I do want to thank-you all those who have now made your contributions and signed up to support Joe Biden and Kamala Harris for President and Vice Presidents of the United States on November 3, 2020 American History will define us all based on the actions in these our "Times."

This nation has now sacrificed enough by outlasting the abuse of American governess and American Democracy by the now Impeached, Incumbent President Donald Trump; the time has come for us the American voter to have our say once again in this nation.

Our people are asking for sanity to our daily lives. We need to seriously get on with the business of surviving a global Pandemic, feeding our people and reorganizing our consumer economy.

Our consumer based economy is based on consumers spending in a free diversified manners.

Whereas as Donald Trump and his Republican Party enablers have now spent over three and a have years giving away America's

Treasury to Corporate welfare entities and to the  those who have and need  no more.

Whereas, the contributors and founders of this nation where the people getting to decide who will be our next President, in the stead of the now Electoral College appointed President Donald Trump.

Never should a yes we can political candidate/Leader compromise the vote of the American people by conceding their election prior to final popular vote count; time elements should never compromise the vote/election of the people as is our American socialist democracy of and for the Constitution of the people United States of North America./ArturoCortez/76541/09/07/2020

**09/08/2020** We now have 60 days to change America, now a land of those of us who have, and a land of those who have not, so we must all pray for all those who have enough to give enough; to give for those who have not, in this our own Capitalist Democracy,

## 09/08/2020

### The Resistance 2020/ Yes we Can Candidates Support List for 2020

I realize we must win this election in a capitalist electoral democracy so I too must swallow my pride and ask for your help once again Resistance warriors for Help as the resistance writer of this massage, with the intent to bring change to the United States Government by utilizing my God given talents/Blessings to influencing the readers of my writings. It is clear to me now that the Resistance will end by popular vote of the people come November 3, of 2020.

It is for this reason that we make a clean break from the time of Donald Trump/POTUS/45; we need to solidify control of our nation/Government under Joe Biden and Kamala Harris.

So it is that by contributing to any one or all of these candidates you will be voting to solidify the Executive Branch, The US Senate, and the United States House of Representatives under a "New" responsible United States government of the people of the United States of America under the new Administration led by the Presidential fiber of Joe Biden and Kamala Harris.

We as the American people must send a clear message to the rest of the world that American democracy is able to tolerate, and overcome Presidential political abuse of our American Constitutional Rights as citizens of this nation.

I ask you all too please vote Blue, this 2020 election in support of political change which will be here come November 3, 2020 with your support for these Community Leaders/Candidates in your communities across this nation.

Cal Cunningham, for the United States Senate in North Carolina is now in early voting and the race is very competitive please vote and/or support Cal Cunningham for the United States Senate in North Carolina with your in-kind contributions and/ or whatever you can monetary contribution to get these leaders you will have done your part to elect the right community leaders to represent the people of this nation in both the United States Executive Branch and the United States Senate, whereas, we did win the United States House of Representatives in 2018. This act on your part will give the people of this nation control of all three branches of the United States Government.

These Candidates will work towards American human dignity and will become the political backbone of our people of this time/ Missionaries of our American recovery in yet to come national political history. We are now living a horrible nightmare life experience which we must all experience ourselves, as one human race before we can continue our human instinct to define human dignity in our globalized diversified American socialist, American society democracy of today. Please, "Please DONATE," to one or all of these Grass-Root community leaders for change.

North Carolina your turn is up, your election is "on" please support Cal Cunningham, to represent you in the United States Senate:

**Joe Biden** for POTUS/46, @ bluestatedigital.com

**Cal Cunningham**, for United States Senator, North Carolina USA @ bluestatedigital.com

**John Ossoff** for United States Senator, Georgia, USA/2020 @ bluestatedigital.com

**Jaime Harris**, for the United States Senate, South Carolina, USA "This race is about right and wrong,"@ bluestatedigital.com

**MJ Hagar**, for United States Senate, a American Yes we Can," Military Hero Texas, USA, @ bluestatedigital.com

**Amy McGrath** for United States Senate, Kentucky, USA @ bluestatedigital.com

**Mark Kelly** for the United States Senate, Arizona, @ USA bluestatedigital.com

**Barbra Bollier** for the United States Senate, Kansas

This List of Resistance supported Candidates will be updated on Thursday of every week until Monday, November 2, 2020 the purpose of this list is to legally remove and replace (R&R) Donald J. Trump  by Popular democratic vote of the people,& to establish control of people over the United States Government / ArturoCortez/76541/09/09/2020

**09/11/2020**
**09/11/2020**

Se Reporta la Senora Hillary de la casa de Clinton,  thank-you for the invitation to meet i must however decline the invite; as a writer of meager means i cannot afford capitalist socialist electoral democracy, so it is that I do what I can, as a man of the lord my God has blessed me with the ability to reach out and move others around me with my writings, so as to give to those around me and myself, self worth in order to move forward as Americans, for one America.

The good news Senora is that I have finished and formatted my writings for the 296 w/p manuscript titled "The Resistance 2016-2019," on time for print and distribution prior to the 2020 General Election.

Although, I did write this book as my personal effort to over through the President of the United States "POTUS/45,  "para q viva la gente como la gente."

As a matter of fact I did enjoy reading our email correspondence of 2016 in the publish editing of the Resistance.

I do find that my Resistance political warriors/ political war machine is not of party rule order my friend even though our goal is the same between a Movement and the Political Campaign.

However, at this point I can predict old Joe the winner and next President of the United States; in 2020 our goal is to take control of the Executive Branch and the United States Senate, we did take the Congress in 2018 we the people of this nation will take our nation back in 56 days.

I have no doubt that the Resistance writings against the governess of today in the manuscript "The Resistance 2016-2019" will soon come to its welcome "end" come November 3, 2020.

Any way this manuscript is now available via traditional publishing methods, you Hillary and Kamala Harris are welcomed to review the manuscript, because you are a part of the book, a critical review of this book is expected to be archived for history in the life and times of ArturoCortez/76541.

Okay, I added my zip coat to my name when you wrote something about to many Arturo Cortez's on face book, to be exact 230 facebook.com Arturo Cortez's. I do not know whether that is good or not so I did add my Texas Zip Code to my on line signature to make things fair to other honorable Arturo Cortez's out there.

Hillary, "tell the party to keep it inclusive with respect to, "Republican Party Resistance Warriors."

In this time an election must be for the best interest of the State a United Vote for our nation/America.

My best to Bill and you have a wonderful day darling/ ArturoCortez/76541/09/11/2020

## 09/12/2020

Day 52 Prior to the 2020 election,

Today I received a request to add Candidate Barbra Bollier for the United States Senate, Kansas to

**"The Resistance 2020/ Yes we Can Candidates Support List for 2020," we now have 7 Resistance Senatorial Candidates/ Community Leaders challenging the Republican Senate for the right to lead the United States Senate and we only need 4 to win:**

North Carolina your turn is up, your election is "on" please support **Cal Cunningham**, to represent you in the United States Senate:

**Joe Biden** for POTUS/46, @ bluestatedigital.com

**Cal Cunningham**, for United States Senator, North Carolina USA @ bluestatedigital.com

**John Ossoff** for United States Senator, Georgia, USA/2020 @ bluestatedigital.com

**Jaime Harris**, for the United States Senate, South Carolina, USA "This race is about right and wrong,"@ bluestatedigital.com

**MJ Hagar**, for United States Senate, a American Yes we Can," Military Hero Texas, USA, @ bluestatedigital.com

**Amy McGrath** for United States Senate, Kentucky, USA @ bluestatedigital.com

**Mark Kelly** for the United States Senate, Arizona, @ USA bluestatedigital.com

**Barbra Bollier** for the United States Senate, Kansas @ USA bluestatedigital.com

We only need 4 of the 7 Resistance community leaders to win to take back the Senate to what it once was, we must stand firm as one America with honorable respect for any and "all who give, and have not, as is the ones who do have, and contributes enough for himself and a few others," your whatever you can donation is what makes our democracy strong, we must take control of the nation in 52 days and our candidates have so much time to spend your contribution before the election/ or the evil extermination of American human will continue regardless of who is in the white house our leadership is no more it is in fact dysfunctional to the human needs of the American people, and only we the American voters can change that in 52days/ ArturoCortez/76541/09/12/2020.

## 09/17/2018

**The Resistance 2020/ Yes we Can Candidates Support List for 2020** 47 days before the 2020 General Election, I am so proud to announce that Mike Bloomberg one of many in this nation who really does have the means, has committed $100,000,000 million dollars to the Joe Biden Campaign to remove and Replacement (R&R) Donald J. Trump POTUS/45 from our administrative government offices of the United States Government, of the people.

Although, we of the many in the Resistance do not have much money to buy American politics for the good of the nation, we do have the human American right to bring those things of Cesar ($) to the Round Table of human dignity, as a capitalist nature/ virtue of human so long as self preservation of our economy is in concerned.

Certainly, one could say, because we do vote for our Community leaders and representatives at the highest levels of our American governmental power by the all mighty American popular vote of the people.

It is the popular vote of the American people which creates and distributes power as our form of a ongoing social revolution within American society which we all know as American Democracy for our diversified American people where as only a sweet water native America can claim to be true Americans, now alien in our own hypocritical land.

Whereas, the Mike Bloomberg that helps Joe Biden in 2020 is making a statement to the economic pillars of Corporate America "now is the time to take our country back from the, "I am the greatest Greats POTUS/45."

Making things perfectly clear to Corporate American human and human of man and woman of this nation, "we are now all in the same boat, with things bound to get worst with Donald Trump who is now creating "Presidential Peter Piper Super Virus Spreader Evens' across our nation inspired by our national Presidential Political Events, whereas; all in a time when, today marks 193,000 deaths to date due to the CoronaVirus Pandemic and know Presidential Leadership.

According to scientist from across the world over 230,000 Americans will be dead or dying from the CoronaVirus by Election Day.

So it is that "We need more Money," from all Corporate Entities in order to grease the American capitalist political machine, in order that it works for us the people of this nation in 2020.

To not have the money to by American politics is no excuse whether one is of the ones who have, or of the ones who have not, our capitalist Presidential Election will be won by those who have the money to influence the Vote as it has always been in American Democracy, for now.

Donald Trump's time will come in 49 days, with or without money when this American Political freedom capitalist Monarchy will come to its end in American politics "or" we could be saying after the election, "We could have put more money into buying our election, and maybe we would not have to deal with Donald Trump and his "Herd Immunity" mentality solution to the CoronaVirus meaning of course that we are now allowing the virus to take all it needs from humanity in order that the CoronaVirus dies off before we as the human victim do, something with our American scientific community to  fight the global Pandemic.

This rallies for Donald Trump political scenario which is now playing out is interesting to me because the Aztec Empire, Leaders Montezuma 1and his nephew Montezuma II would also offer their most faithful subjects to the Gods as a sign of cult faith, there were those in 1519 who would actually volunteer to die for their leader and did, it is then in pri-Columbian History where I assume one would fine the native word "Pendejo" or "Pendejos= more than one," coined.

Mike Bloomberg is simply a American billionaire who remembers who we once were before Donald Trump in American politics and a special friend to the Resistance who challenges Corporate America to give to the Resistance Senatorial political campaigns going on across the country now to (R&R) the United States Senate in 2020, with responsible community leaders who understand their loyalties to the United States Constitution of the people of our nation.

There are 12 seats up for election in the United States Senate and we need all of them or not less than 4 seats to take control of the United States Senate of the people out of 12 seats available, so as to rule by popular vote of the people of this democracy.

We as a American people must not under estimate the damage Donald Trump has done to our American Constitution with the help of what once was the Republican Party now transformed into the Donald Trump Loyalty Party, of today.

Now the voters of the conservative Republic Party must swallow their pride and vote Democrat for the nation along with the rest of us.

Whereas, the recovery and reconstruction after Donald Trump must begin as soon as possible if we are to survive this virus and money is now a means to American Survival of the American untamed beast/the American economy and freedom from Donald Trump's era politics of the people, for now.

To be perfectly clear because of Mike Bloomberg we now have Corporate Capitalist Resistance Warriors for human dignity working for the people as one for this nation to protect our socialist, constitutional democracy.

Welcome to the Resistance Mike Bloomberg, the Resistance is strong within you my friend thank you Sir for who you are and what you do for the people of our nation you Sir make me proud to be American/ArturoCortez /76541/09/14/2020

## 09/17/2020

The Resistance 2020/ Yes we Can Candidates Support List for 2020

North Carolina your turn is on up, your early election is now on" please support Cal Cunningham to represent you in the United States Senate:

Joe Biden for POTUS/46, @ bluestatedigital.com

John Ossoff for United States Senator, Georgia, USA/2020 @ bluestatedigital.com

Jaime Harris, for the United States Senate, South Carolina, USA "This race is about right and wrong,"@ bluestatedigital.com

MJ Hagar, for United States Senate, a American Yes we Can," Military Hero Texas, USA, @ bluestatedigital.com

Amy McGrath for United States Senate, Kentucky, USA @ bluestatedigital.com

Mark Kelly for the United States Senate, Arizona, @ USA bluestatedigital.com

Re-elect Doug Jones for the United States Senate Alabama USA

VOTE American we need these Candidates in public office so we can change things in American Politics / ArturoCortez/76541/09/17/2020

## 09/19/2020

No Conpadre, Bautista i am not flying, not since the herd mentality virus extermination of human in Washington D.C, ideology in Washington D.C. began, i am under Doctors orders to stay at home and away from human of man, for now. Only God knows what he is going to do next with us, stay safe Conpadre our prays are with you Comadre Lupe and the girls and families,

## 09/20/2020

Arturo Cortez Calm down Conpadre, there is reason to believe that Border Patrol Agents from Texas were sent to Oregon to create problems for the Oregonians and other Democratic States and Cities in order to get Donald Trump Elected Law and order President, it is said that President, Donald Trump, is now is now producing Television Shows again with the American people of TV knowledge only, Conpadre i say my chest is not a warehouse, so i just pass it along, Vote for Joe Biden before we all lose family to this virus Raza of the Human Type,

## The Resistance/2020

It is difficult to Honor the Lady's last "Death Wish,"

## 09/20/2020"

We must Honor the Lady's last request, as you would want others to Honor your own last Request," Regardless of who you are you know that Supreme Court Justice, Ruth Bader Ginsburg passed on Friday. The Women's Resistance Movements have lost a humane moral compass. Who departed with instructions on what to do after death,

## 09/23/2020

2008 a Si se Puede vote for the promise of our nation, 2012 a Si se Puede vote to re enforce the promise of our nation/ 2016 A Si se Puede, vote for Hillary or Better/ 2020 The Si se Puede Resistance, to Republican Russian Politics within the United States Government. / "answer' the Resistance is not a "Campaign" it is the "Movement" of the people like me who do not get paid to play politics with the vote of the many people.

"American humanity does not have a choice when playing with the capitalist packing order of the Dramatic Party.

Joe old friend i do have your back, all you have to do is not concede this election until the last popular vote is counted, and the rest we live to Texas History to record.

Rest assured The Resistance has not lost a popular vote of the people since we won in 2008, we need lawn signs and ads in Texas, Texas will turn blue as the Republican GOP House is now crumbling here in Texas/Joe Biden you my friend make me proud to be American. /ArturoCortez/76541/**09/23/2020**

## The first 2020 Nation Presidential Debate, Joe Biden-v-Donald Trump

**09/29/2020**

Never In the history of our United States Democracy has there ever been a President so detached from his responsibilities as President.

Last night the President of The United States (POTUS/45) Donald J. Trump showed a tantrum on global Television by outright attacking old, Joe Biden very time Joe attempted to explain his plan for the nation and its people it seemed as though POTUS/45 was not repaired to debate sleep old Joe Biden, as Donald Trump calls Joe Biden in public. Last night Joe Biden did eat the Presidents lunch by connecting the President to a domestic terrorist organization disrupting peaceful demonstrations and in sighting armed violence in democratic cities for the President.

The President lost the 1st Presidential debate and exposed his plans if any for our future as American subjects of the human kind to what he considers his Donald Trump Presidency.

The President called on White Supremacy Militia groups to "stand down and standby" call to action when needed much as a cheap South American Dictator would do.

Whereas, as if he loses this election, then our National Election of the people is rigged and he will refuse to relinquish and transfer his presidential powers to the next President as American democracy honorably expects him to do.

Now, I must turn our attention to the Resistance 2020.

We all Republicans, Centralist, and Democrats, are now on the same boat and we must Resistance as one Movement for American Democracy we must now feed the capitalist democracy we have created for ourselves if we are to rescue American Democracy from Russian Republican Political Siege of the Executive and Senatorial branches of our American democracy which is now literally in extermination mode of the American.

Whereas well over 250,000 a ¼ million Americans will be dead or dying by election day just for weeks from today over 200,000 dead to date; a topic at the debate preferred not to discuss at the Presidential Debate by President Donald Trump.

The Resistance encourages all its Political Warriors to encourage all your members to give and to give now to Democratic politicians only this election year regardless what Party or ideologue you belong too in American Politics, here is a list of Candidates on the Resistance preferred list.

## The Resistance 2020/ Yes we Can Candidates Support List for 2020

North Carolina your turn is on up, your early election is now on" please support Cal Cunningham to represent you in the United States Senate:

Joe Biden for President of the United States, /46, @ bluestatedigital.com

Cal Cunningham, for United States Senator, North Carolina USA @ bluestatedigital.com

John Ossoff, for United States Senator, Georgia, USA/2020 @ bluestatedigital.com

Jaime Harris, for the United States Senate, South Carolina, USA "This race is about right and wrong,"@ bluestatedigital.com

MJ Hagar, for United States Senate, a American Yes we Can," Military Hero Texas, USA, @ bluestatedigital.com

Amy McGrath, for United States Senate, Kentucky, USA @ bluestatedigital.com

Mark Kelly, for the United States Senate, Arizona, @ USA bluestatedigital.com

Re-elect Doug Jones, for the United States Senate Alabama USA

**Candidates added to the Resistance list by Barack Obama on the 30th day of September:**

John Hickenlooper,
Teresa Greenfield,
Cal Cunningham
Sara Gideon,
Mark Kelly,
Ben Ray Lujan,
As of today I feel very good about this election with 33 day to go, however that is no excuse not to give of yourself and your money to help finance the defeat of Donald Trump and his Republican enablers in the Senate and the Congress with your vote of the $ kind as is our American way as of today. / ArturoCortez/76541/29/0/2020

# CHAPTER 30

**October 2020**

## The Resistance/2020

**10/04/2020**

On Friday the 1st day of October, 2020 @/or about 1:00 AM, the White House announced President Donald Trump and his first lady as well as an administrative aide have tested positive for the CoronaVirus.

Today, four days after nine of the most powerful Republicans in Washington American leadership who attended the political Presidential function to fast tract the appointment of a new Republican Supreme Court Justice to replace the Democrat Lady Justice, Ruth Bader Ginsburg who's last dying wish was to have her seat on the Supreme Court filled after the 2020 General Presidential Election in 28 days from today.

I Arturo Cortez who does pray to Jehovah God, three times a day to protect all people of the human race, from this CoronaVirus, curse on our Humanity of today do pray today God that he forgive and enlighten all Republicans of the simple mind and the same ideological political feather.

I like you as a son of God from a theological perspective have to believe that the "Pass Over" of this pandemic is in our own ability to unite once again as one nation created by all Americans who know that we can win against this virus war if we all wear a mask, for 20 days.

We must all unite as a human Race for this Virus Pandemic to pass. But for this to happen you must have trust, faith and respect for ourselves and others around us, in order to once again be able to glorify ourselves among others as a human virtue as we experience the biblical powers of our lord and creator.

The CoronaVirus has now penetrated the most secure Executive Offices this world, our world has to offer as well a infected over 7,000,000 and killed over 210,000 Americans to date and our President refuses to stand with our doctors and scientist on wearing a face mask for the sake of the American people as we continue to die of in front of him.

The CoronaVirus Pandemic can be perceived as God sent to measure our human ability to see ourselves as one humanity of different colors and diverse cultural beginnings, with one God/ Creator all with his human gift or his curse of knowledge.

Whereas, we the people we must do what is right for our own keen/ kind and others for the sake of our human race.

As for Donald Trump he too like we all is now carrying God's mission in his heart and his own Cross on his back to weigh, balance and measure his place on and under God's earth.  Donald Trump will receive what he has earned as he is now in the good hands of the lord our God, and I do trust that our God is now teaching us all with his powerful deeds, whereas it was not I, but rather a wise carpenter who once said "it will be easier for a camel to walk through the eye of a needle, then it will be for a rich man to enter the gates of heaven." in or about 33 Before his Death 2020 years ago, as for today we tell time by the death of Jesus el Cristo, who like you and I was the human, son of God.

Okay, remember "Wear Your Mask for Human Dignity" to thrive no less than 20 days/ and we beat the virus for good. We can than get on with our diversified lives as it is meant to be.

Now we must deal with the business of the Resistance, we must once again feed our political beast if we are to win the White House, and the United States Senate, whereas the Resistance did establish control of the United States House of Representatives, in 2018.

This is a National Candidates support list which the Resistance encourages you to support, if we are to make change truly happen in our country, please give today to any one of these candidates or all of them if you can if we are to save our human race from extinction:

**The Resistance 2020/ Yes we Can Candidates**
**Support List for 2020**

Joe Biden for President of the United States, /46, @ bluestatedigital.com

Cal Cunningham, for United States Senator, North Carolina USA @ bluestatedigital.com

John Ossoff, for United States Senator, Georgia, USA/2020 @ bluestatedigital.com

Jaime Harris, for the United States Senate, South Carolina, USA "This race is about right and wrong,"@ bluestatedigital.com

MJ Hagar, for United States Senate, a American Yes we Can," Military Hero Texas, USA, @ bluestatedigital.com

Amy McGrath, for United States Senate, Kentucky, USA @ bluestatedigital.com

Mark Kelly, for the United States Senate, Arizona, @ USA bluestatedigital.com

Re-elect Doug Jones, for the United States Senate Alabama USA

**Candidates added to the Resistance list by
Barack Obama on the 30th day of September:**

John Hickenlooper,
Teresa Greenfield,
Cal Cunningham
Sara Gideon,
Mark Kelly,
Ben Ray Lujan,

I have known Joe Biden and Joe is one if not the best at bi-partisan politics he will fight the Virus with everything we have, and he will need these Democratic Candidates at his side, to exterminate this virus Please Donate we only have 28 day to spend your contribution on our lives.

/ArturoCortez/10/05/2020

## 10/06/2020

Well, I did start writing this book to influence the 2020 Presidential Election and the time has come to send my manuscript to the printer; I certainly understand that 27 days may not be enough time to get my book published prior to the November 3, 2020 election.

However, I can now see the end to our Resistance to the Donald Trump's United States Government.

Whereas, the President has now contaminated himself and at least twenty if not if not all of his United States White House leadership staff fact; as well as his closest Republican Senators, and Republican United States Congressmen and women to include members of his own family.

Because of Donald Trump the United States has now been left with literately fatedly leaderless, and venerable as we must now wait for American Democracy to play out the end of Donald

Trump's Democratic Electoral Collage Appointment, in the stead of "The Popular vote of the people," as our national President and leader of the free world in one way or the other must face this truth.

As for the 2020 Resistance to date will end and go to the Printer. I do ask that you continue to follow this story on Television as the ending to this story and or Donald Trump could be days away, one way or another as President of the United States.

As for now, I will tell my story in my historical writings dating back to how the Donald got himself elected United States President in November of 2016, which established the Resistance in or about the seventh hour of 2017 all my writings to date related to the Resistance are achieved in this book.

I ask and encourage all the readers and citizens of our nation to step forward and bring an end to this CoronaVirus, by wearing your face mask when out in public for at least 20 days, for the sake of yourselves, families, and your American communities, and the world we live in. "Enjoy' these writings. / ArturoCortez/76541/10/06/2020

A LA CASA DE CORTEZ PUBLICATION/76541/KILLEEN, TEXAS IN PARNERSHIP WITH GLOBAL SUMMIT HOUSE/PUBLISHING

# *La Resistencia / The Resistance*

## BY ARTUROCORTEZ/76541

Writings/Political Journal for 2020

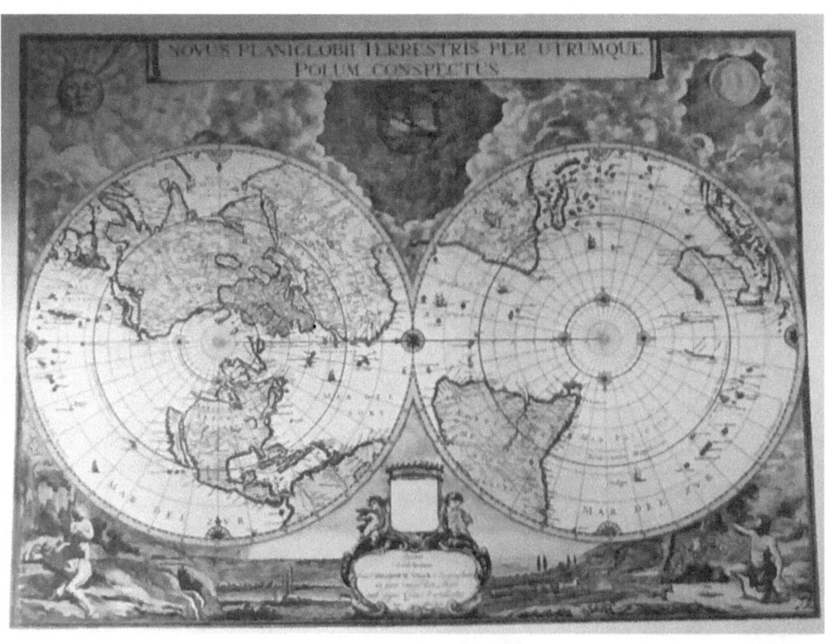

NOVUS PLANIGLOBII TERRESTRIS PER UTRUMQUE
POLUM CONSPECTUS.
MAR DEL SUR
MAR DEL ZUR

# Introduction

"We have now won the popular American vote for the 2020 General Election, now we must fear the Constitutional Political Battles to protect American Democracy which are yet to come,"

It is certainly true I did not vote for Donald Trump, I do not like Donald Trump's elitist ways nor do I like the "Haters" of humans who do not look as they do, for whatever reason.

It is true as well that there are many in our nation who feels they have to like and love our President once elected.

This is not true simply because we do live in America where we are governed by our American constitutional rights which grantees ever American the right to speak truth to power and share our believes with others whether they like it or not.

So it is that I had no choice but to follow and learn the ways of how to deny Presidenual leadership in a respectful manner from a fool Republican United States President, Congress and United States Senate as understood by our global allied partners who have now been humiliated and betrayed by the Republican Party who we can now say, the Republicans as a political party have proudly created treason and attempted political coup over the people of this nation and our American Constitutional rights as the elected political leaders of our nation at this time.

I do believe that American leadership is the right of popular vote in any and all socialist democracies as the framers of our American Constitution meant it to be.

So it is that I as a Writer, Blogger, retired Builder of All Structures, General Contractor, in the construction trades do have the American right to ventilate my personal stories to the American people, in the hope that I can better understand moral human virtue of who we are or think we are to ourselves as one American people, as one American diversified human race.

These colorful writings archived Resistance books do represent five years of my Resistance writings meant to better understand our political place in our own, one of many global democracies of today.

Whereas the first Resistance writings did start coming on the seventh hour of 2017, a time now passed but not forgotten as my mission statement against the Republican United States of North America pro-fascism governess promoted and directed by President Donald's so called popularity at the 2017 Presidenual Inauguration, our first Resistance writings were to deny our United States racist, fascist appointed American President global popularity at his January 20th 2017 Inauguration at a global setting where the world stood shocked and dis-may at what American Democracy was capable of doing to itself under capitalist social rule of the people.

2018, broad us hope as we the Resistance of the American people took back the Unites States House of Representatives from the Grand Old Party "GOP"/Republican Party.

Thus, we had Government over site of the federal offices of the United States once again as our Resistance Battles would now be based on fighting Donald Trump's attempts to globalize our American democratic process as a global Democracy of his foreign government dictator friends.

All this made so by President Trump, to allow the President of the United States Donald Trump {POTUS 45} to continue to rule without the vote or approval or by democratic vote of the American people.

By 2019 Resistance had won the 2018 Mid-Term Elections and established Oversight Authority over Donald Trump, the Republican Party was no longer a political party of the American conservative votes it was then the Donald Trump Party of the American fascist racist separatist and we The Resistance had now become the most powerful American political Movement to Impeach Donald Trump prior to the 2020 Presidenual Elections.

Now here we are today December 2020, a year which will live long in the minds of our nation for century's to come after which we will be judge as the peers of our gifted times within American democratic History.

By 2020 we The Resistance have now, proven to the powers of the world that American democracy does respect democratically appointed presidents to the point of the next election/popular vote of the people.

2020 has now revealed to the Resistance that the United States Presidency is no mans island by way of American political Constitutional rule; as well that it is the doubled edged sword of American Democracy.

We The Resistance now have won the United States Congress, the United States Senate and the Executive Offices of the President of the United States by the will of the popular vote of the people in POTUS/46 Joe Biden.

In 2021the Trump Republican Leaders of the Trump Republican Party and Traitors who signed Covenant and kissed the ring of Donald Trump are still in the Congress and the Senate for now.

The world of today must now realize that we are now in the Battle against the extinction of the human race, whereas, now

Citizen Donald Trump can now claim he only killed 400,000 Americans with his snake oil science solutions over the American people in his time as Republican Dictator over the American people.

The CoronaVirus the first injections began yesterday December 14th 2020 after 300,000 human lives were lost to the virus for lack of Presidenual Leadership during this Covet-19 Pandemic in the most part, or so the story will be told by those of us of the haves, and the have not of this, our time.

I thank you for reading my writings, which I view as a single grain of salt in the political battles of our colorful show time  when the internet exposes and shares our ways within our own personal worlds with others/enjoy& "Stay Safe." ArturoCortez/76541/12/15/2020

# CHAPTER 31

December 2020

**Team admin@turnoutpact.org,**

I certainly cannot speak for a diversified democratic mind however no law enforcement here in Killeen or anywhere in our nation has the American right to take the life of human of man and woman and no American citizen has to pay taxes to be killed by racist law enforcement officers retirement trophy hunters.

No Police Officer should fear doing his or her jobs for the citizens of their local communities. Fear of those you serve is no place for a armed public official, this act alone is but a sickly cowardly excuse to justify insecurity to the point of deliberate murder of any citizen anywhere in America and it must be removed from law enforcement and replaced with equitable multi-racial officials with the tenacity to do their work with community honor and dignity.

Whereas, no American citizen regardless of racial or national identification and or gender identification should ever fear those who he or she pays with their tax dollars for community social security and protection.

Whereas, no Police Officer who has killed the human hand that feeds all Police Departments should be allowed to protect and serve the American citizen's right to life.

Whereas this job requires peaceful solutions and understandings of whom you work; as one of many who's personal ability to protect and serve is sane human virtues regardless of race, gender, and/or national origin.

Whereas, a police officer's job is to protect and serve and should never be viewed as a police officer's right to work, but rather a police officer's privilege to serve the community taxpayer's who can take his job away.

Public financed work services, agreements with community City Councils across this nation must never include positive merits to anyone who has a human kill as a badge of personal honor regardless of who they have killed, or killed for.

I do suppose the question "?" is do I support defunding the police.

My answer therefore is simple, "I do believe that if a law enforcement department of the City Counsil of a City is not consistent with the mission of the City. Than it is the duty and the responsibility of the City Council to remove and replace, and not only police officers but the Department of the City in order to protect and serve with qualified law enforcement personal in a one life lost is too many humane perspective.

The mission of the City is to perform the mission as interpreted by a legally elect City Councilmen and or women.

The City Council does have the responsibility to remove and replace a department of the City here in Killeen, and all across this nation because we are a American socialist capitalist Democracy. And yes I am one who does believe the American citizen does have the American right to defund a police department within our national Constitutional boundaries.

Whereas, the people of his or her community do not have to tolerate those who have violated a humans, human right to exist regardless of race gender or national origin.

Police Officers who crosses the line and kills for whatever reason, must lose the honors and respect which the citizen have entrusted in the Police Officer and his Department.

All life is cheap here in the land of the gun but it is we who must make it clear that for a police officer to kill, is never in the line of duty it is however the fasts way for a law enforcement officer to lose his or her law enforcement careers and benefits as servants in our citizen elected American elected communities.

Solutions:

"Law Enforcement Cross Cultural Community Education and Assessments," of our local community law enforcement.

The development and implementation of local community citizen based, "Community Participatory Processes," in grass-root community policing.

"Remove & Replace {R&R} Police Officers," who have killed a Human of man and woman for whatever reason as the message to law enforcement officials that only bad cops can hurt good cops who have to wear the same colors/Police Unions who train all cops to view citizens on the street as the enemy of a white America must never be allowed to represent American Law Enforcement of and for the American people.

The citizen taxpayers on the streets of this nation are not the enemy but rather the provider of a job to individuals who have the tenacity to honestly serve and protect their community. ArturoCortez/76541/12/01/2020

## May 2020

May 10, 2020 Memo; to the Resistance Political Warriors
From Arturo Cortez/Killeen76541
From this day forward the Resistance stands firm with the Democratic Candidate Joe Biden for President of the United States of North America. I myself have made my personal contribution

to the Democratic Unity Fund and, I respectfully ask that the rest of us of the Resistance do the same. All cyber political Resistance Warriors for/or against American Democracy are now activated to participate in the 2020 General Election to remove American Republicans as we know them today from American political offices across this nation /ArturoCortez/Killeen/05/10/2020

The Resistance writings are my archived writings dating back to the 2016 Donald Trump–v-Hillary Clinton General Election.

This book was written to influence liberal and conservative to vote American in the 2020 Presidential Election, against those who side against American constitutional political dignity.

Where as we the resistance of the people of this nation did take back the United States Congress from the fascist right wing Republicans in 2018, and we will take back the United States Senate, and Executive Branches of the United States Government of the people of this nation by popular vote of the people in 31 days November 3, 2020.

Today is the 2nd day of October 2020, the day President of the United States, Donald Trump announced he and the First Lady Trump, have tested positive for the CoronaVirus, many if not all of the White house Staff are now believers in wearing a mask, for today.

So it is that I pray for old Joe, that Donald Trump and or his clan did not infect him as well, at the First National Debate.

I also pray for all those now selfishly suffering the effects of the CoronaVirus, by political ideology/Pendejismo, at a national Presidential level/ArturoCortez/10/02/2020:

## June 2020

Killeen06/01/2020:
The rule of law is that all men and woman are equals as human of man and woman under American law. Law Enforcement today

is what happens when we as a community fail our own civic responsibilities and community interest concerns. The simple Truth is that we pay the police their salary to protect and serve all peoples of the human kind in the same manner not to select and kill innocent of wrong doing citizens of this nation based on the color of our skin as in the case of George Floyd.

However La Resistencia must encourage all nations of Black Lives Matters to Stand Down on divisive human racial lawlessness, our massage on human dignity has been received around the world, today we must look deep within ourselves and refocus our energy in effecting change to local grass root community Police Department's hiring practices whereas police unions appear to be at the core of police violent inhumane culture.

Police Human Trophy Hunters have no place in law enforcement and/or within our grass root local public service.

The Departments of "Police Human Resources must be "of and for the people of our pueblo/grass root community, where we the people must have the total and complete control over who has the honor of serving and wear our community badge of honor on their chest.

Whereas our communities across this nation are demanding justice and authority over Police Departments across this nation who are killing our American young blood based on our God given color of our skin.

All Resistance warriors are to refocus and infiltrate nationwide "Police Departments of Human Resources" in order to effect police cultural change at a local level, "Stand Down" on the streets, and cash in on the political influence gained necessary to change police culture at local community levels/ArturoCortez/06/02/2020/ Killeen/

By ArturoCortez,

Killeen06/15/2020: Okay, Raza of the human type the King of the Republicans and President of the United States "POTUS",45 Donald Trump is calling on all Republicans to come and rally with him in Tulsa, Oklahoma, the Donald is now playing the Peter Piper political approach on his Russian Donald Trump American Republican Party.

It is also true that the Donald is asking those who will be attending the Trump Rally in Oklahoma to sign papers which would release the Donald from legal responsibility after Republicans get the Corona Virus in Oklahoma.

Certainly this event will translate into political Republican loss of life, meaning of course that Republicans will literally exterminate themselves prior to the November Presidential General Election, whereas the Donald will have something else to blame China for.

However, I do believe the Republicans do have the legal right to commit suicide for the sake of their want to be American King Donald Trump, and my prayers are always with those of simple minds and hopeful conservative political souls. ArturoCortez/06/15/2020

## July 2020

### Arthur Dwayne

Sir, I have presented to you two of my latest books which I have not yet completed prove reading, while at the same time I am attempting to keep up with my 2020 writings which I am still writing for next year. This project today requires:

Immediate third party prove reading, and editing; in your critical review of the 2019 manuscript you make word of grammar, if this is as I understand it, this means to me I can start the formatting process for that book, numbering, page headers, and naming the title of the book, while I wait to hear the word from you for the 2017 manuscript,

We need to find out from the book agent /team member guy whether it is best to release the books one at a time, or all in one.

Please remember that my political writings date back to the first black man elected as the United States President of North America who brought us hope and governmental transparency.

So it is that you have not read the 2018 manuscript yet, and you have not offered me a deal for my work yet, please be advised I do get three to four publishers a day wanting my works; my works will be published sooner or later Sir of that I am sure, I would love to have you and Global Summit House/teams right here with me when the Resistance hits the market places.

If I remember correctly the Title "El Centrolista" published within four weeks from the time I agreed to work with AuthorHouse, the Author House technical teams/ pros seemed to be working for me in the building and construction phase of that book, and/or so it seemed like, back then. Please advice ArturoCortez/08/05/2020

## The Resistance 2020/August 2020

### 08/18/2020

I would say that the Title "The Resistance 2016-2019" is ready for distribution, however I did find a few typos in the first two writings dated 2020 in the beginning of the book, I also had to tighten up the formatting towards the end of the book to make it easier on the printer.

This evening i will go through it one more time and tomorrow i will register it with the Library of Congress, once I have a registration # on the manuscript these is when the manuscript becomes a Book and the final cut of the book from my end so the answer to your question is "the manuscript is not the book until a literary Registration # is on the Title of the manuscript, from La Casa de Cortez, Publication perspective, Sir."

Global Summit House Teams will follow, and I will listen to Global Summit House professional marketing proposals for the Title.

So it is that I again thank you for taking the time to review my work. Sir, if anything I have learned in my time is how to write and build a book, now I am learning how to personally publish & market my own Titles with or without publishers.

## The Resistance /2020

08/22/2020/ 'Joe, Joe you are my friend if you Sir, can't help us with this pendejo than who is it that can.,'/Thank-you Joe for coming out of retirement to protect our American Constitution with proven honorable American Presidential Fiber as the foundation to American grass root personal leadership of American Democracy.

Joe/Sir, you have selected Kamala Harris, a Resistance "Yes we Can Political Warrior," as your running partner Thank-you Joe you make me Proud to be American please advice/ ArturoCortez/76541/08/22/2020

08/23/2020/Whether one is from whatever American political party ideology of today you belong to Donald J. Trump has been given his four years as a "Electoral Collage Appointed Presidency" in the stead of our constitutional American Popular Vote of the American people of this our democratic nation.

Now, Incumbent POTUS/45 and the Electoral College appointee have failed their constitutional presidential responsibilities to the American Constitution as well as to we the people of this nation.

The Executive Offices of the United States is no man's island in our constitutional Democracy.

The United States Congress has now impeached the POTUS/45/Donald Trump. Whereas, Donald Trump has now lost the confidence and trust of the United States Congress meaning he will not be able to conduct his business of the people as a working partner of The United States Congress/House of Representatives, of the people of this nation.

There for, The Resistance/76541/2020 dose encourage all political ideologies to "support the proven, experienced leadership of Joseph R. Biden and Kamala Harris for President and Vice President of the United States of North America.

All Resistance Warriors, from within and without the United States are encouraged to influence their relatives within the United States with the right to vote, to vote early and Vote for Joe and Kamala Harris, Presidents of the United States, simply because it is the right thing to do for this nation and our diversified people of our Nation as Americans of the USA/ArturoCortez/76541/08/23/2020

Tweet/08/24/2020/You are a liar Sir/Donald J. Trump, the Kurdish people are our allied Worrier friends in northern Iraq, and Syria who you betrayed to the Turks: the Kurd's are no longer our friends and they fought and died and won the war against ISIS on the ground for us, under POTUS/44 Barack Obama Administration/

## 08/24/2020

### Global Summit House Teams;

Regarding: manuscript Title "The Resistance 2016-2019", this book is now complete and ready for distribution Mr. Arthur Dwayne, I have attached a copy of the book to this email for your review, the next step belongs to Global Summit House, ,/ArturoCortez/76541/08/24/2020

08/25/2020/Manny Garcia, Ex. Texas Democratic Party, old friend you know as i do that what we need in Texas is for democrats to win in 2020 are yes we can Texano Democratic Candidates Lawn Signs placed in strategic locations, The Texas Republican Party has no political Republican Conservative Platform @ the 2020/ Republican Convention, along with no Republican Presidenual Primaries, there is no Republican Party now, in it's stead is "The 2020 Donald J. Trump family Party," representing nothing but themselves, and not the will of the Republican political ideology or the people of our nation, Donald Trump has now devoured the Texas Republican Party, the now Texas Conservative must draw a line on the Texas historical sand, and vote Democrat for the sake of Texas human life,/ArturoCortez/76541/08/25/2020

## /08/26/2020

Markus Torres/Cordially, thank-you for reading my writings, I am Arturo Cortez the Author, of my 'Si se Puede Title' "El Centrolista 2012-2015"; i am certainly honor that you folks are interested in my book for a possible Movie, so it is that i must advise you i just this week finished formatting my new Title "The Resistance 2016-2019," a follow up to El Centrolista 2012-2015.

The Resistance 2016-2019 is a 296 page word manuscript now formatted into word book form. In this book the Resistance is a Movement of the people who targets POTUS/45, Donald Trump for removal & replacement "R&R".

Whereas, my 2020 writings God willing may be published in 2024, both books are meant to span the moral political times and to appeal to those of us who like to think that we are still a somewhat moral civilized American Democracy, governed by our own domestic American Constitution, Please advise/ArturoCortez if you would like to proceed and thank-you for your interest in the Resistance/Movement/ArturoCortez/76541/08/26/2020

## The Resistance/2020/08/27/2020

Laura Hits the Republican Louisiana, Texas Coast,

Nothing about Hurricane Laura this morning from our fearless Leader POTUS/45, Donald Trump Yet! This Hurricane which hit the Republican States of Louisiana, and Texas @/or about 2:00 AM this morning with winds of 150 miles an hour are now lucky we are not a Democratic States!

Inters Joe Biden who will be a president for all American States in our times of human need, the right man to bring our nation back together; whereas, a puck will always create the problem, and deny the responsibility for extreme action as is Donald Trump the now Snake Oil President, Liar and Impeached, incumbent candidate for President of the United States who is now shamelessly asking for your vote, for another for years of Trump democratic siege and oppression.

The Resistance encourages Black Lives Matters to stand down on demonstrations, and mass gatherings, and instead help us win this 2020 Presidential Election come November 3, 2020 for us all in Joe Biden and Kamala Harris. We are now so close to winning against the now Donald Trump Party, and United States Senate; whereas, we all know where we stand with Donald Trump for now we must stand as one and kick his fine ass out of Public office.

The problem with America today here at home is the President himself, and his self induced social ignorance/evil which is what feeds the beast in American diversified human of man and woman. We must now fight back as one American human race of people to get Joe Biden Elected President in 72 days, I have been told that there are deliberate social civil disturbances planned to disrupt and distract the American people from our Prize, "American constitutional democratic right to Vote," as the same Law to all men and women who contribute to our American tax systems on today's American land.

Yes our best times yet, are almost here in 72 days from today we will be voting on who is the better man to live in the White House for the next four days regardless of political party we will have a new President and we the American people must remember what we once were, as the good thing in our American diversified times/lives, ArturoCortez76541/08/27/2020

## 2020/08/28/2020

Tucker Carlson is a Trump Party "Pendejo" who protects armed Domestic Terrorist, killing Americans exercising their constitutional American right to peacefully protest in Portland Oregon, Whereas, black or white the terrorist is old enough to legally swing from the end of a rope, for Donald Trump,

## By ArturoCortez

08/29/2020/Christian Human Dignity is and always has been a doubled edged sword, with respect to human dignity; find a quite place and thank Jehovah God for who you are and his mission imprinted in your heart, and you will learn it is all about the Human as the only Race,

Conpadre Juan "chill" This year Donald Trump is using the Russian political propaganda dis information tactics once again with the money and tools of the American people to get elected the Donald is now able to produce shows Conpadre he is the president for now, the good thing is that Joe has been in public service long enough to know how to be president to Republican and Democratic States as one America,

08/31/2020 B.O>Do your part for our Constitutional American Democracy and help me publish this Document attached prior to the November 3, 2020 General Presidential

Election, whereas a political campaign is not a, "Movement" but one should complement the other Old Friend, so it is that i will never allow a president to build human cages for my Hispanic people, simply because in American democracy you never know what the next president is going to put in them.

## September/2020

9/01/2020 &63 days left, Donald Trump is now a impeached, appointed, liar United States President, a Corporate Welfare loser from a domestic and international business perspective, and a snake oil salesman from his own understanding of himself, so it is that I must ask you to ask yourself, "what does that make me if he is our President for another four years? Answer, "A willing Pendejo/a Trump Fool."

So I have written, therefore let it be known that we The Resistance proudly made our American stand to win the popular vote in the 2016 Presidential Election; we did support Hillary Clinton for President 2016 and we did win the popular vote.

The Resistance did win the 2018 Mid-Term elections and we now have the Congress exercising our oversight responsibilities as is the responsibility of the United States Congress, The Resistance did have the President of the United States/ Donald Trump impeached prior to this up and coming election.

Let it be said "Donald Trump was given his undeserved Presidential honors and Presidential democratic respect as a legally appointed President for the last four years," which he has now squandered under his believe that he is our democratic King and President for life.

In 63 days Donald Trump will be no more to American's diversified Democracy and we all will be better off for having voted for Joe Biden for President regardless of political ideological differences.

Our only domestic enemy to the United States left after November 3, 2020 will be in the seeds of hate and evil planted by Donald Trump.

Seeds of racial hate and constitutional dismantling of our American diversified society into a fractured conquerable society of dis information and lies in the stead of our American Constitutional moral virtues. All this is now planted in the simple innocent hearts across our American nation, government and the intellectual world of today.

Joe and Kamala are our only hope for the survival of our American constitutional democracy as we knew it to be. Human dignity is always the target for hateful and or evil no matter at what cost, now is the time to stand and vote for what we once were as a democratic plural American society of the popular vote of the people.

Whereas, Joe, Joe you are my friend, thank you for your fifty year of public service to our nation only you as our President can bring back Honor and Respect to American Constitutional Democracy and the offices and departments of the United States governess.

The Resistance/2020 is strong within you my Old Friend; I Arturo Cortez and the Resistance stand firm with you Joe Biden, and Kamala Harris thank-you for what you do for all of us old friend \ ArturoCortez/76541/09/01/2020

## 09/09/07/2020

"Thank-you America, 56 days to go,"

Gracias Raza of the Human Type our Resistance effort to help get Joe and Kamala Harris elect has conservatively yelled $360,000,000 million from one America Resistance liberals,

Centralist, and Conservatives in August, 2020 for the Biden-Kamala Campaign for President, those of you who have, are now working with those of the have not, to take our country back from Donald Trump's Family Party.

It's all Donald Trump's fake news conspiracy a  Russian KGB disinformation propaganda political effort Compadre all to get the Donald re elected in 2020.

Conpadre stay safe at home, the people are saying Donald Trump is attempting to start a race war to get reelected how anyone can feel safe with that here in Texas the American land of the gun is way over my logical head, I think.

On the other hand Donald Trump has now crippled the United States Postal Service which denies me my mail order medications for his personal political reasons.  then we have the covet CoronaVirus by election day in 56 days we will have lost over 200,000 American lives who will die conservative numbers of course because of Presidential incompetence .

As to the Corona Virus there are third world nations Compadre with better numbers on the Virus than we the most advanced nation in the know world of today Donald Trump has failed his most basic responsibilities as our President, the Donald has learned nothing from the Presidency of the United States of North America, Donald Trump's America is literally destroying us as a American people/nation we are now under a minority political siege of our American Constitutional Democracy.

Vladimir Putin the Russian USSR KGB Agent could not have prayed for a better agent then a Capitalist American Republican RX snake oil salesman with no loyalties in the White House of the people of this nation; what better way to make Russia better than Donald Trump who they say owes them Russian money which the Donald is paying back with American Foreign Policy and

American Nationalism with the help of the American Republican Party.

As an Impeached United States President Donald Trump has learned nothing by his abuse of our freedoms allowed to him by our American Democracy, whereas, Donald Trump has now used American Democracy to destroy American Democracy from within itself.

The American honorable Resistance to governmental abuse of human dignity will always be there for all Americans, guaranteed to us by our American Constitutional Rights, as Americans however I do work towards the end of our Resistance against the United States Governess, come November 4th 2020.

American Democracy must never again be compromised or tested by alien foreign government elements/entities of dictatorships, Kingdoms, or other forms of foreign powers.

I do want to thank-you all those who have now made your contributions and signed up to support Joe Biden and Kamala Harris for President and Vice Presidents of the United States on November 3, 2020 American History will define us all based on the actions in these our "Times."

This nation has now sacrificed enough by outlasting the abuse of American governess and American Democracy by the now Impeached, Incumbent President Donald Trump; the time has come for us the American voter to have our say once again in this nation.

Our people are asking for sanity to our daily lives. We need to seriously get on with the business of surviving a global Pandemic, feeding our people and reorganizing our consumer economy.

Our consumer based economy is based on consumers spending in a free diversified manners.

Whereas as Donald Trump and his Republican Party enablers have now spent over three and a have years giving away America's Treasury to Corporate welfare entities and to the  those who have and need  no more.

Whereas, the contributors and founders of this nation where the people getting to decide who will be our next President, in the stead of the now Electoral College appointed President Donald Trump.

Never should a yes we can political candidate/Leader compromise the vote of the American people by conceding their election prior to final popular vote count; time elements should never compromise the vote/election of the people as is our American socialist democracy of and for the Constitution of the people United States of North America./ArturoCortez/76541/09/07/2020

09/08/2020We now have 60 days to change America, now a land of those of us who have, and a land of those who have not, so we must all pray for all those who have enough to give enough; to give for those who have not, in this our own Capitalist Democracy,

## 09/08/2020

The Resistance 2020/ Yes we Can Candidates Support List for 2020

I realize we must win this election in a capitalist electoral democracy so I too must swallow my pride and ask for your help once again Resistance warriors for Help as the resistance writer of this massage, with the intent to bring change to the United States Government by utilizing my God given talents/Blessings to influencing the readers of my writings. It is clear to me now that the Resistance will end by popular vote of the people come November 3, of 2020.

It is for this reason that we make a clean break from the time of Donald Trump/POTUS/45; we need to solidify control of our nation/Government under Joe Biden and Kamala Harris.

So it is that by contributing to any one or all of these candidates you will be voting to solidify the Executive Branch, The US Senate, and the United States House of Representatives under a "New" responsible United States government of the people of the United States of America under the new Administration led by the Presidential fiber of Joe Biden and Kamala Harris.

We as the American people must send a clear message to the rest of the world that American democracy is able to tolerate, and overcome Presidential political abuse of our American Constitutional Rights as citizens of this nation.

I ask you all too please vote Blue, this 2020 election in support of political change which will be here come November 3, 2020 with your support for these Community Leaders/Candidates in your communities across this nation.

Cal Cunningham, for the United States Senate in North Carolina is now in early voting and the race is very competitive please vote and/or support Cal Cunningham for the United States Senate in North Carolina with your in-kind contributions and/ or whatever you can monetary contribution to get these leaders you will have done your part to elect the right community leaders to represent the people of this nation in both the United States Executive Branch and the United States Senate, whereas, we did win the United States House of Representatives in 2018. This act on your part will give the people of this nation control of all three branches of the United States Government.

These Candidates will work towards American human dignity and will become the political backbone of our people of this time/ Missionaries of our American recovery in yet to come national political history. We are now living a horrible nightmare life experience which we must all experience ourselves, as one human race before we can continue our human instinct to define human dignity in our globalized diversified American socialist, American society democracy of today. Please, "Please DONATE," to one or all of these Grass-Root community leaders for change.

North Carolina your turn is up, your election is "on" please support Cal Cunningham, to represent you in the United States Senate:

Joe Biden for POTUS/46, @ bluestatedigital.com

Cal Cunningham, for United States Senator, North Carolina USA @ bluestatedigital.com

John Ossoff for United States Senator, Georgia, USA/2020 @ bluestatedigital.com

Jaime Harris, for the United States Senate, South Carolina, USA "This race is about right and wrong,"@ bluestatedigital.com

MJ Hagar, for United States Senate, a American Yes we Can," Military Hero Texas, USA, @ bluestatedigital.com

Amy McGrath for United States Senate, Kentucky, USA @ bluestatedigital.com

Mark Kelly for the United States Senate, Arizona, @ USA bluestatedigital.com

Barbra Bollier for the United States Senate, Kansas

This List of Resistance supported Candidates will be updated on Thursday of every week until Monday, November 2, 2020 the purpose of this list is to legally remove and replace (R&R) Donald J. Trump  by Popular democratic vote of the people,& to establish control of people over the United States Government / ArturoCortez/76541/09/09/2020

## 09/17/2018

The Resistance 2020/ Yes we Can Candidates Support List for 2020 47 days before the 2020 General Election, I am so proud to announce that Mike Bloomberg one of many in this nation who really does have the means, has committed $100,000,000 million dollars to the Joe Biden Campaign to remove and Replacement (R&R) Donald J. Trump POTUS/45 from our administrative government offices of the United States Government, of the people.

Although, we of the many in the Resistance do not have much money to buy American politics for the good of the nation, we do have the human American right to bring those things of Cesar ($) to the Round Table of human dignity, as a capitalist nature/ virtue of human so long as self preservation of our economy is in concerned.

Certainly, one could say, because we do vote for our Community leaders and representatives at the highest levels of our American governmental power by the all mighty American popular vote of the people.

It is the popular vote of the American people which creates and distributes power as our form of a ongoing social revolution within American society which we all know as American Democracy for our diversified American people where as only a sweet water native America can claim to be true Americans, now alien in our own hypocritical land.

Whereas, the Mike Bloomberg that helps Joe Biden in 2020 is making a statement to the economic pillars of Corporate America "now is the time to take our country back from the, "I am the greatest Greats POTUS/45."

Making things perfectly clear to Corporate American human and human of man and woman of this nation, "we are now all in the same boat, with things bound to get worst with Donald Trump who is now creating "Presidential Peter Piper Super Virus Spreader Evens' across our nation inspired by our national Presidential Political Events, whereas; all in a time when, today marks 193,000 deaths to date due to the CoronaVirus Pandemic and know Presidential Leadership.

According to scientist from across the world over 230,000 Americans will be dead or dying from the CoronaVirus by Election Day.

So it is that "We need more Money," from all Corporate Entities in order to grease the American capitalist political machine, in order that it works for us the people of this nation in 2020.

To not have the money to by American politics is no excuse whether one is of the ones who have, or of the ones who have not, our capitalist Presidential Election will be won by those who have the money to influence the Vote as it has always been in American Democracy, for now.

Donald Trump's time will come in 49 days, with or without money when this American Political freedom capitalist Monarchy will come to its end in American politics "or" we could be saying after the election, "We could have put more money into buying our election, and maybe we would not have to deal with Donald Trump and his "Herd Immunity" mentality solution to the CoronaVirus meaning of course that we are now allowing the virus to take all it needs from humanity in order that the CoronaVirus dies off before we as the human victim do, something with our American scientific community to  fight the global Pandemic.

This rallies for Donald Trump political scenario which is now playing out is interesting to me because the Aztec Empire, Leaders

Montezuma 1and his nephew Montezuma II would also offer their most faithful subjects to the Gods as a sign of cult faith, there were those in 1519 who would actually volunteer to die for their leader and did, it is then in pri-Columbian History where I assume one would fine the native word "Pendejo" or "Pendejos= more than one," coined.

Mike Bloomberg is simply a American billionaire who remembers who we once were before Donald Trump in American politics and a special friend to the Resistance who challenges Corporate America to give to the Resistance Senatorial political campaigns going on across the country now to (R&R) the United States Senate in 2020, with responsible community leaders who understand their loyalties to the United States Constitution of the people of our nation.

There are 12 seats up for election in the United States Senate and we need all of them or not less than 4 seats to take control of the United States Senate of the people out of 12 seats available, so as to rule by popular vote of the people of this democracy.

We as a American people must not under estimate the damage Donald Trump has done to our American Constitution with the help of what once was the Republican Party now transformed into the Donald Trump Loyalty Party, of today.

Now the voters of the conservative Republic Party must swallow their pride and vote Democrat for the nation along with the rest of us.

Whereas, the recovery and reconstruction after Donald Trump must begin as soon as possible if we are to survive this virus and money is now a means to American Survival of the American untamed beast/the American economy and freedom from Donald Trump's era politics of the people, for now.

To be perfectly clear because of Mike Bloomberg we now have Corporate Capitalist Resistance Warriors for human dignity working for the people as one for this nation to protect our socialist, constitutional democracy.

Welcome to the Resistance Mike Bloomberg, the Resistance is strong within you my friend thank you Sir for who you are and what you do for the people of our nation you Sir make me proud to be American/ArturoCortez /76541/09/14/2020

## 09/17/2020

The Resistance 2020/ Yes we Can Candidates Support List for 2020

North Carolina your turn is on up, your early election is now on" please support Cal Cunningham to represent you in the United States Senate:

Joe Biden for POTUS/46, @ bluestatedigital.com

John Ossoff for United States Senator, Georgia, USA/2020 @ bluestatedigital.com

Jaime Harris, for the United States Senate, South Carolina, USA "This race is about right and wrong,"@ bluestatedigital.com

MJ Hagar, for United States Senate, a American Yes we Can," Military Hero Texas, USA, @ bluestatedigital.com

Amy McGrath for United States Senate, Kentucky, USA @ bluestatedigital.com

Mark Kelly for the United States Senate, Arizona, @ USA bluestatedigital.com

Re-elect Doug Jones for the United States Senate Alabama USA

VOTE American we need these Candidates in public office so we can change things in American Politics / ArturoCortez/76541/09/17/2020

## 09/19/2020

No Conpadre, Bautista i am not flying, not since the herd mentality virus extermination of human in Washington D.C, ideology in Washington D.C. began, i am under Doctors orders to stay at home and away from human of man, for now. Only God knows what he is going to do next with us, stay safe Conpadre our prays are with you Comadre Lupe and the girls and families,

## 09/20/2020

Arturo Cortez Calm down Conpadre, there is reason to believe that Border Patrol Agents from Texas were sent to Oregon to create problems for the Oregonians and other Democratic States and Cities in order to get Donald Trump Elected Law and order President, it is said that President, Donald Trump, is now is now producing Television Shows again with the American people of TV knowledge only, Conpadre i say my chest is not a warehouse, so i just pass it along, Vote for Joe Biden before we all lose family to this virus Raza of the Human Type,

## The Resistance/2020

It is difficult to Honor the Lady's last "Death Wish,"
09/20/2020" We must Honor the Lady's last request, as you would want others to Honor your own last Request," Regardless of who you are you know that Supreme Court Justice, Ruth Bader Ginsburg  passed on Friday. The Women's Resistance Movements have lost a humane moral compass. Who departed with instructions on what to do after death,

## 09/23/2020

2008 a Si se Puede vote for the promise of our nation, 2012 a Si se Puede vote to re enforce the promise of our nation/ 2016 A Si se Puede, vote for Hillary or Better/ 2020 The Si se Puede

Resistance, to Republican Russian Politics within the United States Government. / "answer' the Resistance is not a "Campaign" it is the "Movement" of the people like me who do not get paid to play politics with the vote of the many people.

"American humanity does not have a choice when playing with the capitalist packing order of the Dramatic Party.

Joe old friend i do have your back, all you have to do is not concede this election until the last popular vote is counted, and the rest we live to Texas History to record.

Rest assured The Resistance has not lost a popular vote of the people since we won in 2008, we need lawn signs and ads in Texas, Texas will turn blue as the Republican GOP House is now crumbling here in Texas/Joe Biden you my friend make me proud to be American. /ArturoCortez/76541/09/23/2020

The first 2020 Nation Presidential Debate,

Joe Biden-v-Donald Trump

## 09/29/2020

Never In the history of our United States Democracy has there ever been a President so detached from his responsibilities as President.

Last night the President of The United States (POTUS/45) Donald J. Trump showed a tantrum on global Television by outright attacking old, Joe Biden very time Joe attempted to explain his plan for the nation and its people it seemed as though POTUS/45 was not repaired to debate sleep old Joe Biden, as Donald Trump calls Joe Biden in public. Last night Joe Biden did eat the Presidents lunch by connecting the President to a domestic terrorist organization disrupting peaceful demonstrations and in sighting armed violence in democratic cities for the President.

The President lost the 1st Presidential debate and exposed his plans if any for our future as American subjects of the human kind to what he considers his Donald Trump Presidency.

The President called on White Supremacy Militia groups to "stand down and standby" call to action when needed much as a cheap South American Dictator would do.

Whereas, as if he loses this election, then our National Election of the people is rigged and he will refuse to relinquish and transfer his presidential powers to the next President as American democracy honorably expects him to do.

Now, I must turn our attention to the Resistance 2020.

We all Republicans, Centralist, and Democrats, are now on the same boat and we must Resistance as one Movement for American Democracy we must now feed the capitalist democracy we have created for ourselves if we are to rescue American Democracy from Russian Republican Political Siege of the Executive and Senatorial branches of our American democracy which is now literally in extermination mode of the American.

Whereas well over 250,000 a ¼ million Americans will be dead or dying by election day just for weeks from today over 200,000 dead to date; a topic at the debate preferred not to discuss at the Presidential Debate by President Donald Trump.

The Resistance encourages all its Political Warriors to encourage all your members to give and to give now to Democratic politicians only this election year regardless what Party or ideologue you belong too in American Politics, here is a list of Candidates on the Resistance preferred list.

The Resistance 2020/ Yes we Can Candidates Support List for 2020

North Carolina your turn is on up, your early election is now on" please support Cal Cunningham to represent you in the United States Senate:

Joe Biden for President of the United States, /46, @ bluestatedigital.com

Cal Cunningham, for United States Senator, North Carolina USA @ bluestatedigital.com

John Ossoff, for United States Senator, Georgia, USA/2020 @ bluestatedigital.com

Jaime Harris, for the United States Senate, South Carolina, USA "This race is about right and wrong,"@ bluestatedigital.com

MJ Hagar, for United States Senate, a American Yes we Can," Military Hero Texas, USA, @ bluestatedigital.com

Amy McGrath, for United States Senate, Kentucky, USA @ bluestatedigital.com

Mark Kelly, for the United States Senate, Arizona, @ USA bluestatedigital.com

Re-elect Doug Jones, for the United States Senate Alabama USA

Candidates added to the Resistance list by Barack Obama on the 30th day of September:

John Hickenlooper,
Teresa Greenfield,
Cal Cunningham
Sara Gideon,
Mark Kelly,
Ben Ray Lujan,


As of today I feel very good about this election with 33 day to go, however that is no excuse not to give of yourself and your money to help finance the defeat of Donald Trump and his Republican enablers in the Senate and the Congress with your vote of the $ kind as is our American way as of today. / ArturoCortez/76541/29/0/2020

# CHAPTER 32

**October 2020**

## The Resistance/2020

**10/04/2020**

On Friday the 1st day of October, 2020 @/or about 1:00 AM, the White House announced President Donald Trump and his first lady as well as an administrative aide have tested positive for the CoronaVirus.

Today, four days after nine of the most powerful Republicans in Washington American leadership who attended the political Presidential function to fast tract the appointment of a new Republican Supreme Court Justice to replace the Democrat Lady Justice, Ruth Bader Ginsburg who's last dying wish was to have her seat on the Supreme Court filled after the 2020 General Presidential Election in 28 days from today.

I Arturo Cortez who does pray to Jehovah God, three times a day to protect all people of the human race, from this CoronaVirus, curse on our Humanity of today do pray today God that he forgive and enlighten all Republicans of the simple mind and the same ideological political feather.

I like you as a son of God from a theological perspective have to believe that the "Pass Over" of this pandemic is in our own ability to unite once again as one nation created by all Americans who know that we can win against this virus war if we all wear a mask, for 20 days.

We must all unite as a human Race for this Virus Pandemic to pass. But for this to happen you must have trust, faith and respect for ourselves and others around us, in order to once again be able to glorify ourselves among others as a human virtue as we experience the biblical powers of our lord and creator.

The CoronaVirus has now penetrated the most secure Executive Offices this world, our world has to offer as well a infected over 7,000,000 and killed over 210,000 Americans to date and our President refuses to stand with our doctors and scientist on wearing a face mask for the sake of the American people as we continue to die of in front of him.

The CoronaVirus Pandemic can be perceived as God sent to measure our human ability to see ourselves as one humanity of different colors and diverse cultural beginnings, with one God/ Creator all with his human gift or his curse of knowledge.

Whereas, we the people we must do what is right for our own keen/ kind and others for the sake of our human race.

As for Donald Trump he too like we all is now carrying God's mission in his heart and his own Cross on his back to weigh, balance and measure his place on and under God's earth.   Donald Trump will receive what he has earned as he is now in the good hands of the lord our God, and I do trust that our God is now teaching us all with his powerful deeds, whereas it was not I, but rather a wise carpenter who once said "it will be easier for a camel to walk through the eye of a needle, then it will be for a rich man to enter the gates of heaven." in or about 33 Before his Death 2020 years ago, as for today we tell time by the death of Jesus el Cristo, who like you and I was the human, son of God.

Okay, remember "Wear Your Mask for Human Dignity" to thrive no less than 20 days/ and we beat the virus for good. We can than get on with our diversified lives as it is meant to be.

Now we must deal with the business of the Resistance, we must once again feed our political beast if we are to win the White House, and the United States Senate, whereas the Resistance did establish control of the United States House of Representatives, in 2018.

This is a National Candidates support list which the Resistance encourages you to support, if we are to make change truly happen in our country, please give today to any one of these candidates or all of them if you can if we are to save our human race from extinction:

**The Resistance 2020/ Yes we Can Candidates Support List for 2020**

Joe Biden for President of the United States, /46, @ bluestatedigital.com

Cal Cunningham, for United States Senator, North Carolina USA @ bluestatedigital.com

John Ossoff, for United States Senator, Georgia, USA/2020 @ bluestatedigital.com

Jaime Harris, for the United States Senate, South Carolina, USA "This race is about right and wrong,"@ bluestatedigital.com

MJ Hagar, for United States Senate, a American Yes we Can," Military Hero Texas, USA, @ bluestatedigital.com

Amy McGrath, for United States Senate, Kentucky, USA @ bluestatedigital.com

Mark Kelly, for the United States Senate, Arizona, @ USA bluestatedigital.com

Re-elect Doug Jones, for the United States Senate Alabama USA

**Candidates added to the Resistance list by Barack Obama on the 30th day of September:**

John Hickenlooper,

Teresa Greenfield,

Cal Cunningham

Sara Gideon,

Mark Kelly,

Ben Ray Lujan,

I have known Joe Biden and Joe is one if not the best at bi-partisan politics he will fight the Virus with everything we have, and he will need these Democratic Candidates at his side, to exterminate this virus Please Donate we only have 28 day to spend your contribution on our lives.

/ArturoCortez/10/05/2020

## 10/06/2020

Well, I did start writing this book to influence the 2020 Presidential Election and the time has come to send my manuscript to the printer; I certainly understand that 27 days may not be enough time to get my book published prior to the November 3, 2020 election.

However, I can now see the end to our Resistance to the Donald Trump's United States Government.

Whereas, the President has now contaminated himself and at least twenty if not if not all of his United States White House leadership staff fact; as well as his closest Republican Senators, and Republican United States Congressmen and women to include members of his own family.

Because of Donald Trump the United States has now been left with literately fatedly leaderless, and venerable as we must now wait for American Democracy to play out the end of Donald

Trump's Democratic Electoral Collage Appointment, in the stead of "The Popular vote of the people," as our national President and leader of the free world in one way or the other must face this truth.

As for the 2020 Resistance to date will end and go to the Printer. I do ask that you continue to follow this story on Television as the ending to this story and or Donald Trump could be days away, one way or another as President of the United States.

As for now, I will tell my story in my historical writings dating back to how the Donald got himself elected United States President in November of 2016, which established the Resistance in or about the seventh hour of 2017 all my writings to date related to the Resistance are achieved in this book.

I ask and encourage all the readers and citizens of our nation to step forward and bring an end to this CoronaVirus, by wearing your face mask when out in public for at least 20 days, for the sake of yourselves, families, and your American communities, and the world we live in. "Enjoy' these writings. / ArturoCortez/76541/10/06/2020

**A La Casa de Cortez, Publication**

**November 3, 2020**
**The Resistance 2020 "Judgment Day,"**

For our present United States Presidential Administration, and Election Day 2020 is the will of the American people after the American people will make their Democratic choice for president today.

Today the Resistance will put its political weapons' down, and respect the will of the American Vote as is, what it is, to be American.

On the 20th day of January we take over the United States Presidency and establish a much needed new direction for this nation and the End of the Resistance of the people of this nation against the now loser President, Donald Trump.

Today I call on all Texano constitutional Republicans and Democrats to go Vote and go early as the Resistance Patriots of our American constitution in Texas and outside Texas vote Blue down the ballet.

Whereas we will take our nation back from Russian KGB Capitalist influence within the United States government rule of our time with this 2020 vote for America.

2020 Resistance Warriors, we have now accomplished our mission to establish "Human National Unity" to Remove and Replace POTUS/45, whereas over 100 million early resistance voters have already voted for change to the "Donald Trump Reality Show" in Washington, District of Columbia, {D.C.}.

American Democracy has been compromised unfortunately "in fact" and deliberately by Donald Trump and his Trump Party Republicans enablers from across this nation in order to favor the Russian Dictatorship capitalist interest by Donald & Melania Trump who are now Impeached at the United States House of American Representatives.

As for me I want to thank you all who read my Resistance writings much in the same way as a national ideological grain of American Salt democratic constitutional reset confident that we have left nothing for luck/ the Electoral College to claim from this Election for the direction of our nation.

This Election will be remember as a time in anti-human American Republican governess, versus human American Science and all will have no doubt as to where I American Resistance stood with respect to American human dignity blessed with intelligence wisdom and knowledge as our blessings and/or our course in this election.

## ArturoCortez/76541/11/03/2020

Arthur my friend all of my books are based on a yearly basis. 2021 starts a new book as though to the end of my time.

Sir, "The Resistance" itself does consist of my archived writings for 2016, 2017, 2018, 2019, and 2020.

The title "The Centralist," does consist of my archived writings for the reelection of Barack Obama/POTUS/44 between 2012, 2013, 2014, and 2015.

And yes it is true that each year could be marketed as a separate book.

What is different for me in 2020 is that in the "Centralist 2012-2015" I was able to share the writings my teams who shared with me, making me the conduit between the political world that rules and true human reality, Sir.

The "Centralist" did publish with the registration approve #'s of The United States Library of Congress which did include Correspondence writings from Hillary Clinton, Barack Obama, and Joe Biden as well as many, many others in the business of political power.

I have now removed correspondence letters from the title "The Resistance " and I can see a moral humble narcissist, of man and woman as a sign of old age Mr. Dwayne.

The mission of the Resistance was to take back the United States Government from the Fascist Russian influence from the Presidency of Donald Trump because, I willed it so in these writings or so it reads.

Arthur as we talked once before whether to release "The Resistance" before or after the 2020 Presidential Election, as it has turned out the public did not need my book to do the right thing simply because my stories had already been share on line.

At this point the quality of the product is my only concern.

It looks as though I will be doing more work on the "Resistance" and I am looking at the middle of January 2021 if not later for release of the Resistance books.

Please, ask the Global Summit House Teams to stand down for now, as I will be making some major changes to the manuscript with Georgia on my mind.

Thank-you and stay well my friend, thank you for what you do for the Resistance my friend, have a wonderful holiday season. / ArturoCortez/76541/12/02/2020

## A La Casa de Cortez, Publication

@9:30 AM/Central Texas Time

By Arturo Cortez

It is my Sincere Honor here at La Casa de Cortez, Publications/76541 to confidently predict Vice President, Joseph R. Biden our next "President Elect" of the United States of North America.

We do expect legal challenges from the now loser Presidential Candidate Donald Trump Republican Party but in fact we the American people of this nation have won by way of fair and equitable national popular election/vote, by way of American Democracy who has now won this 2020 Presidential Election to Remove and Replace (R&R) Impeached POTUS/45 Donald Trump.

I would like to thank my friend Joe Biden, for coming out of retirement to lead us all as Americans out of yesterday and into tomorrow as one nation under God.

From this day forward The Resistance/La Resistencia/and the Resistance 2020 along with Resistance allied Organizations across this nation and all Resistance Warriors are asked to stand down on offensive acts against any and all political ideologies' the American people have made their will known and the Resistance will now Honor and respect the will of the people of American Democracy and put its anti-government weapons down, for now.

Gracias, "To the New" President Elect Joe Biden, you old friend make me proud to be American /ArturoCortez/ 11/06/2020/ Killeen/..

When the great white democratic hope do dose not turn out as planed it always blames the other races, the fact is this nation is divide by racial cultural deference, and yes it was in 1824 when Mexican General Santana and Stephen Austin negotiated the first colonial English colonies in the wilderness of than Central Texas; the Texanos of that time in Central Texas knew the English new comers to Texas as the new Mexican Americans in the Independent State of Texas by God's own truth.

"Endorsement"

11/07/2020/ "I agree," The Resistance will continue its whatever we can contributions to support the Honorable Reverend, Raphael Warnock of Georgia, for United States Senator, Rev. Raphael Warnock is a Resistance Warrior consistent with our mission to take total and complete control of the United States governess of the people, of the United States of North America of and for the people, of our Nation.

Today I call once again on all Americans to contribute your time and your money in effect to give national unity an opportunity to reconstruct our national political democratic systems, back to a one American Vote for the nation, and two political parties for the people.

This nation of the people has been under political siege by foreign Republican capitalist influences/enablers/in the White

House and now seeded and germinating treason in our national governess infrastructures.

It is our responsibility as the Resistance to hand Joe Biden and Kamala Harris, a clean American slate to American Democracy, as responsible Americans of our diversified American people of this nation.

Please Donate to Georgia's own, Raphael Warnock for United States Senator.

By, Arturo Cortez/76541/11/08/2020

## A whatever contribution to the nation,
## By Arturo Cortez

11/11/2020/"Hey Joe" Arturo here, I know you are busy so I will make it quick my friend. I can understand your email and all of that, but what I can't understand is what in the world it has to do with me, now.

Whereas, the Resistance has won the 2020 Presidential election in your favor my friend, with the exception of the total Popular Vote count as of yet of course for now. So it is I now have no Resistance to the Executive Branches of the United States, which was a part of the mission of the Resistance, the other part of my mission is for you to have say so over the United States Senate which is my only concern at this time, whereas my only concern at this time is with the Georgia run-off Elections your fundraisers need to find a way to make our case for money to the nation as you now belong to the bi-partisan nation who elected you as the President of all Americans as is or should be.

You're paid fund raising Presidential Staff now have to get the socialist capitalist democratic support of all Americans as it should be in our capitalist, socialist, American Democracy.

To be perfectly clear you are now a President Elect by Electoral College vote as of today/ you now have political capital and the political experience and knowledge to use it, before you lose it.

Congratulations Old Friends, everything you say and do now is political to be used as a double edged sword for or against you and those who have and those who have not, and so it is you are the right man for the job by luck alone my friend, whereas you now have a re-election coming up if you are to institutionalize any changes you might make in your time as President/ please advise if you feel the nation can use my service/ whereas, no one is real in American Capitalist politics unless we get paid for what we do, whereas getting played is always part of the political games of the winners, and the losers in American politics.

The Lord our one God has blessed us all with you in command of our nation, Joe, you do make me proud  to be Arturo Cortez, your friend, please take this text as a humble gift from me to you much as a "grain of salt.": /ArturoCortez/11/11/2020

## A La Casa de Cortez, Publication/

The Resistance/
By ArturoCortez/Killeen, Texas 76541
12/10/2020
Querida, Eva Longoria La Resistencia/"The Resistance/the American people does support its Resistance Warrior's Reverend, Raphael Warnock, and Jon Ossoff both candidates for the Georgia United States Senate and we have been doing so throughout their campaigns to get elected as Senatorial representatives of the people of Georgia in the United States Senate.

Please be advised and please advice others that the Resistance of the people did win the 2016 popular vote for President of the United States, but it was the Presidential Democratic Candidate Hillary Clinton who did betray the will of the American voters by forfeiting the Presidential Race prematurely to then Presidential Republican Candidate for President Donald Trump based on information data from the United States Electoral College, which today rules in the stead of the American popular vote of the American Voter.

The Resistance did win the United States Congress in 2018, and we did get President Donald Trump Impeach prior to the 2020 Election and of course we did win the United States Presidency in now 2020 in the same manner we won the 2008 election of President Barack Obama/Hope and Promise.

This year we do intend to win both Senate seats in Georgia for total and complete control of the House of Representatives/the United States Congress, the United States Senate and the Executive branches of the United States Government of the American people of our nation for the National Democratic Party of our nation, for lack of a better democratic United States Political Party.

Although American democracy has now been tested fascist and fascism must never again be allowed to stand as a part of our American diversified political fabric.

So it is that I now call on all capitalist American Corporate organizations of the private and the private types to stand as one and be counted on the side of our American constitutional government in support our President Elect, Joseph Biden and Kamala Harris by making your contributions to the Resistance Democratic Senatorial Political Georgia Warriors, Jon Ossoff and Reverend, Raphael Warnock.

The Resistance/The People of this nation must have total and complete control of our American political systems in place to honor and protect our United States of American Constitution of the American people.

The Resistance must now once again ask those who do have to stand for all Americans who have made it possible for American Capitalism to co-exist as an essential part of our socialist American political governess of the people.

The Resistance does ask those of the have not, to give whatever you can, and do whatever it is you can do within the legal limitations of our Capitalist Socialist Democracy to assist both Reverend, Raphael Warnock and Jon Ossoff to get elected to the United States Senate, by popular vote of the American people of this nation, ArturoCortez/76541/12/10/2020

### "The End of the four year Resistance"

I suppose the time has now come to begin the fumigation of the White House of the diversified peoples of this nation, the writings that follow are all about the political war games the Resistance played to became what it is to be a winner and not a loser in American politics of today.

Thank you all Resistance Warriors for what you all did to be viewed as one American race of the human kind.

Thanks to all of you we have now won the White House, the United States Senate and the United States House of American Representatives/ the Congress for the people of our nation.

Thank-you all for reading my writings and enjoy this now Historical personal political testament to American Democracy, it was all real.

### The End of 2020

NOVA TOTIVS TERRARVM SIVE NOVI ORBIS TABVLA, auct. G. Blaeu
BLAEU WALL MAP